READER'S DIGEST DIY

FIX
YOUR HOME
FOR LESS

Published by The Reader's Digest Association, Inc.
LONDON • NEW YORK • SYDNEY • MONTREAL

contents

order of work

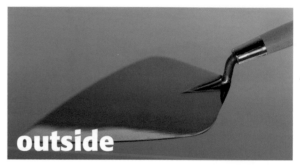

outside

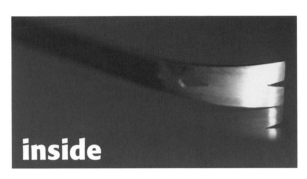

inside

doors & windows

plumbing

electrics

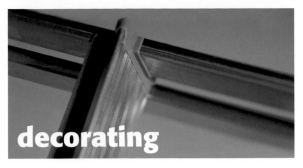

decorating

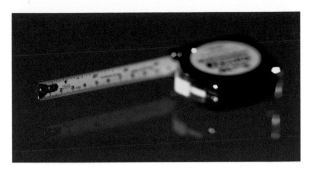

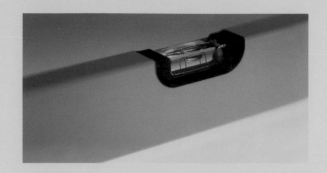

about this book

Your home is probably your greatest financial asset, and to ensure it holds its value and remains safe and comfortable for your family, it's essential to keep on top of repairs before small faults become big, expensive problems.

Fix Your Home for Less gives you all the advice, information and and step-by-step know-how you need to carry out repairs and improvements quickly – and at a fraction of the cost – so you won't need to spend a fortune calling in the professionals.

Inside you'll find everything the do-it-yourselfer can tackle, including basic repairs and maintenance, simple plumbing and electrics, flooring, plastering and decorating. Whether you're an experienced DIYer or just keen to save money, *Fix Your Home for Less* will act as a professional helping hand whenever and wherever you need it.

Each chapter focuses on a key area of your home, highlighting potential problems and providing quick, inexpensive solutions that you can be sure will last for years to come. All tasks or projects are easy to follow, with clear instructions and illustrations. Special hints and tips offer essential, expert advice throughout.

Order of work shows you how to identify areas of your home that need attention or improvement, and explains how to avoid and manage common problems such as damp and condensation.

Outside takes you on a tour of your roofs, gutters and walls, and shows how simple maintenance routines will help you avoid costly repairs in the future.

Inside explains how your rooms are constructed, from floor to ceiling. Whether you want to re-tile a floor, fix a loose board or build a new internal wall, you'll learn how here.

Doors and windows are key when it comes to keeping up the value of your home, and need to be maintained for your home's security. See how you can make basic repairs, and find out how to replace doors and windows where needed.

Plumbing guides you through your home's water supply and shows you how to change a tap, clear a blockage, fix a radiator – and most importantly how to avoid emergency call-out charges.

Electrics is an area where you'll need the services of an electrician for many jobs, but there are things you can do yourself. Find out how to identify and fix common problems such as a blown fuse, how to change a plug or switch and how to install a light fitting.

Decorating takes you project-by-project though the jobs you need to do to keep your home looking good. Learn how to strip wood, paint a range of surfaces, tile kitchens and bathrooms and put up wallpaper like a professional.

order of work

construction How your home was built

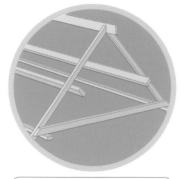

TRADITIONAL TIMBER ROOF

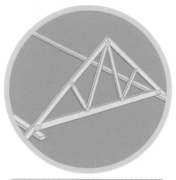

TRUSSED TIMBER ROOF

Generation of change

The age of your home will dictate how it has been built. The construction of houses built in the past half-century differs markedly from those put up before about 1920. Houses built during the intervening generation of change incorporate both traditional house-building techniques and some of the new methods of construction that were being introduced.

Before picking up the tools

Knowing how your home is built before embarking on DIY jobs can save you time and money. Understanding how the roof, walls and floors are put together and what they're made of will help you to plan improvements and alterations, and to deal with any faults that may develop as time goes by.

Look in the loft

A glance in the loft will tell you what sort of roof you have. Traditional timber roofs, assembled on site, have open space below the rafters for storage. Roofs constructed in the past 50 years usually have roof trusses—prefabricated timber frames incorporating rafters and ceiling joists. These are factory-made so the roof structure can be erected quickly, but the design and number of the trusses leaves little room for storage.

Save boarding on a roof

If you live in an older house with a boarded roof—one with planking laid across the tops of the rafters—don't have it stripped off if you ever have a new roof put on the property. The boarding insulates the roof space far better than a layer of roofing felt alone, and areas which are rotten can be replaced easily with sections of new pressure-treated wood.

Strong enough to bear the weight?

Old roofs are usually covered with natural slates or clay tiles, and were designed to take the weight of these. Before you replace them with concrete tiles, which are usually much heavier, ask an expert whether the roof timbers will need to be strengthened. If the timbers do need reinforcing, the cost is likely to cancel out any saving you might make by re-roofing with manufactured tiles—in which case, you're better off leaving the roof structure alone and replacing like with like.

Two kinds of external brick walls

SOLID WALL CONSTRUCTION

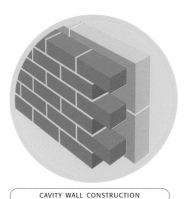

CAVITY WALL CONSTRUCTION

Solid all the way through

The bricks in solid walls are laid in patterns known as bonds. What they all have in common are headers–bricks laid end-on so that they pass right through the wall to give it strength. A solid wall will be as thick as the length of a brick (215 mm) plus the thickness of plaster inside and any rendering outside. You can measure the wall at a door or window opening.

A cavity in the middle

Only the long faces of bricks, known as stretchers, are on view if your house has cavity walls. The walls are a minimum of 255 mm thick (two single leaves of brickwork, each 102.5 mm thick, separated by a 50 mm wide cavity) and more if the cavity is wider or the internal leaf is built of thicker blockwork.

Drier and warmer

Cavity walls have several advantages over solid ones. Any rain that penetrates the outer leaf of brickwork cannot bridge the cavity and instead runs down its inner face to ground level, so that the inner leaf stays dry. Interior wall surfaces are warmer because the air in the cavity acts as an insulator, and extra insulation placed in the cavity during or after building makes them warmer still.

Timber-framed houses have an inner leaf consisting of load-bearing wooden wall panels clad with external plywood sheathing and filled with insulation.

construction

construction Suspended and solid ground floors

SUSPENDED TIMBER FLOOR

SOLID CONCRETE FLOOR

What lies beneath your feet?

Ground floors in houses built before about 1950 are usually covered with floorboards laid over timber joists which are suspended over an underfloor airspace. In the past 50 years solid concrete ground floors have become the norm, although they may be overlaid with timber strip flooring or chipboard. **Accessing and altering plumbing** and heating pipework under a timber floor is a relatively simple matter; getting at pipes buried in concrete is much more difficult.

No more damp and better insulation

Concrete floors in the kitchens and sculleries of old houses are prone to rising damp because they were laid straight onto the earth, with no separating damp-proof membrane (DPM). Inherent dampness in a solid floor also makes it cold and so liable to condensation. Where concrete floors have been laid next to wooden ones, they can hinder ventilation of the underfloor space, increasing the risk of rot in the wood floor. Nowadays, Building Regulations ensure that concrete ground floors are underlaid with a DPM of heavy-grade polythene, and since 1990 they have also had to be insulated.

Prone to rot and draughts

In older homes, the ends of the joists supporting timber ground floors are embedded in external walls, making them prone to rot if the walls are damp. The square-edge floorboards used until the 1930s let in underfloor draughts—a problem largely cured by the use of tongue-and-groove boards, although at the cost of making the boards more difficult to lift (see page 58).

home survey Assessing the condition of your property

Get your priorities right

Carry out a survey to make sure your home is weathertight, safe and thief-proof before you do anything else. There's no point in decorating if the roof is letting in rain, or installing new light fittings if the wiring is dangerous and needs replacing. And if the house isn't secure, filling it with expensive fixtures and fittings before making sure that all the exterior doors and windows have good locks is also getting your priorities wrong.

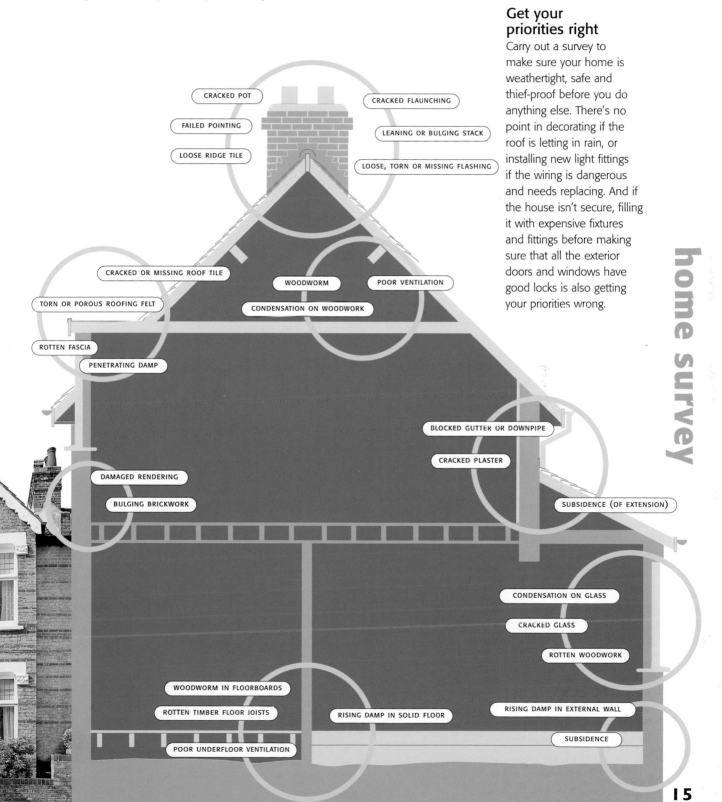

- CRACKED POT
- CRACKED FLAUNCHING
- FAILED POINTING
- LEANING OR BULGING STACK
- LOOSE RIDGE TILE
- LOOSE, TORN OR MISSING FLASHING
- CRACKED OR MISSING ROOF TILE
- WOODWORM
- POOR VENTILATION
- TORN OR POROUS ROOFING FELT
- CONDENSATION ON WOODWORK
- ROTTEN FASCIA
- PENETRATING DAMP
- BLOCKED GUTTER OR DOWNPIPE
- CRACKED PLASTER
- DAMAGED RENDERING
- BULGING BRICKWORK
- SUBSIDENCE (OF EXTENSION)
- CONDENSATION ON GLASS
- CRACKED GLASS
- ROTTEN WOODWORK
- WOODWORM IN FLOORBOARDS
- ROTTEN TIMBER FLOOR JOISTS
- RISING DAMP IN SOLID FLOOR
- RISING DAMP IN EXTERNAL WALL
- SUBSIDENCE
- POOR UNDERFLOOR VENTILATION

home survey Assessing the condition of your property

Take it from the top

Start your home survey with the roof. A pair of binoculars is useful for inspecting it without having to climb a ladder. If you can't see the whole roof surface from your garden or the street, ask to view it from a neighbour's property.

Stacks of trouble

Chimneys are the most exposed part of your house, so check them closely for signs of damage. Look for cracks in the pots and in the flaunching–the mortar bed in which the pots are embedded. If a stack is built against an outside wall, examine it for straightness. The combination of coal gases condensing inside the flue and rain soaking through the mortar joints can set up a chemical reaction which makes the brickwork bulge outwards. Repointing the brickwork (see page 49) and lining the flue can arrest the problem, but a severely damaged stack may have to be completely rebuilt.

Check the controls

Before you start any DIY, make sure you know where the water and gas stoptaps and main electricity supply switch are located. Keep a torch by the electricity meter, plus some fuse wire if the system has fuses (see page 174). Locate all drain inspection chambers (manholes) and check that the covers can be lifted easily if a drain becomes blocked (see page 138).

Look for overflows

Check the gutters and downpipes for blockages (see page 44). Stains on the house walls can reveal where previous overflows have occurred. The next time it rains, check where gutters are overflowing or where water is leaking from downpipe joints.

Include the garden

Remember to survey the garden at the same time as the rest of your home. Fences may be in poor condition, a shed roof may be leaking, garden paths may need lighting, and nearby trees may be undermining boundary walls. A gate or door into the garden might need a lock ftting to it.

Inspect the loft

Go into the loft to inspect the underside of the roof. Look for water stains on the timbers, or wait until there's a heavy downpour and then look for signs of rain getting in. There should be ventilators along the eaves, at the ridge, in gable walls or on the roof slope. Shine a light along the eaves if there are none to be seen, because a badly ventilated roof space can be liable to dry rot, and this often sets in along the eaves. Lastly, examine the roof timbers for woodworm.

Is the woodwork sound?

Prod the external woodwork with a bradawl to detect rot under the paintwork (see page 82) and look round the edges of door and window frames for gaps where rainwater can penetrate—especially on north and west-facing walls, which are the most exposed to the weather.

That sinking feeling

Subsidence is the most serious problem you might detect. It occurs most commonly on clay soil, which expands when wet and then contracts as it dries out. Look at the corners of your house and at the door and window openings. Are they vertical and square?

Zigzag cracks running down the walls from the corners of door and window frames, and between the main house and an extension, are signs of possible subsidence. Inside, doors and windows may start jamming for no apparent reason, and wallpaper can crease or tear.

Barriers to rising damp

Look for a damp-proof course (DPC)—visible outside between the second and third courses of brickwork above ground level. This is a horizontal band of slate, bituminous felt or black polythene. In an older house built before DPCs were introduced, you may see a row of small mortar or rubber plugs indicating that a chemical DPC has been injected into the walls in recent years.

Where the air gets in

Airbricks or grilles are built into the outside walls, just above ground level, in houses with suspended timber ground floors. These allow air to circulate in the underfloor space, helping to keep it dry and to discourage rot. Make sure they are not blocked or obstructed in any way.

Testing timber floors

Jump up and down on timber ground floors. If they sag noticeably, the joists may be rotten because their ends are built into walls suffering from rising damp. Prod the skirting boards with a bradawl to see if they're rotten—another indication that there may be problems beneath the floor.

Safe and secure

As you work your way around the house checking the woodwork, look at how windows and external doors are secured. You may need to fit new locks or upgrade existing ones (see pages 98–103).

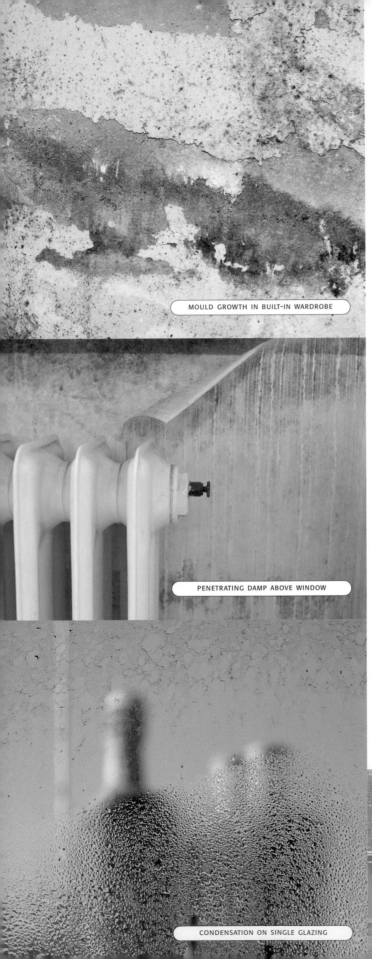

MOULD GROWTH IN BUILT-IN WARDROBE

PENETRATING DAMP ABOVE WINDOW

CONDENSATION ON SINGLE GLAZING

Diagnosing damp and tracing the causes

Find the reason before trying a remedy

Damp problems in a house can be due to a number of causes–rain getting through the walls or roof, moisture being absorbed from the ground, condensation settling on cold surfaces, or a mixture of these. Make sure you know what the cause of dampness is before trying to cure it, otherwise you may be dealing only with part of the problem, or even adopting the wrong remedy for the sort of damp involved.

Spot the tell-tale semicircles

In an old house with a slate damp-proof course (DPC), slight movement of the building can crack the slates, allowing damp from the ground to rise into the masonry above the crack. A single point failure will cause a semicircular patch of damp up to 1m (3 ft 3 in) or so across, while multiple cracks will lead to an almost continuous band across the affected wall.

Try the foil test

If you're not sure of the cause of a damp patch on a wall, try the foil test. Dry the wall surface with a fan heater, then tape some kitchen foil tightly over the damp area. If the surface of the foil is wet after 24 hours, you have condensation. If the foil is dry but the wall surface beneath it is damp, you have rising or penetrating damp. Discount rising damp if the moisture is more than 1m above outside ground level.

Getting through the gaps

Patches of dampness on walls around windows and doors are usually caused by rain getting through gaps between their frames and the surrounding masonry. Where the damp is below the opening, it may be because there is no drip groove to stop the water creeping under a projecting sill or threshold. If there is a drip groove, make sure the rain is not crossing it because it is blocked with paint or mortar (see page 51).

Suspect condensation

If the roof isn't leaking but the timbers and loft insulation are damp, the likely culprit is condensation. This is caused by warm moisture-laden air rising into the loft from the rooms below and condensing on cold surfaces within the loft space. In serious cases, roof timbers can start to rot and saturated insulation materials can stain ceilings.

Looking for a leak in the roof

Discovering exactly where a pitched roof is leaking can be difficult. Rain can trickle down the roofing felt and then along the sides of rafters before it drips onto the loft floor. Look for clues such as dampness on a party wall or chimney stack in the loft, which might indicate that flashings are defective or missing (see page 35). Getting someone to play a hose on the roof, area by area, while you remain inside the loft can also help to reveal where the water is getting in.

Woodworm at work

At the same time as checking lofts, underfloor spaces and built-in cupboards for signs of dampness, inspect structural timbers and joinery for evidence of woodworm, which thrives in slightly damp environments. Look for the small flight holes made by the beetles when they emerge from the wood and the fine wood dust created by the pest. Check the untreated backs of all freestanding chests and wardrobes, and the unpainted top and bottom edges of doors at the same time.

home survey Diagnosing damp and tracing the causes

Prod the paintwork
Use a bradawl to test the soundness of skirting boards if there are signs of damp in downstairs walls or the underfloor space. The backs of skirting boards are usually left unpainted, so they readily absorb moisture from the masonry. However, severe deterioration of the boards is often not apparent because of paint applied to their face sides.

Crossing the bridge
If you think you have rising damp in your house, locate the damp-proof course (DPC) and make sure it isn't covered by a flowerbed, path, drive or patio. Look for rendering that has been applied over the DPC. Check whether there is a vertical DPC sandwiched between the house wall and the end of a garden wall built up against it. Curing these common causes of rising damp will solve the problem for little or no cost, saving you from incurring an expensive bill from a professional damp-proofing firm.

Check out the plumbing
Leaks in plumbing and central-heating pipework can cause damp patches which could be misinterpreted as rising or penetrating damp. This is especially common where the pipes are run beneath a floor or are buried in wall plaster. Here a pinhole leak or a weeping fitting can release surprisingly large volumes of water as time goes by, especially if it has no chance to dry out naturally.
If this is the cause of the problem, you have two possible courses of action. You can either expose the fault and then replace the affected pipes, which will cause a lot of disruption. Alternatively, you can simply leave them where they are and bypass them by installing new ones.

Letting off steam
The kitchen and bathroom are the main sources of condensation in the home. Bathing, cooking and washing up, and washing and drying clothes all pour large volumes of steam into the air. Portable gas space heaters and paraffin stoves also create a lot of moisture.
The problem is made worse by poor room ventilation and over-efficient draught-proofing, both of which stop warm moisture-laden air inside the house being replaced with cooler drier air from outside.
Unventilated fitted cupboards built against outside walls can suffer badly from condensation. This can lead to unsightly mould growth, which will quickly spoil clothes stored there.

inspirations Prepare a plan and visualise your options

Measure and draw

Experiment with ideas for alterations by drawing a floor plan on graph paper or using a home design software package on your computer. An ultrasonic estimator is the most accurate tool for quickly taking measurements. The larger the scale of the drawing or model, the more detail can be included on it.

Some home design packages offer walkthroughs and the ability to incorporate plumbing and electrical infrastructure; most offer multiple views.

Mark which way doors open—it has a vital effect on the positioning of light switches—and include other features on your plan such as radiators, light fittings and socket outlets too.

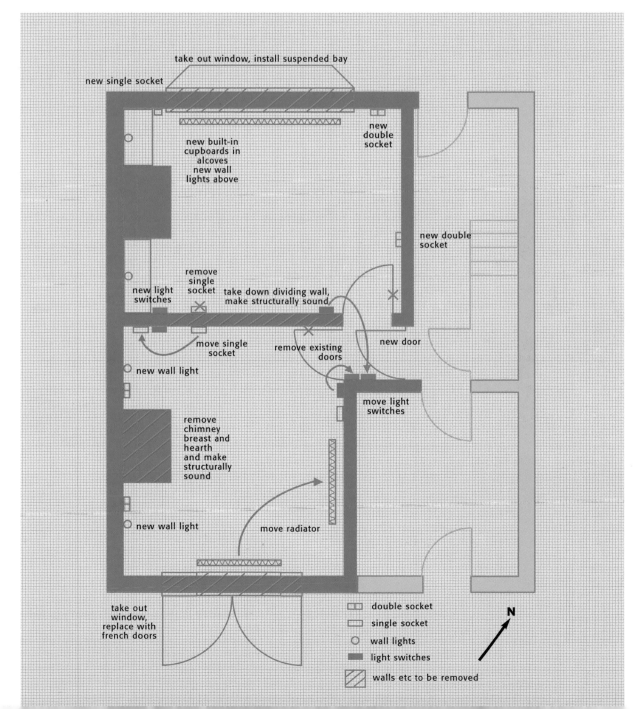

take out window, install suspended bay

new single socket

new double socket

new built-in cupboards in alcoves
new wall lights above

new double socket

remove single socket

new light switches

take down dividing wall, make structurally sound

new door

move single socket

remove existing doors

new wall light

move light switches

remove chimney breast and hearth and make structurally sound

new wall light

move radiator

take out window, replace with french doors

double socket

single socket

wall lights

light switches

walls etc to be removed

N

inspirations Prepare a plan and visualise your options

A sense of direction

Find out in which direction north lies and mark it on your plan. Aspect can be vital if you're thinking of building a conservatory, or having skylights or new windows put in the house—all of which need to face south or west to get most sunshine and daylight.

Illusions of space

Several design tricks can be used to make a room feel bigger than it really is. For example, brightly lit rooms with pale walls, bare floors, simple furniture and sheer curtains feel spacious. Strategically hung mirrors also add an illusion of extra space, reflecting what lies through a window, around a corner or beyond an open doorway.

Envisage the impact

If you decide to have new openings made in a wall, or an existing one enlarged, you can get an idea of the overall impact by sketching them full-size on sheets of lining paper, then taping these in position on the wall surface.

That shrinking feeling

A room can be made to feel smaller too. Dark walls and ceilings seem to advance. A picture rail also makes a ceiling feel lower, especially if the wall above the rail is painted to match the ceiling colour. Heavy, patterned fabrics, dark furniture and focused lighting emphasise the shrinking effect.

Change without disruption

Instead of altering the dimensions of rooms by knocking them into one another to create bigger spaces or putting up stud walls to make them smaller, consider creating change by illusion. Using colour, lighting, furniture and furnishings to create different effects is cheaper and less disruptive than undertaking building work.

Consider the alternatives before you start making changes

Structural considerations
Make sure a dividing wall is non-loadbearing before you knock it down to turn two rooms into one. One way to tell is to look at floorboards in the room above–if they run parallel to the wall, the joists they're laid on must be supported by the wall–but seek expert advice if you're in any doubt.

Counting the potential costs
One room made from two will have more light if both the originals had windows, but the bigger area will be more expensive to heat. A sense of comfort may be lost if the enlarged room feels too long, too narrow or too low. In addition, there will now be space where there were two surfaces to stand furniture against and hang things on.

New uses for existing areas
You can make your home suit your lifestyle better by changing the way you use rooms. For example, an understairs cupboard could be converted into a downstairs toilet. You could house the washing machine, tumble drier and airer in an old walk-in larder and increase food storage in the kitchen.

An integral garage is an obvious candidate for conversion into a playroom, a home office or a teenager's room if you're prepared to leave the car on the drive or street.

Rooms with a view
Glass creates an impression of space. Glazing a solid door at the end of a claustrophobic hall introduces a view of the outside or into a room, lets in light and makes the hall feel more spacious. Creating or emphasising a view of the garden through a window or french doors makes a room appear larger, especially if tall plants are kept away from the other side of the glass.

Lofty thoughts
Don't forget the loft when you're looking for extra space. Although the roof trusses used in most houses since about 1950 usually involve too much structural work to make loft conversion practical, the roof spaces in older properties can often be turned into an extra room (see page 12).

solutions Making the most of your abilities

Risks not worth the saving

Always err on the side of caution if you're not confident about your DIY skills—especially if the job involves working at height. All the equipment needed for carrying out roof repairs and alterations can be hired (see page 32), but if you are unsure about whether you can do the job safely, paying professional contractors is preferable to risking injury or worse.

Opportunity to tackle other tasks

Scaffolding forms a substantial part of the total cost of having a house re-roofed. Try to take advantage of it by having other jobs, such as painting the outside woodwork or repointing the brickwork, carried out while the scaffolding is in place. It will have to satisfy the requirements of different tradespeople (for example, providing planking and access ladders for painters). **You will probably have to pay extra** to keep the scaffolding beyond the four weeks usually negotiated by roofers. Remember that you will not be covered by the contractor's insurance if you work from the scaffolding yourself.

A sensible division of labour

Many building jobs involve an element of unskilled work. For example, having a room replastered involves hacking off and carting away the old plaster. Tradespeople will often agree to you doing this sort of work yourself to save money before they come in to carry out the skilled part of the job.

Time and patience

Before you tackle a large project yourself, estimate how long it will take and how disruptive it will be. Can you and others living in the house put up with a long period of disorder if you're able to devote only weekends to the project?
Nothing kills enthusiasm more quickly than apparent lack of progress. You may conclude that the solution is to employ others to do the major disruptive work while devoting your input to just the finishing stages.

Get an expert opinion

Consult a professional surveyor or building engineer if your home survey alerts you to a serious problem–subsidence, for example– that could require major structural work. An expert will assess whether the problem has stabilised and requires no action, can be arrested without major building work, or requires extensive remedial work.

Strategies to combat damp problems

Let your house breathe

There are a number of simple but effective remedies for condensation. Open windows when the weather is suitable so that drier air can get in. Fit extractor fans with humidity detectors in kitchens and bathrooms to remove moist air automatically, or else plug in a dehumidifier. Lastly, remember that sealing up doors, windows and unused flues to eliminate draughts will increase the likelihood of condensation.

Is a guarantee required?

Installing a damp-proof course (DPC) in an older house usually involves drilling holes into the second or third course of brickwork above outdoor ground level, then pumping a chemical waterproofer into the walls. You can hire the equipment and do the job yourself if you don't need the guarantee.

Easy ways to cut humidity

Create less moisture by drying clothes outdoors whenever possible. If you have a tumble drier, vent it to the outside.
Keep lids on boiling saucepans and shut bathroom and kitchen doors to stop steam spreading through the house.
Use dehumidifiers in damp, enclosed areas and avoid heaters that run on paraffin or oil–both fuels produce large quantities of water vapour when they are burned.

solutions

solutions Strategies to combat damp problems

Allow time for drying out
If your home needs a DPC, schedule it into the order of work as early as possible. The plaster on damp walls will have absorbed salts from the masonry and will have to be hacked off to a height of about 1m (3 ft 3 in) before the DPC is installed. Then the masonry will need to be left bare for several months so that it can dry out before the walls are re-covered—either with a traditional sand and cement plaster, or with one recommended by the damp-proofing company.

Raising the floor
Always seek advice about the best way to tackle rising damp in a solid floor, which is caused by the absence or failure of a damp-proof membrane (DPM) between the floor and the ground beneath.

Low levels of damp can be tackled by coating the floor with a heavy-duty damp-proofing liquid to create a new DPM, then applying a thin sand and cement screed on top. **If you cannot afford to raise the floor** level much, you can lay a self-levelling compound instead of a traditional screed to provide a new floor surface. If, however, the damp problem is very severe, you may be advised to have the whole floor lifted and replaced.

Made to absorb moisture
Decorate kitchens and bathrooms with paint specially made for these rooms. Ordinary emulsion paint will flake or develop mould if it gets damp frequently, but anti-condensation paint is designed to absorb moisture from damp air and release it back into the atmosphere when the air is drier.

Damp-proof plaster
If condensation is severe, on north-facing walls for example, have them replastered with an anti-condensation plaster. Like kitchen and bathroom paint, this product absorbs moisture when the atmosphere is damp and releases it when it is dry. The plaster also contains small air bubbles which insulate the surface, helping to further reduce the risk of condensation.

Try small adjustments first
You can hold condensation at bay by spending more on keeping the house warm—turning up the central heating and improving the insulation. Often, however, marginal adjustments—slightly more ventilation combined with a low but constant level of background heat—are just as effective, and cheaper.

safety first Solutions for accident black spots

Minimise fire danger

Buy a fire blanket and keep it somewhere accessible in the kitchen, which is where most fires start. Fit smoke detectors in the hall and on landings. Don't store tins of paint or other flammable materials under the stairs; move them to a garage or shed so they won't pose a risk to a main line of escape if you're unlucky enough to have a fire. Finally, if there are locks fitted to patio doors or upstairs windows, keep the keys nearby and make sure that everyone knows where they are.

Lighting the way

Falls tend to occur at entrance doorways, on stairs and in kitchens and bathrooms, often because people cannot see clearly where they are going. **Wire in two-way light switches** so that nobody has to negotiate the stairs in the dark (see page 195). Put up a hand rail if necessary (see page 83) and if there are babies or toddlers in the house, fit stair gates at the top and bottom of the flight. Fit outside lights to illuminate the route to your front door at night (see page 201).

Stop slipping and sliding

Put down non-slip mats in shower cubicles and in baths used for showering. Fit wall-mounted grab handles in the bathroom for extra safety, especially if you have someone elderly or disabled living in the house.
A fabric bath mat soaks up water and stops the bathroom floor from being slippery when wet. If you are replacing the bathroom flooring, choose a slip-resistant material.

Warning sticker

Place a colourful label at eye level on patio doors to warn people of their existence. It's easy to walk into the glass, especially in fine weather when you might expect the doors to be open. Replace ordinary glass with toughened or laminated glass in all full-length glazed timber doors. Since 2002, all replacement windows (and replacement doors with more than 50 per cent glazing) have needed Building Regulations approval. In order to meet the requirements of Part L (conservation of fuel and power), replacement windows need a 'U' value of 1.6 W/m²K (1.8 for glazed doors).

safety first Solutions for accident black spots

Wear the right gear

Assemble a safety kit before embarking on DIY. For many jobs you'll need safety goggles, a face mask, a hard hat, a pair of tough gloves and some sturdy footwear. Different items offer varying degrees of protection. A dust mask, for example, won't protect you against solvent vapours and fine droplets of paint in the air, so buy a specialist spray mask or a respirator made to at least approved standard EN405 if you're going to tackle jobs such as respraying car bodywork. If you anticipate using noisy power tools such as a concrete breaker or floor sander for long periods, buy some ear defenders too.

Invest in a first-aid kit for your workshop that meets Health and Safety Executive standards for workplace use. These are available from tool and equipment hire shops.

Remove or tape down

Loose rugs laid on polished wooden hall floors and landings pose a serious hazard, especially near the top of stairs. Either remove them, or fix special non-slip tape to the underside.

Fit castor cups

Move chairs and sofas fitted with castors away from patio doors and other low-level glazing, so there's no chance of them being propelled through the glass when people sit down on them. Alternatively, fit castor cups beneath the castors to stop the furniture from moving so easily.

Secure shelves

If you have an adjustable shelving system on an open wall, rather than in an alcove, secure the shelves to their brackets with screws. This will stop an accidental collision from dislodging a shelf or its contents. It is also a good idea to round off any sharp shelf corners in this situation.

Use tools safely

Many DIY tools need sharp blades or powerful motors to be able to do their jobs properly. This means that they can cause injury if they are not used correctly and with care. When using bladed tools, keep them sharp so they will cut without effort, and make sure that your hands are behind the cutting direction and out of the cutting line. Read the instructions before using any power tool for the first time, and never bypass or de-activate any safety guard that is fitted to the tool.

Backs against the wall

Secure the tops of tall bookcases and display units to the wall with L-shaped brackets so they cannot topple over if they are unevenly loaded or if a child tries to climb up the shelves.

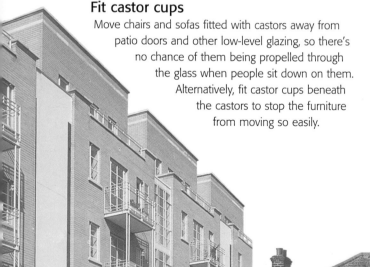

Reducing the risks from power in the home

Make an appointment

If you have no record of when a gas or oil-fired central-heating boiler or water heater was last serviced, arrange for a service straightaway. This will ensure that the appliance burns its fuel properly and is adequately ventilated.

If you experience drowsiness or headaches in the room when an appliance is on, don't use it until it's been checked.

Avoid trailing flexes

Flexes from appliances such as toasters and kettles hanging over the edge of a worktop can be dangerous if you have children or boisterous animals. You can shorten the flex by cutting through it and fitting a new plug to make things safer. Never plug appliances into a cooker point with a socket such that the flex trails over a hob or hotplate.

Baby-safe sockets

Plug socket guards into all unused electric sockets if you have small children in the family; this prevents tiny fingers or metal objects from being poked into socket holes. It is also worth making sure that all plugs have sleeved live and neutral pins, so they are safe even if partly pulled out of their sockets.

Prevent a heat surge

The water temperature in a shower can rise suddenly and cause scalding if a cold tap is turned on elsewhere in the house. You can eliminate the risk by replacing the shower mixer with a thermostatically controlled model or by fitting a mains-fed electric shower unit (see page 148).

Fully bonded

For total electrical safety, all exposed metalwork in the bathroom should be linked (bonded) to earth by special cables covered in green-and-yellow PVC insulation (see page 124). If there is no evidence of these vital links in your home (they may have been concealed under the floor, for example), call in an electrician to find out and to install them if necessary.

safety first

29

outside

ladders Make safety your top priority

Get a good grip
Hold the rungs, not the ladder sides, when you climb or descend a ladder. If you miss your footing, you will automatically grab them and so avoid a fall. If you hold the sides and you slip, you will get skin burns from a metal ladder and splinters from a wooden one. Don't hug the ladder; climb with your arms straight and your body upright.

Stand well away
Fit a stand-off to the top of your ladder to hold it away from overhanging eaves and allow you to work on the gutters. You may crack a plastic gutter if you rest a ladder against it.

Change to cordless
Power cables hanging from ladders are a potential safety hazard; use cordless power tools whenever you can.

Don't climb too high
Use the top four rungs of a ladder as handholds only. If you try to stand on them and grab something higher up for support, such as a gutter or sill, you are quite likely to fall.

Secure a firm foothold

If a ladder is going to be in one position for a lengthy job, tie it to sturdy pegs driven into the ground on each side of the uprights to prevent it slipping. On hard surfaces, or when you need to move the ladder frequently, get someone to stand on the bottom rung of the ladder and anchor it in place. On soft ground, stand the ladder on a board to stop it from sinking. Screw a batten to the board to prevent the ladder from sliding outwards, then tie and stake it. Alternatively, you can hire a ladder safety foot, which has a high-friction base.

Get an extra pair of hands

Someone of average height can push up the top section of an extension ladder by only about 2m (6 ft 6 in) once it is in position. To extend the ladder further, lay it on the ground with its foot braced against the wall, then pull out the extension to the required length. Don't forget to turn the ladder over before raising it, so the right side faces outwards. Triple extension ladders are available with cord-and-pulley operation. These can be extended single-handed, but you will need help to control the ladder while setting it in position.

Dress for comfort and safety

Wear thick-soled shoes with a good grip and, if you're going to be standing on one rung for long periods, fit a hook-on platform to the ladder to prevent sore feet. Trousers and long-sleeved tops protect you from knocks and scratches, and a safety helmet protects your head.

Keep off the glass

Lash a length of timber at least 75 x 50 mm across the top of a ladder to enable you to paint or glaze a window. The timber rests on the masonry at each side of the opening and holds the ladder safely away from the glass.

1 Carry ladder upright to work site unless there are overhead electricity cables or other obstacles in the way

2 To erect ladder, jam its feet against base of wall, then lift top end over your head and walk towards wall

3 Ladder is at correct angle when, with toes touching bottom of ladder and arms and back straight, you can grasp rung at shoulder height

ladders

33

ladders Stepladders and platforms

A prop to stop a topple
Clamp or screw a 50 x 25 mm batten, long enough to reach the ground, to the back of a stepladder at an angle of around 45°, to make it more stable.

A grip to stop a drop
Stretch strong elastic bands round the platform of a stepladder so you can tuck tools under them and prevent them rolling off. A magnetic strip stuck to the platform edge will do the same job for loose nails and screws.

Improvise a platform
Use the components of a slot-together platform tower to make a mobile low-level work platform. Lock the wheels once the platform is in position.

Handy holdall
Never climb a ladder with your hands full. Instead, raise and lower tools and other items in a small bucket tied to a length of rope, making sure the load is well balanced and not too heavy. Then hang the bucket on an S-hook—available from hardware shops and DIY stores—suspended from a rung.

Check before you climb

The three-rung test
With the ladder set up, climb three rungs and jump up and down, then lean out to each side to check that it won't settle. Reposition the ladder on firmer ground or on a board if it moves.

Look for the label
By law a new ladder must carry a label stating its safe load rating. Many also have a sticker, designed to be used with a spirit level, that enables you to set up the ladder at a safe angle.

Ladder health check
Before using an aluminium ladder, check that all the rungs are secure and that it is not dented or deformed. Inspect a wooden ladder for splits, broken rungs, missing or damaged reinforcing stays under the rungs, and rot and woodworm. Protect it with varnish or clear wood preservative. Do not use paint, which hides defects. Check that hinges and stays on stepladders are securely attached. If a stepladder is an old wooden one, make sure the restraint cords are sound.

roofs Giving your roof the once-over

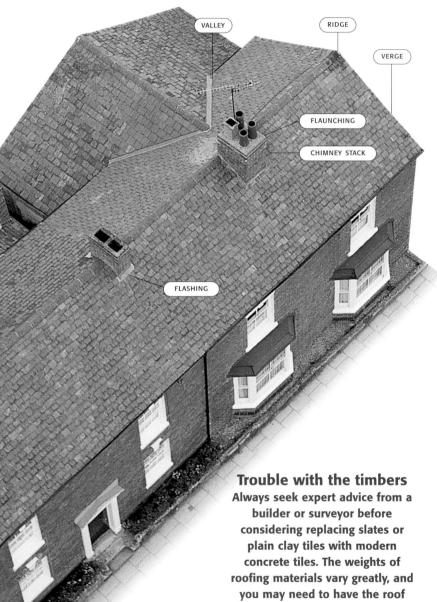

VALLEY

RIDGE

VERGE

FLAUNCHING

CHIMNEY STACK

FLASHING

Looking for faults

Carry out a thorough inspection of the roof surface and any chimney stacks on a regular basis, looking for the faults described here, then problems can be fixed before they cause serious damage. However, unless you are happy to work on your roof and to carry out necessary repairs yourself, it's best to call in a builder or a specialist roofing contractor to do the work for you.

Stacks of trouble

Start at the top of each chimney stack, checking that the pots and the mortar layer (flaunching) holding them in place on the stack is intact. Then inspect the brickwork and the pointing, noting any frost-damaged bricks or missing mortar. Consider having unused flues capped.

Keep flashings flat

Lead or aluminium flashings waterproof the join between a chimney stack and the roof surface. Make sure their upper edges are held securely in the mortar between the bricks, and that their lower edges lie flat on the roof; if they're not, rain can get behind and the roof will leak. Replace mortar fillets with metal flashings because mortar cracks.

Trouble with the timbers

Always seek expert advice from a builder or surveyor before considering replacing slates or plain clay tiles with modern concrete tiles. The weights of roofing materials vary greatly, and you may need to have the roof structure strengthened–a potentially expensive and highly disruptive job.

Ridge tile healthcheck

Most houses have ridge and hip tiles set in a continuous mortar bed, and when this cracks up the tiles can be dislodged by high winds, allowing water to get in and rot the timbers. Check that yours are all secure, and identify any loose ones with a chalk cross so they can be lifted and re-bedded securely.

Slipping slates mean rusty nails

Large numbers of slates slipping out of position indicate that the nails securing them to the battens have rusted through. The slates themselves may be sound enough to be re-fixed, but you will probably find some that need replacing. Secure the slates with copper nails that will not rust.

Stay off the tiles

Roof tiles can be lifted and cracked, or even removed completely, by high winds. However, a more likely cause of damage is someone climbing onto the roof and standing directly on the tiles. Never do this yourself; one slip could be fatal. Use a roof ladder or crawl boards at all times.

35

roofs Getting on top of the problem

Sound ring test
Test a secondhand slate by tapping it lightly with a hammer. You'll hear a ringing sound if it's in good condition, and a dull sound if it's cracked. Look at the underside, too; it's usually the first surface to powder and crumble.

Inspect the valleys
Valleys–the internal angles where two roof slopes meet–are usually lined with a metal tray secured to wooden boards that are themselves supported by the roof rafters. Keep them clear of wind-blown debris so they can't overflow and soak the woodwork. Check them for splits or tears too; any you find can be waterproofed temporarily by sticking on some self-adhesive flashing tape.

Watch the verges
At gables, the end tiles of each row may project beyond the face of the wall to form what is known as a verge. This overhang is supported on plain tiles, slates or strips of fibre cement sheet bedded on top of the sloping masonry. Check that the mortar forming the verge is intact. If it's cracked or missing, high winds could lift and dislodge the tiles.

Spread the load safely
Convert your ladder for roof work with a ridge hook, if you can obtain one which fits it. For extensive work on a roof, however, hire crawl boards, which are much more comfortable than an ordinary ladder. They also spread weight more evenly and reduce the risk of tiles or slates being cracked.

Wear the right safety gear
For maximum safety, wear a hard hat when working on a roof. Strong work gloves will protect your hands from sharp edges. A tool pouch makes sure you have both hands free and reduces the chances of tools sliding down the roof. Always wear stout boots with solid soles, so the rungs don't cut into your feet, and add knee pads if you wish for extra comfort.

Safe and secure

When you've built the tower up to the required height, fit a handrail and a set of toe boards all around the platform. Hire stabilisers for towers with platform heights up to 6 m (20 ft), or tie them securely to the building at eaves level.

Using an access tower

A slot-together access tower is the safest way to reach the roof. You'll need one with a platform height of about 5 m (16 ft) to reach the eaves of a two-storey building. Choose a narrow-width tower (above) if space is restricted, such as between houses. Make sure the base of the tower is standing level and square, and spread the load on soft ground by putting boards under the legs. Fit lockable castors if the tower is on hard level ground, to make it secure, but easily moved.

Firm base for the feet

One of the most useful accessories for improving ladder safety is a base stabiliser, which can be bought or hired. The high-friction base resists slipping when the ladder is standing on a hard surface. It also spreads the load and stops the feet of the ladder from sinking into soft ground.

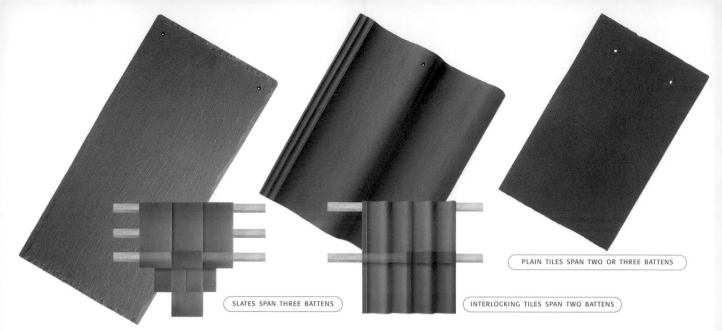

SLATES SPAN THREE BATTENS

INTERLOCKING TILES SPAN TWO BATTENS

PLAIN TILES SPAN TWO OR THREE BATTENS

roofs Replacing damaged tiles and slates

Nibs, nails or clips

How you replace a broken tile depends on how it is fixed to the underlying batten. Most plain tiles are made with nibs projecting from their top back edge, that hook over the batten and are nailed in place every fourth or fifth row. Interlocking tiles are often held with nails, or by clips nailed to the batten. But you won't be able to tell just by looking, unless you can see the underside of the tiles from the loft space.

Ripping through rusty nails

Hire a tool called a slate ripper to hook round and cut through the nails that secure slates and tiles to their battens. Most tiles are not nailed in place but all slates are fixed with two nails—usually around half-way up, but sometimes at the top.

Work from the underside

Hire a slate cutter if you need to trim a lot of slates to size. Work with the top surface of the slate downwards, so that the edges break away slightly along the cutting line. This creates a bevel like the weathered edges of the existing slates on the roof surface.

Alternatively, hold the slate bevelled side down on your workbench and align the cutting line with the bench edge. Then chop it with a bricklayer's trowel, using the bench edge as a guide.

Release single lap tiles

Try to push up the tiles in the course above the broken one (far left). Then lift the edge of the tile overlapping one neighbour and twist it to disengage the interlock with the other.

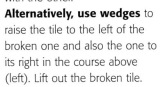

Alternatively, use wedges to raise the tile to the left of the broken one and also the one to its right in the course above (left). Lift out the broken tile.

To remove a plain clay tile, tap wedges under the two tiles in the row above it. Then slide a bricklayer's trowel under the broken tile so you can lift its nibs off the batten over which they are hooked. Slide the new tile into place and remove the wedges.

If any of the tiles are nailed, free them first with a slate ripper (above centre).

1 Slide slate ripper under damaged slate, hook barb round nail and give tool a sharp blow to cut through nail. Remove slate

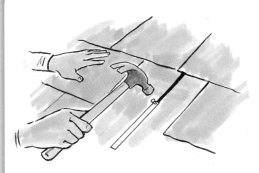

2 Locate timber batten visible between slates exposed by removed slate, and fix tingle with galvanised nail

3 Slide new slate into place. Fold end of tingle over bottom edge of slate, then double it back on itself to stop snow and ice forcing clip open

roofs

roofs Replacing damaged tiles and slates

Cut and fit a tingle

As you can't nail a replacement slate in place, use a tingle—a narrow strip of lead or zinc—instead. Cut it to the length of the exposed area of slate plus about 50 mm (2 in), and nail it to the tiling batten between the exposed slates. Its lower end is then folded up to hold the replacement slate in place.

Drill holes for nails

Use a masonry bit to make nail holes in a new slate. Lay the slate on a scrap of board or a bed of sand and drill from the underside. When the bit breaks through, it will chip off a bit of slate and form a countersink for the nail head.

More grip for ridge tiles

Before you bed a loose ridge tile on fresh mortar, brush on some PVA adhesive to improve the bond. If you can't chip off the old mortar that bedded the loose tile without damaging the tiles beneath, stick it back to the old mortar with roof and gutter sealant. Don't fill the gap at the apex of the roof with mortar. This space ensures that air can circulate round the ridge board and keep the timber dry.

Hide conspicuous replacements

If you're replacing a slate or tile on a conspicuous part of the roof and the new one is a poor match, borrow an existing one from an unobtrusive part of the roof and use that instead. Fit the new tile in place of the borrowed one.

Sealing cracked slates

Squeeze roof-and-gutter sealant from a cartridge gun into cracks in slates or tiles (far left). Alternatively, cover them with self-adhesive flashing tape. Brush some flashing primer onto the slate first. Then cut the tape to size, peel off the backing paper and press it in place. Run an old wallpaper seam roller over the tape to bed it down firmly (left).

A new lease of life

Extend the life of an old flat roof with a repair kit. There are several available, all of which involve sandwiching a layer of reinforcement fabric between coats of liquid waterproofer. The roof surface must be dry and as dust-free as possible. Apply a generous coat of waterproofer with an old soft-bristled broom. Then unroll the fabric, overlapping the edges of adjoining lengths, and brush on a second coat of waterproofer. Let this dry before applying a third coat (and a fourth one if it's recommended). Wear old shoes for the job—along with the broom, they'll only be fit for throwing away afterwards.

roofs Fast fixes for felt roofs

Save the stone chippings

The chippings on a flat roof protect the felt from overheating in the sun and the degradation caused by sunlight. Over time they tend to get washed into the gutter and then down the drain. Cover the top of the downpipe with a fine mesh to prevent this, and rescue chippings from the gutter to scatter over any bald patches on the roof surface.

Solar-reflective coating is an alternative to chippings, but needs renewing periodically to maintain its effectiveness.

Stand on boards

Flat roofs are generally not designed for access. If you have to climb onto one to clean windows or to paint an exterior wall, lay boards down to spread your weight. Don't walk on the unprotected roof–your weight will push the chippings through the felt—and take care not to drop heavy tools. If you stand a ladder on a flat roof, rest its feet on a board, with a batten screwed along the outside edge to stop the feet sliding outwards.

Tape over a split

Scrape chippings from the surrounding area (far left) and get rid of any moisture trapped in the split, speeding up the process with a hot-air gun if you have one. Fill the split with bituminous mastic, then prime the area round the split with a bitumen primer and allow it to dry. Cover the area with a piece of self-adhesive roofing repair tape.

Bed the tape down firmly by running an old wallpaper seam roller over it a few times (left). If you suspect that the split lies directly over a joint between underlying decking panels, continue the repair all the way to the roof edge.

roofs Fast fixes for felt roofs

Stick down the seams
Loose seams in roofing felt can be lifted and torn by high winds. Use roofing mastic or cold-applied felt adhesive to stick them down before this happens.

Release chippings with heat
Use a wide scraper to remove loose chippings from areas needing repair. If they are stuck to the felt, a hot-air gun will release them.

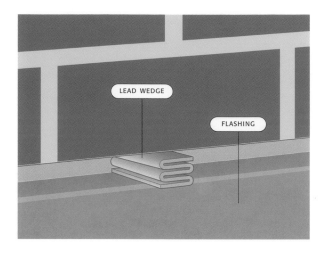

Mending blisters in felt
Use a trimming knife to make a cross-cut over the blister, taking care not to cut through the layer of felt below. Peel back the flaps and thoroughly dry the area underneath using a hot-air gun. Spread cold-applied felt adhesive to the exposed area and press the flaps back into place. When bonded, seal the cuts with a heavy-duty bituminous mastic and replace the chippings.

Secure loose lead flashings
A lead flashing waterproofs the join between, for example, a porch or lean-to and a wall. The top edge of the flashing should be wedged into a brickwork joint, then mortared in place. If a flashing needs refixing, replace any missing wedges before repointing. Cut small strips of lead and fold them concertina-fashion, then tap them into place with a mallet.

Protect a metal roof
If you live in a house with a flat roof covered in lead, zinc or copper, prevent acid attack from moss or lichen by treating it regularly with a fungicide. Patch any splits in the metal sheet with self-adhesive flashing strip.

Two ways to insulate
Flat roofs can rot from below as well as above. Warm air from the room below condenses in the ceiling space, attacking the underside of the decking panels. The solution is to insulate the roof, after carrying out any necessary remedial work to the deck, and this can be done in two ways.
A 'warm' roof is formed by laying rigid polystyrene sheet insulation over the existing decking and then adding a new layer of decking and roofing felt on top. It is the better option if the existing roof deck is still relatively sound.
A 'cold' roof has insulation beneath the roof deck, plus a ventilation gap to ensure that air can reach the underside of the deck. This can be installed only if the deck has to be completely replaced or if the ceiling below is removed.

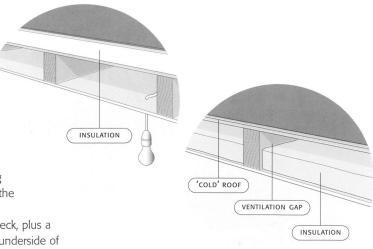

Mending a corrugated plastic roof

Cutting corrugated plastic

To hold the sheet you are sawing securely, support it on a pile of other sheets. Alternatively clamp it between two lengths of wood positioned parallel and close to the cutting line. In cold weather, bring the sheets indoors for sawing as the plastic becomes brittle and may crack in low temperatures.

Don't crack the sheet

Avoid cracking plastic sheets when you screw them down by drilling the holes a little oversize–through the corrugation ridges, not the valleys. Then make sure that the washers and any spacers are properly positioned, and don't overtighten the screws.

Making screw holes

Drilling holes for the fixings can be tricky, since the drill bit tends to slip on the curved surface of the corrugated sheet. Provide a little friction for the bit by sticking a small piece of masking tape over the drilling position.

Replacing a damaged sheet

Remove the fixings, slide the damaged sheet out and push a wooden wedge between the rafter and the adjacent sheet that overlapped it. Slide the new panel under the raised sheet, allowing an overlap of two corrugations.

Weatherproofing joints with walls

Use matching prefabricated flashing units to weatherproof the junction between the roof and a wall. Their hinged upstands can be adapted to any gradient and are designed to be lapped by a conventional metal or felt flashing (right).

Seal the eaves against draughts and water penetration by fitting flexible foam plastic filler strips between the bottom edge of the sheet and the top of the beam supporting it.

roofs

gutters Escape routes for rainwater

Don't ignore the problem

The weight of trapped water can bring a gutter crashing down—a real danger if it is a cast-iron one. Deal with blockages as soon as you see an overflow.

Make a gutter scoop by cutting the bottom from a suitably shaped plastic motor-oil container and use the spout as a handle—it will hold much more than a garden trowel. Empty debris into a bucket hung from the ladder.

Bung a rag temporarily into the top of the downpipe to prevent rubbish being swept into it as you scoop.

Extra brackets cure a sag

Install extra support brackets if a gutter is sagging. They should be fixed about every 600–900 mm (2–3 ft). Scoop out any water lying in the gutter. Then, with the aid of a string line or straightedge, position and fix extra brackets on the fascia making sure that they are in line with the existing ones.

Test the fall by pouring water into the gutter at its highest point. If puddles form, the brackets need adjusting.

Free the downpipe

Water seeping from a joint on a section of downpipe indicates a blockage in the pipe somewhere between the affected joint and the outlet. Try unblocking the pipe from ground level first. Cover the gully to keep debris out, then push a length of stiff wire or a running garden hose up the pipe to shift the rubbish. If this doesn't work, unblock the pipe from the top using drain rods.

A wire mesh excluder fitted at the top of the downpipe will stop potential blockages such as leaves, moss and tennis balls from getting into the pipe in the first place.

Reach out with a rake

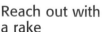

To avoid having to move the ladder frequently, make a gutter rake. Cut a small piece of 9 mm or 12 mm plywood, or solid wood, to match the shape of the gutter. Use a screw to fix this to the end of a length of broom handle, about 1.2 m (4 ft) long, then attach a loop of cord to the other end to secure it to your wrist. Finally, drill some holes in the end piece of the rake for water to escape through.

Keep autumn leaves out of gutters by fitting plastic mesh leafguards if trees overhang the roof, but if you do need to put up a ladder to clean them, make sure it is fitted with a stand-off (see page 32) and do not rest it on the guttering.

Cast-iron hints and tips

Heavy metal

Cast-iron gutters and pipes are heavy—don't try to manhandle them from the top of a ladder. They also shatter if dropped, and corrode to sharp edges, so wear sturdy gloves.

Use a scaffold tower, and knock some 150 mm round wire nails into the fascia as temporary gutter supports, angling the nails so that the gutter cannot slip off them. Get help to remove and replace long lengths of gutter.

Marrying new to old

If only part of the cast-iron guttering has corroded, you can buy new—for a price—or scour architectural salvage yards for a matching replacement. Alternatively, ask a builders' merchant if a plastic adaptor is available for joining on some plastic guttering with a similar profile.

Clean and seal

Putty was traditionally used to seal the joints between sections of cast-iron and aluminium guttering, but a suitable sealant is far better for the job. If you're renovating either of these gutter types, use an old chisel to remove the putty. Then make sure the area is dry before you re-make the joint with the sealant.

Have a hacksaw handy to dismantle sections; the nuts and bolts securing them are usually rusted and seized. Saw through nuts and punch bolts out from below—but take care, cast iron is brittle. Replace them with mushroom-head plated gutter bolts and nuts.

STAGES IN
FITTING A PLASTIC GUTTER

1 Drive nail into fascia board at top end of gutter run, about 25 mm (1 in) below edge of tiles. Attach string line and allow fall of 6 mm (¼ in) for every 1 m (3 ft) of eaves length

2 Stretch string line between bracket and nail as a fixing guide for remaining brackets

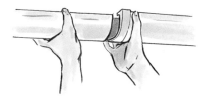

3 Fix brackets, remove line and insert gutter in brackets, back edge first. Snap-fit into retaining clips on brackets

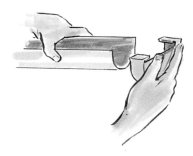

4 Cut last section of gutter so that it extends beyond end of roof by about 50 mm (2 in). Fit stop-end before fixing section in place

HALF-ROUND GUTTER

HALF-ROUND GUTTER

HALF-ROUND GUTTER

RUNNING OUTLET

CLIP

90° ANGLE

SUPPORT BRACKET

OFFSET BEND

DOWNPIPE

STOP-END

gutters Putting up a new system

OFFSET BEND

DOWNPIPE

Centre option splits the load

On a long roof, consider placing the downpipe halfway along the eaves. This halves the weight of water that the gutter has to carry. It also halves the gap between the gutter and the edge of the tiles or slates, created by the fall of the gutter, so there is less chance of wind driving rain onto the wall in the gap between the edge of the roof and the gutter.

PIPE CLIP

RAINWATER SHOE

Water for the garden

Diverter kits, available from garden centres and DIY stores, enable you to fill a rainwater butt from the downpipe. The diverter returns water to the downpipe before the butt overflows. **Raise the butt** on bricks or a stand, so a watering can will fit under the tap.

Cutting it fine

Always cut lengths of plastic guttering and downpipe at ground level. Use a hacksaw or tenon saw, and remove the burr with a file, so that it can be neatly joined to another length. To cut round pipe squarely, wrap a piece of paper around it so that the edges line up, then stick it down with tape. The edge of the paper provides a cutting guide.

Fixed and replaceable seals

The rubber seals on gutter unions eventually perish. Sometimes they are bonded and you have to buy an entire new union to stop the leak, but with some brands the seal can be detached from its groove and replaced separately.

Cure dislocated joints

Plastic gutters expand in the heat—you can hear them creaking in the sun—and sometimes sections come apart at the unions. Check the joints after a spell of hot weather. Tap the end of the gutter back into place with a mallet if it has pulled out of a union.

brickwork Facelifts for outside walls

Turn a damaged brick about-face

Frost-damaged bricks should be replaced, but if you cannot find a matching one turn the damaged brick around. Use a power drill, on hammer action, and a masonry bit to make holes in the joint all around the brick to its full depth. Chip away the remaining mortar with a plugging chisel, prise the brick out, then mortar it back into the hole, back to front.

Give salt the brush-off

A white powdery deposit, called efflorescence, is common on new brick walls. It is caused by salts in the bricks reacting with rainwater. Don't try to wash it off or you will make the problem last longer. Instead, brush the affected area with a dry bristle brush until it stops recurring.

Avoid harsh measures

Think hard before you have the outside of your home sandblasted or cleaned with acidic chemicals. Although the results can look effective, both methods are harsh because they remove a layer from the surface of the walls. Like a piece of old furniture that has been rubbed down and lost its patina, your house could lose some of its character if you try to make the old bricks look like new.

Lock out moisture

Flakes of brick lying along the foot of a wall in winter are a sure sign of frost damage. The longer the problem is ignored the worse it will get, so as soon as the weather warms up apply a colourless, microporous water-repellent sealant, which will allow the bricks to breathe but will keep out moisture. If you're going to apply it with a spray gun, choose a still day, wear a respirator, and cover up to keep the fluid off your skin.

Treat the whole wall because the waterproofer can alter the colour of the bricks very slightly. Otherwise, the wall will look patchy, with treated areas being darker.

Water works

You can remove years of grime from bricks with nothing more elaborate than a stiff bristle brush and a running hose. Work in horizontal bands from the top to the bottom of a wall, inspecting the pointing as you go. Use a solution of household ammonia—about half a cup in a bucket of water—on really grimy areas. Wear goggles and rubber gloves to protect your eyes and hands.

Draw stains with a paste

Remove stubborn stains like tar and oil with a paste made from fuller's earth or ground chalk, mixed with paraffin or white spirit. Wipe over the stain with a little of the solvent used to make the paste, then spread a layer of paste over it (below left). Finally, tape a plastic bag or a piece of aluminium foil on top to stop the poultice drying out (below right). Over a few days the paste will draw the stain out and you can wash the bricks clean.

WEATHERSTRUCK JOINT

BUCKET-HANDLE JOINT

FLUSH JOINT

A profile for the elements

The way pointing is finished is crucial to repelling rain.
Weatherstruck and bucket-handle joints are best, although
flush joints often look best when you want to disguise small
areas of new pointing.

brickwork Patching up the joints

Make a mortarboard

A scrap of 6 mm or 9 mm external plywood makes a good
mortarboard. Ideally, you want a piece about 400 x 400 mm
(16 x 16 in). Drill a hole for a screw in the centre of the
piece and fix it to the end of a short length of broom handle.
Hold the board tight against the wall, directly below the joint
being repointed. This minimises the amount of wet mortar
getting on the face of the bricks or dropping on the ground.

Making a bucket-handle joint

Traditionally, bricklayers used a short piece of
metal bucket handle to 'tool' a bucket-handle
joint. You can imitate the effect by dragging
a short piece of hosepipe along the joint.

Stick to the recipe

Buy a bag of premixed mortar containing a plasticiser for a small area of repointing. Otherwise, it's more economical to make your own; mix 1 part of ordinary Portland cement or masonry cement into 6 parts of clean building sand. Add the recommended volume of a liquid mortar plasticiser or 1 part of hydrated lime if you're using Portland cement (masonry cement contains a plasticiser). Don't use washing-up liquid instead of lime or plasticiser, it is detrimental to the mortar.

Adding extra cement will make the pointing too hard, so that bricks absorb moisture more readily than the mortar, making them liable to frost damage. Adding extra water to a mix that is going dry will weaken it, although it is a good idea to flick a little water into the raked joints with a brush, to stop the mortar drying out before you can achieve a neat finish.

Fashion a frenchman

Bricklayers use a bladed tool called a frenchman to trim away wet mortar neatly from the base of weatherstruck joints. You can make one for yourself from a strip of thin metal. Bend about 25 mm (1 in) at one end over at an angle of 90°. Wear goggles in case the metal snaps.

Make a guide from a straight piece of 75 x 25 mm planed timber about 600 mm (2 ft) long to use with the frenchman. Pin two small pieces of hardboard or thin plywood on one side of the piece of wood, near the ends. These allow clearance for the tip of the frenchman between the guide and the wall. Fix a handle on the other side of the guide.

STAGES IN REPOINTING A WALL

1 Rake out old mortar to a depth of about 12 mm (½ in), using a plugging chisel. Hire a hammer drill and mortar-raking chisel for large areas

2 Load mortar onto board with trowel. Wet joints, then push mortar into joints, filling vertical ones first

3 Finish joints with pointing trowel or special pointing tool

4 Before mortar dries, blend new pointing with old using a sponge. Carefully clean face of brickwork with soft dry brush

rendering Repairs to a faulty coating

Tap and listen
The bond between rendering and the wall fails when moisture seeps between the two and freezes. Tap the wall with the handle of a screwdriver, to establish how large an area sounds hollow and needs stripping off and replacing.

Testing for subsidence
Cracks in rendering could be a sign of subsidence. Call in a surveyor, who will stick glass strips across the cracks at several points with epoxy adhesive. If any strips break because the crack is widening, subsidence is the likely cause.

Paint over fine cracks
Fill hairline cracks in rendering with a coat of exterior masonry paint. If the surface is powdery, brush away loose material and seal the area with stabilising primer before painting.

Improve the bond
Scratch base coats of render to provide a key for subsequent ones to bond with. You can do this with the edge of a trowel or by making a 'scratch comb'. Drive a row of nails through a short length of batten so that the points project by about 6 mm (¼ in). Allow about 20 minutes for the render to start drying before scratching it.

Undercut for a strong key
Chop loose rendering off the wall with a brick bolster and club hammer. When you reach sound material, undercut the edges so that the new render will key well with the old coating and resist fracturing along the join as it dries.

Reinforce with metal lath
If, when you remove loose rendering, the brickwork below has deteriorated, fix a piece of expanded metal lath over it with galvanised or masonry nails before applying the new render.

A better bond

New render will stick on the wall better if you paint on a coating made up of 1 part cement and 1 part sharp sand mixed into PVA sealer, diluted with an equal volume of water. Use a stiff brush to 'stab' the mixture onto the masonry. When it dries, the surface of the wall should feel like coarse abrasive paper, providing a key for the new render.

Repairing a bottom edge
If the bottom edge of rendering breaks away from the wall, nail a temporary batten across the gap to maintain a straight line and support the wet render while it dries. Make sure the rendering does not cover the damp-proof course (DPC), otherwise a 'bridge' will be created for moisture absorbed by the wall from the ground.

Restoring a corner

Repairing broken render around an external corner is a two-phase operation. Fix a batten to contain the edge of the wet render at the corner while you fill the gap on one wall. Then reposition the batten on the repaired side of the corner and fill the adjoining wall.

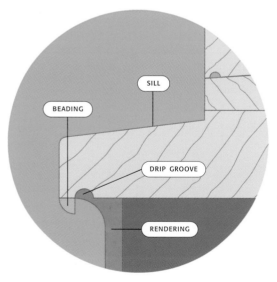

SILL
BEADING
DRIP GROOVE
RENDERING

Keep sills clean

Careless rendering can block the drip groove under projecting windowsills, allowing water to creep all the way under the frame. For a quick solution, pin a strip of quadrant beading under the front edge of the sill. In the longer term, unblock the drip groove.

1 Cut away loose material to a sound edge. Brush away dust, then prime bare brickwork with PVA adhesive sealer

2 Apply first coat using steel float, finishing about 6 mm (¼ in) below surface of the surrounding render

3 After about 20 minutes, scratch first coat with trowel or scratch comb to provide key for finishing coat

4 After 12 hours, apply finishing coat with wood float and rule off. Blend into existing surface using a damp sponge

rendering

rendering Repairs to a faulty coating

Blending new with old

Overfill the area you are patching, then use the edge of a length of timber—a piece of an old floorboard is idea—to 'rule' or scrape off the excess. Push the piece of board across the wet render with a sawing action until the repaired surface is flush with the old render, knocking the end of the board on the ground to remove the waste that gathers on it.

Use a wood float to finish the rendering; a steel one brings water and cement, and lime particles to the surface, causing fine cracks to form in the rendering as it dries.

Recipe for a successful finish

The right ratio

A good rendering mix consists of 6 parts plastering sand (also called rendering sand or fine sharp sand) to 1 part cement and 1 part hydrated lime. Mix the cement and lime together first, then blend in the sand before adding water. A liquid plasticiser is an alternative to the lime; add the recommended volume to the water. Masonry cement already contains a plasticiser. Mix it in a ratio of 1 part of cement to 5 parts sand.

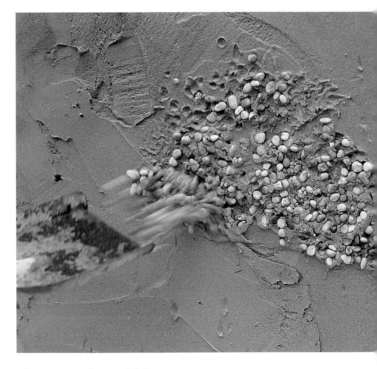

Appropriate additives

Give yourself longer to work with wet render in hot weather by adding a drying retardant to the mix. If there's a risk of freezing, add a frost-proofing additive to the mix.

Economy mix

A small bag of dry ready-mixed mortar may be adequate for a small rendering job. For larger areas, save money by buying the cement and rendering sand separately and making the mix yourself.

Throw on the pebbles

Pebbledashing is fairly easy to patch. Buy some matching pebbles from a builders' merchant, wash and drain them then, with a coal shovel or dustpan, throw a scoopful at the wet render. Wash any pebbles that fall off at the first attempt before reusing them. When an adequate layer is sticking to the wall, gently press the pebbles in with a wooden plasterer's float.

Colour match cement

Add a powder pigment to dry cement in a colour to match your paint to reduce the number of coats of paint required. Use white cement if you're going to paint the rendering white.

cladding Boarding exterior walls

SINGLE-FIXED   DOUBLE-FIXED   HIDDEN NAILING   SHIPLAP   TONGUE AND GROOVE

Five ways to nail boards

There are several ways of nailing wood cladding to the framework of timber battens that supports it on the house wall. Which method you choose will depend on what type of cladding you're fitting and whether you want the fixings concealed or not.

Single-fixed boards are secured by nails driven through their faces and missing the board below.

Double-fixed boards are fixed by nails that pass through the board below too.

Hidden nailing involves driving the nails in close to the top edge of each board so the nail heads are hidden by the bottom edge of the next board. This technique provides good protection to the nail head but offers little resistance to the board being levered off.

Beware of moisture barriers

Wooden cladding is often used as an external wall finish on a timber-framed house, and a moisture barrier of building paper may be fitted beneath the battens to which the boards are secured. Keep an eye out for it when you are replacing damaged boards, and take care not to puncture it.

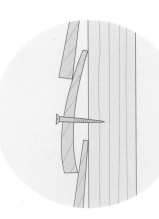

Flattening a bulge

To flatten warped and bulging boards, insert corrosion-resistant woodscrews along their centre line and into the batten behind. Drill clearance holes through the boards first to avoid splitting them. Countersink the screws and cover their heads with exterior grade filler, or with a coloured wood stopper if the boards are stained rather than painted.

cladding Boarding exterior walls

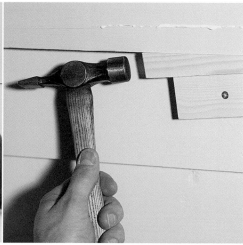

Doing the splits

To repair a split in timber cladding, lever the split open and squeeze in some exterior PVA woodworking adhesive (left). Tape may be strong enough to hold the split closed while the glue dries. Otherwise, screw a small block to the board below and drive a wooden wedge between it and the bottom edge of the repaired board (right).

Removing damaged timber

Reaching hidden nails

Gain access to a nail securing the board above the one you're replacing by driving in two wedges. Then slide in a mini-hacksaw and cut through the nail.

Cutting a broken board

Saw through a damaged board directly above the centre of a support batten. Drive two wooden wedges under the edge of the board on either side of the batten. This provides clearance for the saw as you cut through the board. Then wedge a piece of scrap wood into the gap so that it covers the face of the good board below, protecting it from the saw blade. **Cut as far as possible** with the tenon saw. Then wedge up the board above the cut board and finish the cut with a padsaw (keyhole saw).

'Popping' exposed nails

To remove exposed nails, use a crowbar to lever up the bottom edge of the board, resting it on a piece of scrap wood to protect the face of the board below. Then hold the crowbar blade beside the nail head and tap it to push the board back and pop out the nail.

Fixing tricks for a professional finish

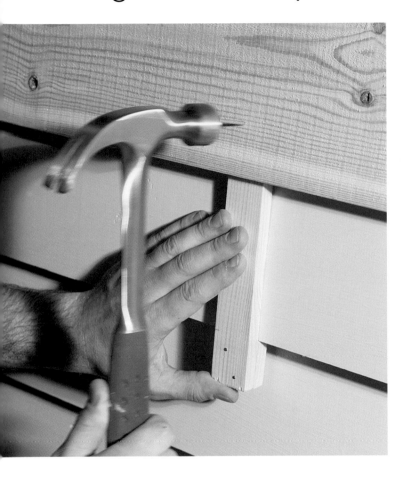

A spacer for an even overlap
Keep the overlap of the boards the same by making a spacer from a couple of pieces of scrap wood. Mark the overlap you want on the longer piece and pin the smaller offcut to it.

Avoid stains from rusty nails
Use galvanised roundhead nails to fix the boards. They won't corrode and cause rust stains as steel nails do. Punch the nail heads in slightly and fill the dimple with exterior filler.

One-handed trick
If you don't have a spare hand to hold a nail, tuck it firmly into the claw of the hammer, point facing outwards, and drive it into the board. Then unhook the claw and finish driving the nail.

Add some insulation
If you have to strip a large area of cladding, fit sheets of rigid polystyrene insulation between the battens and cover them with waterproof building paper before fitting new boards.

Avoid a patchwork look
Replace whole boards rather than small sections if rot is widespread, to avoid creating a patchwork of repairs.

Protect before fixing
Treat every surface of a new board with preservative or wood primer before fixing it in place. This will delay the onset of rot in the future.

A support while you start to nail
If you are working on your own, bend a narrow strip of soft sheet metal into an S shape and hook it over the top edge of the previous board to support one end of the next board while you nail up its other end. This will not work if you are fixing cladding between projecting masonry piers, however, as they will prevent you from slipping the hook out for re-use after nailing up each board.
Use old cut pieces of board you remove from around openings, fixtures or other obstructions as templates when cutting replacements to size.

Prevent split ends
You can stop the wood splitting when nailing near the end of a board by drilling pilot holes first. For fixings elsewhere, blunt the nails first by hammering their points on concrete.

cladding

inside

floors Discover what lies underneath the boards

Open the airways

Clear rubbish from the crawl space beneath a suspended timber ground floor. It can block the airbricks in outside walls and obstruct the voids in the honeycombed walls that support the floor joists, preventing air from circulating freely.

Preservation in a pellet

In older houses the ends of the joists are often built into the external walls. Check their condition carefully. If the timber is sound, drill a hole in the top of each joist and insert a wood preservative pellet in it, as close to the wall as possible.

Always cover the hole

Replace floorboards loosely if you have to interrupt work. Hang a sign on the outside of the room door warning of loose boards until you have replaced them permanently.

Are the joists dry?

Hire a moisture meter to assess the condition of the joists. If the reading is over 20 per cent, there is a risk that rot could set in or may have done so already, and underfloor ventilation should be improved as soon as possible. Use a torch to illuminate the underfloor void, and a mirror fixed to the end of a stick to spot any signs of deterioration in the timbers.

Locate the services

Hire a cable and pipe detector to locate underfloor services before nailing or screwing down loose floorboards. Services often run immediately below the boards—in notches cut across the tops of the joists—making them very vulnerable to accidental damage.

Easy underfloor access

For access to essential fittings such as a stoptap, cross-cut the overlying board between adjacent joists. Support the replaced section on battens secured to the sides of the joists with screws.

While the carpet is up

If you're going to have a fitted carpet replaced, rip up the old one well in advance. Then you can check the condition of your floorboards before they become inaccessible again.

Marked for future reference

Take the opportunity to record the routes of cables and pipes while a floor is up. You can mark their positions straight onto the boards, unless you intend to leave them bare.

Raise the temperature

If all the boards in a downstairs room have to be lifted, take the chance to increase warmth and lower heating bills by installing underfloor insulation. There are two types available.

Lay nylon garden netting across the joists to support the same type of glass fibre insulation blanket that's used in lofts (see page 170). Wear gloves, safety goggles and a mask when working with this material. Draw the netting up tight before nailing down the boards (left), so that the blanket does not sag and allow cold air to get past it.

Cut rigid insulation, made from light polystyrene foam, to fit snugly between joists. Support the slabs on battens nailed to the sides of the joists (below).

Solutions for sagging floors

If a timber ground floor moves noticeably when you jump up and down on it, the ends of built-in floor joists may be rotten due to damp in the walls. Cure the problem by lifting the boards and sawing through the joists at least 600 mm (2 ft) beyond the last signs of rot. Bolt new preservative-treated wood to the sawn joists, using toothed timber connectors. Support the ends in joist hangers—galvanised steel shoes secured to the walls.

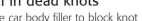

Fill in dead knots

Use car body filler to block knot holes in boards before laying vinyl sheet flooring. If you don't, pressure from chair legs and similar objects could pierce and damage it.

floors

59

floors Ways to hide gaps and silence squeaks

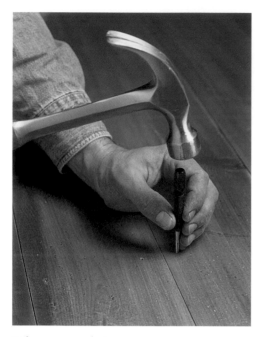

Quieten with a shim

If you can get at the underside of a squeaky board from below—to the ground floor from a cellar, for example—tap a thin wooden shim dipped in woodworking adhesive into the gap between the board and the joist, to quieten it.

Take a punch to the heads

A squeaky board can sometimes be cured by driving the nails a little deeper with a nail punch. Locate the punch carefully so it doesn't skid off the nail and scar the board when you strike it.
Talcum powder or chalk dust, brushed into the joints between squeaky boards, usually silences them temporarily.

Tap a wedge into a gap

You can fill wide gaps between boards with thin lengths of square-edge moulding, bought at a timber merchant or DIY store. Plane them to a slight wedge shape, then apply a little woodworking adhesive before tapping them into the gaps, thin edge first. Plane them down to floor level when the adhesive has set, then stain them to match the boards.

Exchange nails for screws

Stop squeaky boards by replacing nails with screws. Use the old nail holes and choose screws the same length as the nails but thicker, so they bite into the joist but don't go any deeper. You don't want to puncture a hidden pipe or cable.

When the boards have to be taken up

Ripping off the tongues

Before lifting a tongue-and-groove (t & g) floorboard, you will need to cut through the jointed edges. The best tool for the job is a circular saw because you can set the blade depth. Lock the depth gauge to 15 mm to avoid cutting into a joist, pipe or cable. If you need to remove just a short length of board, a handsaw will do the job; hold it at a low angle so the blade does not project too far into the underfloor space.

Crosscut beside a joist

A floorboard saw is designed for cutting out a section of floorboard without marking the ones on either side. Make the cut alongside a joist (look for the nailing lines that mark the centres of the joists). Then use a straightedge and sharp trimming knife to score a guideline for the saw. Angle the saw slightly off the vertical so that the cut is bevelled; this makes the sawn line less noticeable when the board is replaced. **A jigsaw can also be used,** although you will have to drill a hole through the board to admit the saw blade. Make sure there are no cables or pipes in the way of the blade.

What sort of boards?

Find out whether you've got square-edged floorboards (butted up against one another) or tongue-and-groove ones by trying to insert the blade of a knife between the boards. With square-edged boards, there won't be any obstruction. If the knife won't go down more than about 6 mm (¼ in), it's because the blade has found a tongue.

floors

floors Laying down the floor

Mark it from the gap
When fitting a new length of board, lay it the right way up over the gap left by the old board. Mark the ends of the gap across the edges of the new board with a pencil and try square. Join the marks across the top of the board with a straightedge and trimming knife, then saw along this guideline.

The right nail for the job
Traditional cut brads are still the best nail for fixing floorboards. The shanks grip the joists better than oval or lost-head nails and the heads can be driven just below the board surface. The length of the brads should be two-and-a-half times the thickness of the floorboards.

Tiling onto a suspended floor
Ceramic tiles can be laid over old floorboards if the boards are covered first with 15 mm exterior grade plywood; otherwise the natural movement of the boards will cause the joints between the tiles to crack. Make sure that the joists are strong enough to bear the extra weight, and remember that the floor level will be raised by the thickness of the ply, adhesive and tiles.

A batten for the end
Screw battens to the joists to support the ends of the replaced board. They should fit tight under the boards on either side, to ensure the replaced board is level with its neighbours.

Grouped for effect
If you are laying new floorboards right across a room and intend to varnish them, try to group the boards so that the grain pattern and colour of the wood disguises the joins.

Tailor boards, not joists
If a replacement board is thicker than the existing ones, take the waste out of the board, not the joists. Measure the difference exactly, then use a saw and chisel to notch the underside of the board where it is supported on joists.

Driving the boards together tightly

Floor cramps can be hired for driving boards together tightly before nailing. Alternatively, a pair of wedges can be used—either wooden ones sawn from offcuts or the tough plastic sort sold in DIY stores. Lay three or four boards loose, with the grooved edge exposed if they are the tongue-and-groove type. Then nail a spare length of board across the joists to retain the wedges. Tighten the boards by driving the wedges against each other, preferably using two hammers.

Put down hardboard first

The joins between floorboards can show through the surface of floorcoverings such as linoleum, vinyl and cork, spoiling their appearance. Prevent this by covering the old floor with hardboard after first sinking any protruding nails with a nail punch. Fix the sheets down with hardboard pins, driving their diamond-shaped heads in flush with the hardboard.

Lever edge boards into place

Leave an expansion gap of about 9 mm (⅜ in)—which will be covered by the skirting board—between edge boards and walls. To get an edge board tight against the one next to it, insert a batten into the gap and use it to lever the board into place. Then maintain the tension on the batten by tapping a wooden wedge between it and the wall while you nail the board down.

Save the ceiling

Old ceilings can crack when boards are nailed down on the floor above. If yours are fragile, screw boards down instead, countersinking the screw heads and hiding them with wood plugs or dowels if the boards are being left bare.

Secret nailing for exposed floorboards

Tongue-and-groove floorboards can be secret-nailed, leaving the floor surface unmarked by fixings. If you are laying a complete new floor, hire a floor nailer (below) to help you finish the job more quickly. To drive a nail from the tool's magazine, simply strike the plunger with the mallet supplied.

floors

floors Laying coverings on concrete and boards

Combating rising damp

Old concrete floors were often laid straight onto the ground and can be damp as a result. If the damp is not too bad, it may be possible to keep the floor dry by coating the surface of the concrete with an epoxy resin or rubber/bitumen coating, but have the problem assessed by an expert first.

Levelling uneven concrete

An uneven concrete floor surface can be treated with a self-smoothing compound, which will raise the floor level by about 10 mm (⅜ in). Remember: you need to trowel the finish out quickly to achieve good results.

Test for dampness

If you suspect that a concrete floor is damp, try this test before laying a floor covering over the top. Leave a solid object on the floor overnight so that air can't get at the area covered; if there's a dark patch when you move it the next day, there is damp in the floor.

You can hire an instrument called a hygrometer to measure the moisture content of the floor. Knowing how damp the floor is will help you to choose the appropriate treatment.

Remove with a spade

A spade is a good tool for removing old floor tiles that have been stuck to the sub-floor. File a sharp edge on the blade, then slide it under the tile edges and lever them up.
Hire a floor-tile stripper for removing large areas of flooring. The machine has a vibrating blade that can be adjusted to suit the old floor covering and the strength of the adhesive.

Incentives for hard labour

Break up an old concrete floor yourself if you are having a new floor laid and want to save money. Locate water and gas pipes before you start. Hire a concrete breaker to make the job easier; one with vibration damping will be less tiring to use and you won't get 'vibration white finger'. Wear ear defenders, work gloves, goggles and steel-toed footwear.

Conceal board edges

Cover old floorboards with hardboard sheets before laying vinyl on top. Condition the sheets by brushing 500 ml of water onto the mesh side of each one, then stacking them flat in the room, mesh sides together, for 48 hours. Then nail them mesh side up.

Stiffen floors before tiling

Cover floorboards with 15 mm exterior-grade plywood before laying ceramic or quarry tiles. Without this, the natural movement of the boards will cause the tile joints to crack. Seal the ply with wood primer first. Remember that the thickness of ply, adhesive and tile will raise the floor by up to 40 mm (1½ in).

Buy all tiles together

Purchase all the floor tiles you need at the same time, and ensure that batch numbers match, otherwise you may encounter colour variations.

The professional's tool

A notched steel trowel is well worth buying if you have a large floor to cover. It enables you to spread the adhesive much more quickly and evenly than you can with the small plastic spreader included with flooring adhesives.

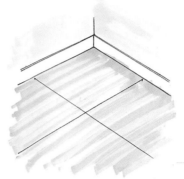

1 Snap chalk lines between midpoints of opposite walls to find centre of room. Check that they cross at right angles

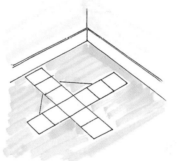

2 Dry-lay rows of tiles along chalk lines. Then adjust row positions so cut tiles at room perimeter are equal and of reasonable size. Mark chosen starting point on floor

3 Stick down tiles in pyramid pattern, beginning at centre of room and working outwards towards each wall in turn. Then cut and fit border tiles

floors

floors Buying and storing sheet and tiles

Options in vinyl

It takes less time to lay vinyl sheet than vinyl tiles because it doesn't need adhesive, except perhaps in doorways, or careful measurement to find the centre of the room. However, packs of tiles are easier to carry, there's less wastage and cutting mistakes are usually limited to one tile (if you make an error when cutting vinyl sheet, the whole piece may be wasted). Spare tiles are also easier to store than sheet offcuts.

Storing flexible flooring

Keep vinyl and cork tiles flat in boxes and weigh down unpacked ones to stop them curling up at the edges. Store rolls of vinyl flat on the floor, not on end.

Cutting coverings to fit

Invisible seams

When joining vinyl sheet or lino, lay one piece over another, align the pattern and cut through both layers using a straightedge and a sharp trimming knife. Plan joins at 90° to windows; the seam will reflect less light and be less obvious than one parallel to them.

Avoid joins in doorways, where shoe heels are likely to catch, lift and tear the edges, and try not to place seams in line with the edges of floorboards or chipboard flooring panels. Any slight movement in the floor structure will immediately open up such a seam.

Tackling thick tiles

A professional tile cutter will cut most quarry tiles, but very thick ones may call for a power tile saw or angle grinder. The saw creates less dust and vibration, but the grinder is more useful for cutting irregular shapes. Remember to wear goggles, a mask and sturdy gloves when using either tool.

Patching sheet coverings

To repair damage to flexible sheet vinyl flooring, use an offcut saved from when the flooring was laid, or steal a patch from somewhere it won't be missed, such as under the fridge. Cut the patch oversize, lay it over the damaged area, align the pattern and tape it to the floor. Then cut through both layers using a straightedge and a sharp trimming knife. Lift out the damaged piece and insert the patch, which you may have to stick down with double-sided tape.

Replacing flexible tiles

Before trying to lift a damaged soft or flexible floor tile stuck to the floor, use a hot-air gun to heat the surface and soften the adhesive, or lay kitchen foil on top and heat it with an iron. Cut across the middle of the tile, then slide a scraper into the cut and lever the tile up—you'll be less likely to damage the edges of adjoining tiles. Keep the blade of the scraper hot and use it to remove the old adhesive from the floor.

floors Tips for a perfect finish

Checking the gaps

Maintain even joints between hard floor tiles by using a tiling gauge marked with the right gap, or fit tile spacers—either bought or cut from hardboard or ply. Mass-produced tiles are usually laid with a very narrow joint between them. Disguise size variations that occur in handmade floor tiles with wider joints—say, 9 –12 mm (⅜ –½ in).

Adhesive alert

Take great care when using flammable flooring adhesives. Follow instructions on the container, and don't nip into the next room to warm up beside a fire because clothing absorbs fumes and could burst into flames. Air work clothes outdoors when the job is done.

Follow curves closely

Make a paper template as a guide for fitting flexible tiles or sheet vinyl flooring around curves. Cut slits in the paper so you can fold the tongues up against the surface around the curve. Cut off tongues at the crease lines, then lay the template over the tile, mark the curve and cut it with a sharp knife.

Accurate holes for pipes

Fit vinyl flooring round radiator pipes by punching holes through it with a pipe offcut of the same diameter. Use a round file on the inside of the pipe to sharpen the cutting edge, then strike the other end with a hammer. Make a cut from the hole to the edge of the sheet so you can fit it around the pipe.

Allow for expansion

When laying wood strip or parquet flooring, leave an expansion gap round the perimeter of the room. Fill this with proprietary cork strip (usually sold along with the flooring) when you've finished, then hide it by pinning quadrant moulding to the skirting board. If you're fitting new skirting boards round the room, these will hide the cork strips.
In a very large room, extra expansion gaps may be needed at intervals across the floor. Ask your flooring supplier if this will be necessary.

Guard against staining

Seal porous quarry and terracotta tiles before laying them. This will prevent them becoming stained later on by the grout. Buy a branded sealer, or make up your own by mixing 2 parts of boiled linseed oil to 1 part of white spirit.
Once the tiles are laid and grouted, give them as many additional coats as they can absorb, allowing each to dry before applying the next one. Consult a specialist tile supplier about waxes and other preparations that will protect the seal and enhance the tile colour.

Brush vinyl flat

Use a soft-bristled broom to flatten vinyl sheet across a floor before you start to cut it to fit. This will press out any air trapped under the sheet.

Seal blocks first

Before laying a woodblock floor, seal the individual blocks. If you seal them after laying, the sealer is likely to stick the blocks together. Future shrinkage will then result in gaps opening up along the weakest joints (above).

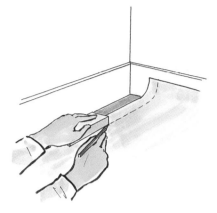

1 Pull sheet about 50 mm (2 in) away from longest wall. Then slide the block and pencil against the skirting to scribe the wall profile onto the sheet

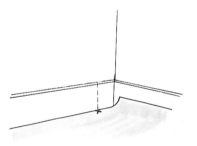

2 Cut and fit sheet against longest wall. Draw reference mark on skirting and matching mark on edge of sheet

3 Pull sheet away from next wall and mark it again in line with reference mark. Measure distance between marks, cut block to match this exactly and use block and pencil to scribe edge along next wall. Repeat for other walls

floors

plastering First steps that ensure a perfect result

What sort of construction?

Repairs to plasterboard and lath-and-plaster call for different techniques, so if you're not sure what the wall or ceiling is made of, make a small hole with a bradawl. Plasterboard is either 9.5 mm or 12.5 mm thick and can be penetrated easily; lath-and-plaster is thicker, and the timber laths are not easily pierced.

Sounding the surface

Determine the extent of loose plaster before deciding whether to patch it yourself or call in a professional. Tap the surface with your knuckles, listening for the hollow sound that indicates the plaster has 'blown' (lost its adhesion to the masonry behind). Then you can mark out the full extent of the repair.

The stud detective

If you can't work out where wall studs or ceiling joists are, drill a small angled hole through the surface and feed in a length of wire until you feel it hit the timber. Grip the wire at the point where it enters the hole, then pull it out and measure the distance to the end. Studs are normally about 50 mm thick, so add 25 mm to determine the distance from the hole to the centre of the timber.

The usual measurement from the centre of one stud or joist to the centre of the next is 400 mm, but you may find other spacings in old houses.

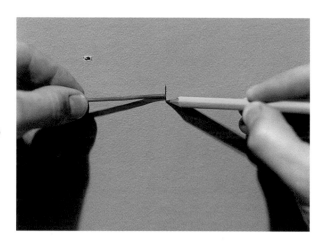

Whisk up the mix

A chef's hand whisk is the best tool for mixing up plaster. Aim for a consistency resembling thick whipped cream for the undercoat and just-melted ice cream for the finishing coat. Once it's right, don't keep on whisking; you will encourage the plaster to start drying.

Rely on the trowel

Aim to get the plaster smooth while it is still wet, rather than rubbing it down with abrasive paper after it has dried. As you apply the plaster to the wall, press the trowel hard at a shallow angle. Then spray on a fine mist of water from a garden spray gun to stop the plaster from drying too quickly, and finish off with a series of light strokes with the trowel held almost flat.

Reduce the suction

Flick some water over the area you are going to plaster. If it soaks in quickly, reduce the suction by brushing some diluted PVA sealer over the surface. This will also help the plaster to bond.

Keep it clean

The container in which you mix plaster, any implements used to mix it, and the water itself must be absolutely clean. Wash and rinse between mixes, so that no lumps of setting plaster or other impurities get into the next mix.

Add plaster to water, not the other way round. Sprinkle the plaster in gradually and keep stirring the mix until the consistency is right.

Fixing damaged wall and ceiling surfaces

Cover-up options for crumbling plaster

One way to tackle plasterwork that's in poor condition is to cover it up. You can fix new plasterboard over old, but you need to use long stainless-steel twinfast screws to fix the new sheets to the wall or ceiling timbers. A false ceiling can be suspended below the old one and walls can be covered with, for example, timber cladding fixed to battens secured to the old wall. Bear in mind that all these solutions make the room slightly smaller and lower. Even if this won't spoil the dimensions of the room, many fittings, especially electrical ones, will have to be removed and repositioned on the new wall or ceiling surface.

A patch on a string

Square off the sides of a small hole in a stud wall or ceiling using a padsaw. Then patch the damage with an offcut of board small enough to pass through the hole on the diagonal. Thread string through its face and tie it to a nail. Next, spread filler or a plasterboard adhesive on the outer face of the patch and push it through the hole. Rotate it and pull on the string so it presses against the inner face of the wallboard. Hold the string for a short while until the filler or adhesive gets a grip. Leave it to set hard, then cut off the string and plaster over the patch.

1 Hack away all loose plaster, using a club hammer and sharp brick bolster

2 Prime laths with a coat of diluted PVA sealer, then mix up undercoat plaster

3 Apply undercoat to a level about 3 mm below existing surface. Leave it to set

4 Mix up and apply finish plaster. As it dries, spray on a little water and then polish surface with steel float

plastering

plastering Fixing damaged wall and ceiling surfaces

Repair a damaged corner

The easiest way to patch a damaged external corner is to use a planed timber batten as a plastering guide. Pin the batten flush to one edge of the corner with masonry nails, leaving their heads projecting so you can remove it easily. Then plaster up to the batten. When the plaster has dried, remove the batten carefully and repeat the process from the other side of the corner. Finish by rounding off the new corner with some fine abrasive paper.

Cut back to the timbers

If you need to repair a big hole in a partition wall or ceiling, square up the damage with a multi-purpose saw, cutting back to the edges of the studs or joists on each side of the hole. Nail 50 x 25 mm battens to the joists or studs, then cut a patch of plasterboard to fit and nail it to the battens. Cover all the joints with plasterboard tape before plastering over the patch.

For a ceiling patch, skew nail 50 x 50 mm square supports between the joists at each side of the hole and nail the cut edges of the existing and new plasterboard to them.

What type of plaster?

You can apply finish plaster to minor blemishes and knocks needing a layer up to 3 mm thick. For deeper patches, apply an undercoat of browning plaster first. If there is any risk of dampness, use a render made from sand and cement with added plasticiser rather than a gypsum plaster.

Fixing bulging plaster

On a lath-and-plaster ceiling, the plaster may sag away from the laths. Vacuum up any loose plaster in the ceiling void. Push the sagging plaster back up against the laths with a piece of board and a prop. Return to ceiling void and pour a runny mix of bonding plaster over the area, leaving the board and prop in place until the plaster has set.

stud walls Planning the structure of a new wall

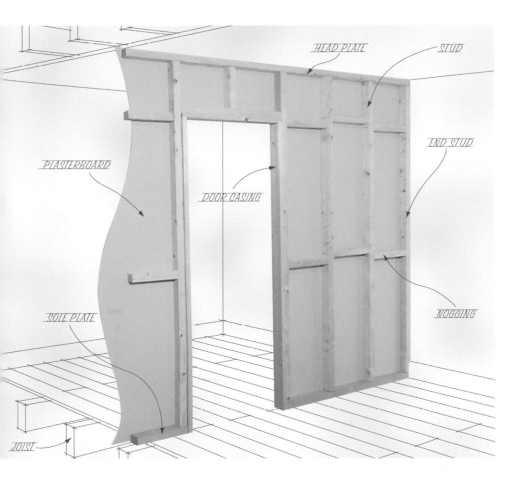

HEAD PLATE

STUD

PLASTERBOARD

END STUD

DOOR CASING

SOLE PLATE

NOGGING

JOIST

The anatomy of a stud wall

A stud wall, also known as a timber-framed partition wall, gets its name from the vertical timbers (studs) that are fitted between the horizontal head and sole plates. This simple framework provides a sturdy support for the sheets of plasterboard that are nailed to it. The only other components involved are horizontal braces called noggings fitted between the studs. These stop the studs twisting, give the plasterboard extra support and provide fixing points for shelves, wall cupboards and the like.

If the wall includes a door opening, the sole plate is cut away and an extra nogging is fitted above the door to act as a lintel. The door opening is lined with a casing, which protects the cut edges of the plasterboard. The door is then hung within the casing.

Providing light and services

If you intend to build a stud wall, plan its position with care and get your plans approved by your local authority to ensure that they comply with building regulations. Bear in mind that, although each room needs natural light (unless it is a kitchen or bathroom), regulations do not allow you to erect a wall which intersects an existing window, so a new window may be needed. You will also have to arrange lighting, heating and possibly plumbing in each new room.

Coping with high ceilings

If a room is more than 2.4 m high—the length of a sheet of plasterboard—you'll need to make up the height with cut-to-size pieces of board. Fit extra noggings between the studs to support them.

Building the new wall

Beware of cables and pipes

Before drilling any holes in your walls, ceilings and floors, use an electronic detector to check for hidden electricity cables and water or gas pipes.

stud walls Building the new wall

The right timber for the job

Use 75 x 50 mm sawn timber for walls up to about 2.4 m (8 ft) high. For rooms with higher ceilings, use 100 x 50 mm timber. Wood shrinks as it dries, so make sure your supply is well seasoned. If it is not, the resultant shrinkage in the structure can cause cracks to appear in the plaster, where the stud wall meets the adjacent wall and ceiling surfaces. Check also that all the wood you buy is straight; you cannot build a satisfactory stud wall with warped timber.

Beefing up the insulation

Stud walls are poor sound insulators. You can improve their performance by using 12.5 mm plasterboard instead of the standard 9.5 mm—or, better still, by using a double layer of 9.5 mm boards. Fix the second layer with 50 mm nails and stagger the joints so they don't coincide with those in the first layer. After cladding one side of the wall, jam 100 mm thick glass-fibre insulation batts between the studs, then clad the second side.

Choose the best fixings

To minimise the risk of cracking existing ceiling plaster by hammering, use screws rather than nails to secure the head plate to the ceiling joists and the sole plate to the floor joists. No.10 screws 3½ in long are ideal.

Fasten the end studs to masonry side walls with 100 mm long frame fixings or 4 in No.10 screws and wall plugs. Then use 100 mm round wire nails to skew nail the rest of the studs to the head and sole plates, and to secure the noggings and other frame members, such as door casings.

A handy block

Nail an offcut of wood temporarily to the sole plate to hold each stud in position while you skew nail it in place.

Finding the joists

Secure the head and sole plates to each joist they cross. Locate the floor joists by looking for the lines of nails in the boards. The ceiling joists always run in the same direction as the floor joists; you can locate these initially by tapping the ceiling surface (a dead sound indicates a joist), then more accurately by making test drillings or using a joist detector.

If the new wall runs parallel to the joists, position it so it stands on top of a joist. You might need access to the ceiling void above so you can insert noggings and screw the head plate to them if ceiling and floor joists are not exactly aligned.

Bracing the studs with noggings

Stagger noggings that are acting solely as braces for the studs so you can nail through the side of the stud into the end of each one. If the noggings must be in line—to provide a fixing for a row of cabinets, for example—cramp a block to the stud under each nogging to support it as you skew nail it in place.

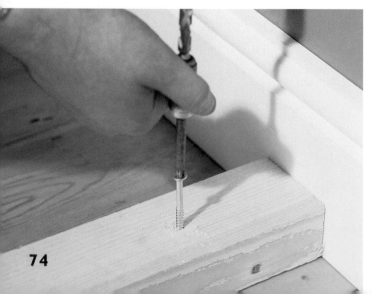

Leave clear stud marks

When all the studs are in place, mark their centre lines on the ceiling and floor along both sides of the wall as a guide when nailing on the plasterboard.

Room for manoeuvre

Don't drive the fixing screws fully home into the sole plate until the first stud is in position and you've checked whether it is truly vertical with a spirit level. If it's not, you can then adjust the sole plate position before driving in the screws.

On solid ground floors, drill clearance holes through the sole plate but don't fix it down until you've positioned the first stud on top of it and checked that it's vertical. Then you can drill and plug the holes in the floor and fix it in place.

Vary the spacing

If you are fixing 12.5 mm plasterboard, or using a double thickness of the thinner 9.5 mm board, space the studs at 600 mm (2 ft) centres. If you're using a single thickness of 9.5 mm board, space the studs at 400 mm (16 in) centres.

Supporting heavy weights

Plan the exact position of a heavy fixture, such as a wall cupboard or a washbasin, as you assemble the wall framework. Then you can include extra studs or noggings to support it before you nail up the plasterboard.

Running cables and pipes

Drill holes through the centres of the studs and noggings to run cables and pipes vertically and horizontally within the wall. Don't run cables and pipes through the same holes, though.

Mount sockets and light switches on special plastic mounting boxes that fit flush in a hole cut in the plasterboard. You can get single and double boxes.

Run electric cables inside PVC conduit clipped to the studs and noggings if the wall cavity will be filled with insulation. This will prevent them from overheating.

Cut notches for waste pipes. Drill a hole, then saw out the wedge (left). Replace the cut-out or fit bridging pieces to strengthen the wood.

STAGES IN ASSEMBLING THE FRAMEWORK

1 Use an offcut to mark position of each end of head plate on ceiling. Screw plate to joists

2 Use plumb line to position sole plate directly below, then screw it to floor. Screw end studs to side walls of room

3 Use offcut to mark stud positions. Cut and fit studs

4 Insert noggings for stiffness and casings for door openings

plasterboard Handling plasterboard

Basic requirements

There's more to plasterboard than meets the eye. For lining ceilings and cladding stud walls, you need standard plasterboard. This has one side faced with smooth ivory-coloured paper and the other with rougher grey paper. Tapered-edged boards allow you to tape and fill the joints between boards neatly (see pages 79-81). The standard thickness is 9.5 mm, but 12.5 mm boards are also available.

Special situations

There are several types of plasterboard made for special purposes. Foil-backed boards are designed to stop water vapour passing through wall and ceiling surfaces—for example, into a loft, where it could cause condensation and make the roof timbers rot. Boards backed with a layer of expanded polystyrene provide insulation for dry-lining cold external walls that are liable to condensation.

Standard board sizes

The standard 2400 x 1200 mm board size is convenient to use because the ceiling height in many houses is just under 2400 mm. However, sheets of this size are quite heavy and difficult to manoeuvre in tight spaces, and they can be easily damaged if they are knocked or bent, so get help when moving or fixing them. Smaller size boards are also available and are ideal for repair work.

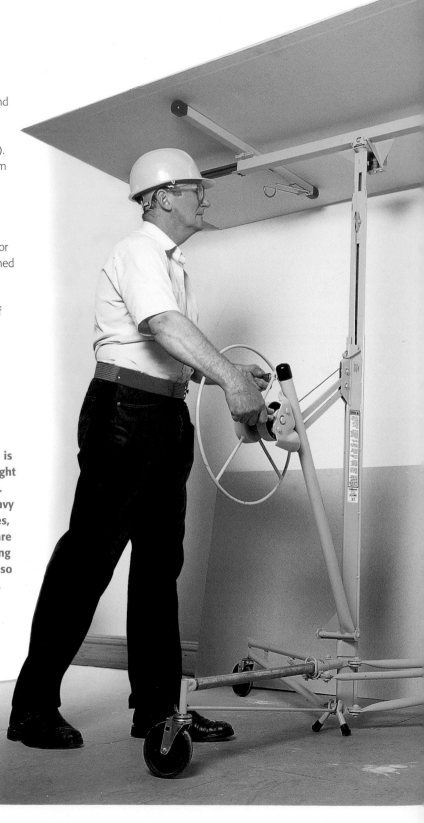

Hire a pair of extra hands

Standard-size sheets of plasterboard are too heavy and unwieldy to fix on a ceiling single-handed. If you have to work on your own, hire a panel lifter (main picture) to raise the boards into place and hold them there while you drive in the fixing nails. The machine can support panels while they are fixed to walls and sloping ceilings too.

If you have help, make a T-support from a plank and batten (left). Then use the propped plank to hold the board tightly against the ceiling joists while driving the nails into place.

Cutting it fine

Use a long straightedge and a sharp trimming knife to cut plasterboard (left). Cut through the paper and into the core of the board on the side that will face outwards. Then snap the cut open by bending the board along the cut line (below). To finish, cut through the paper on the other side.

To make a cut-out in plasterboard, drill a hole within the waste area to admit a padsaw blade, then saw carefully out to and around the cut-out line.

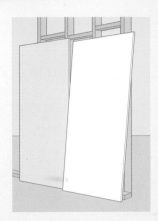

Which side is which?

The grey side of plasterboard is turned to the wall; the ivory side, covered with a higher quality paper, is designed for direct decoration with paint or wallpaper as well as skimming with plaster. The boards are fragile so store them with care. Pair ivory faces against one another to protect them, especially if you wish to decorate straight onto the board.

plasterboard

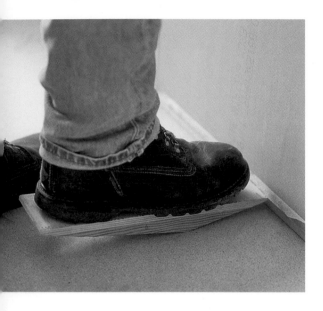

Make a rocking wedge

This simple rocking wedge or foot lifter will hold boards tightly up against the ceiling while you drive in the nails. Cut a piece of 100 x 50 mm wood about 350 mm (14 in) long, and draw a line across one face 150 mm from the end. Then draw a line on each edge, linking the ends of the first line to the opposite corners of the block, and saw off the two triangular waste sections. Slide the rocker under the base of the board and press down on it with your foot. The seesaw effect will lift the board.

Leave a narrow gap

Boards should be about 12 mm (½in) less than room height. If this means cutting them, support cut edges on the rocking wedge and lift the boards to the ceiling. Both edge and gap will then be hidden by the skirting board.

Hammer in the nail heads

You can buy a special hammer with a domed head for nailing plasterboard. It enables you to drive in the nails until their heads dimple the surface of the board, without tearing the paper facing.

Choose the right nails

Plasterboard nails are galvanised or zinc-plated so that they won't rust and spoil decorations, slightly jagged for better grip, and countersunk so that they indent the paper surface of the board. Use 30 mm nails for 9.5 mm board and 40 mm nails for 12.5 mm board, spaced about 150 mm (6 in) apart, and at least 9 mm (⅜in) in from the board edges. **Stick a band of insulation tape** around your hammer handle, 150 mm from the end, to make a handy nail spacing gauge.

The horizontal option

Plasterboard doesn't have to be fixed vertically. The dimensions of the wall may make it more practical to fix the boards horizontally. Work from the top downwards. Nail a temporary support to the studs to hold each board while you nail it in place, fitting the first board tight up against the ceiling.

Filling joints and turning corners

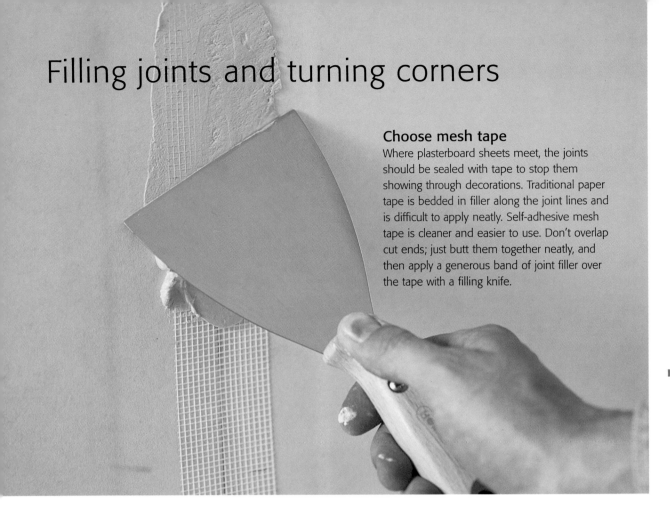

Choose mesh tape
Where plasterboard sheets meet, the joints should be sealed with tape to stop them showing through decorations. Traditional paper tape is bedded in filler along the joint lines and is difficult to apply neatly. Self-adhesive mesh tape is cleaner and easier to use. Don't overlap cut ends; just butt them together neatly, and then apply a generous band of joint filler over the tape with a filling knife.

Feather with a sponge
A damp sponge is the best tool for feathering (smoothing the edges of) joint filler so it blends smoothly with the surface of the board. When the filler is completely dry, you can smooth it further with a fine sanding block for a totally invisible joint.

Make a tape dispenser
Once you begin taping plasterboard joints, you will find it useful to keep the roll of tape to hand, so make a simple dispenser from a wire coat hanger, bent into a V-shape and hooked onto your tool belt.

Protective seal
Leave joint filler to dry for at least two days. Then apply a coat of plaster primer to the ivory face if you plan to hang wallpaper. This evens out the suction between the raw board and the taped-and-filled joints, and also stops the board surface from tearing when the wallpaper is next stripped.

plasterboard Filling joints and turning corners

Tidy up the edges
Board edges that have been cut by hand can be rather ragged. Before applying joint tape, trim off any torn or loose paper facing and repair the board surface with filler.

Keep the filler clean
Clean the blade of your filling knife by drawing it across a piece of scrap wood rather than over the rim of the bucket in which you mixed the filler. If you scrape it on the bucket, you'll end up with a lot of gritty bits in the unused filler.

Reinforce the corners
Cover all corners with joint tape. If an external corner is especially vulnerable, use zinc-plated metal angle bead, nailed in place or bedded in with joint filler. Then skim the walls with plaster.

Plasterboard on solid walls

Give warmth to walls
A plasterboard lining on a solid outside wall provides extra insulation. Use foil-backed board to prevent condensation. Traditionally timber battens are put up first, and the boards nailed to them but so long as the wall is straight and flat, you can apply a series of dabs of plasterboard bonding compound to the wall or board (depending on the manufacturer's recommendations), then press the boards into place.

Horizontal bands of the bonding compound spread along the top and bottom of the wall reduce the airflow, improving the insulation, and provide a solid base for fixing skirting boards and cornices. Insert wedges at the bottom of the sheets of board to keep them tight to the ceiling while the compound dries.

Raid the offcuts box
You will need pieces of packing in different thicknesses to fill the gaps between the battens and the wall surface. Offcuts of hardboard and thin plywood are ideal; cut them into strips about 50 mm wide and apply a little woodworking adhesive before tapping them into place behind the battens.

Finding the high spots

If the wall is uneven, you need to put up a truly flat framework of battens to support the plasterboard. Lay a batten flat on the floor against the wall and draw a line on the floor along its outer face. Then hold the batten vertically against the wall, at intervals, and make a mark on the floor wherever its bottom end projects beyond the first line. Draw a second line parallel to the first one

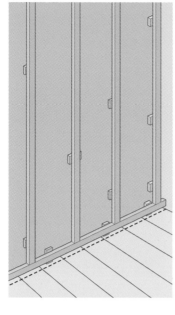

through the outermost of these marks. Fix the floor-level batten so its outer face is aligned with the outer line. Fix the vertical battens so their faces align with the batten at floor level, using packing where necessary. Finish off by fixing a horizontal batten at ceiling level.

Use frame fixings

The quickest way of fixing battens is to use frame fixings—all-in-one screws and wall plugs (see page 350). Drill holes through the battens and use them as a template to drill into the wall. Insert the fixing and hammer the screw home.

Frame window reveals

Fix battens all round window and door openings to support the board edges. Make sure they align with the other battens horizontally and vertically, and use packing where necessary.

1 Cut sheet of board about 13 mm (½ in) less than floor to ceiling height. Start fixing boards in a corner

2 Fix board tight to ceiling. Nail to vertical studs, to head and sole plates and to any noggings fitted

3 Drive nails in roughly every 150 mm (6 in), keeping them at least 9 mm (⅜ in) in from board edges. Tape all joints

4 Apply joint filler over tape and use it to fill nail holes too

plasterboard

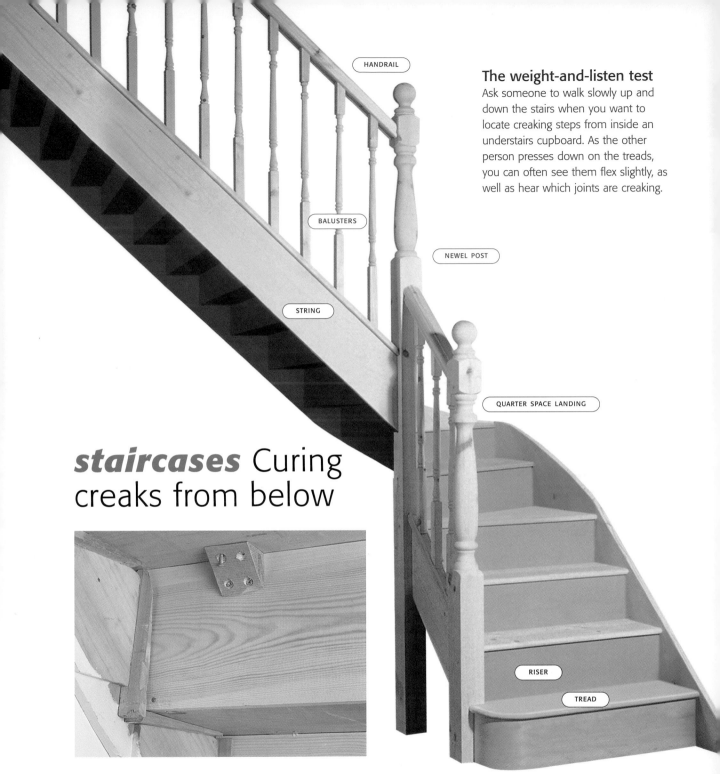

HANDRAIL

BALUSTERS

NEWEL POST

STRING

QUARTER SPACE LANDING

RISER

TREAD

The weight-and-listen test
Ask someone to walk slowly up and down the stairs when you want to locate creaking steps from inside an understairs cupboard. As the other person presses down on the treads, you can often see them flex slightly, as well as hear which joints are creaking.

staircases Curing creaks from below

Replace angle blocks
Small triangular blocks of wood under the stairs stiffen the joints between treads and risers. Replace any missing ones, otherwise the stairs may creak. Apply PVA adhesive to the blocks and rub them in place until they stick. Then secure the blocks with screws long enough to pass through the blocks and into the underside of the stairs, but not right through them.

Silenced with talc
Try brushing some talcum powder or chalk dust along the tread and riser joints of stairs which creak. It often cures the problem temporarily.

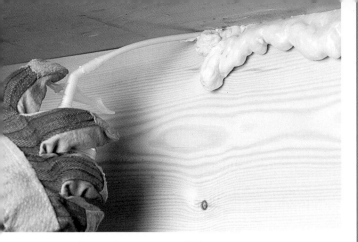

Try filling the gap with foam

For a quick fix, squirt polyurethane foam filler into any gaps between treads and risers from under the stairs. The foam stops creaks by preventing the wood surfaces from chafing.

Tighten loose wedges

If there are wooden wedges under the stairs holding the treads and risers tight in the strings, check they're not loose. If any are, squeeze some glue onto the tips and tap them back into place.

Reinforcing a slack joint

To close up the joint between the back of a tread and the bottom of a riser, squeeze some PVA adhesive into the gap. Then drive three evenly spaced screws upwards, through the tread and into the riser. Position screws 12 mm (½ in) from the back edge of the tread.

1 Use spirit level to mark wall at least 900 mm (3 ft) above front edge of every tread. Join marks using a straightedge

2 Fit brackets to underside of handrail. Align top of rail with drawn line and mark fixings for top bracket

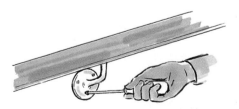

3 Secure top bracket with one wall plug and screw. Pivot rail and fix bottom bracket in same way. Mark all the screw holes. Then remove handrail and drill for wall plugs before permanent installation

staircases

mouldings
Fixes from above

Repairing the edge of a tread

When repairing the front edge or nosing of a tread, cut the repair as shown above. The dovetail or wedge shape counteracts the weight put on it, so the repair does not depend on glue and screws alone for its strength.

Stiffen joints with brackets

When you cannot get at the underside of the staircase to reinforce loose joints, pull back the carpet and fix metal brackets into the angle between treads and risers—two on each step will be enough. The metal brackets are thin enough not to show through the carpet when it is replaced.

Remedies for broken and loose balusters

Bind up the break

If you've got all the pieces, it's possible to mend a broken baluster invisibly. Spread adhesive on the broken ends, squeeze them together and bind the repair together tightly with insulating tape. Temporarily wedge the baluster between two blocks of wood nailed to a work surface. These will keep the broken ends squeezed together while the adhesive dries. Use a fine grade abrasive paper to remove hardened glue after you have removed the tape.

Take out for stripping

Before starting to strip an intricate balustrade by hand, see if the balusters can be removed without too much trouble. If they can, take them out and pay to have them stripped. You can then concentrate on making the newel posts and handrail look like new.

Tap in a shim

Cut a shim—a slim wooden wedge—to fix a loose baluster. Spread adhesive on both sides of the shim, then use a pin hammer to tap it into the gap where the baluster is joined to the handrail or the string. When the glue has dried, use a sharp trimming knife to tidy up the repair so that the shim does not show.

Strategies for removal

Balusters are secured to the handrail and string in different ways. If they are simply nailed to the top edge of the string, free them by using a fine nail punch to drive the nails right through the ends of the balusters, rather than trying to prise them out.

If the outer string is 'open' (cut to follow the line of the treads and risers), prise off the cover moulding on the side edge of each tread. Then gently tap the bottom ends of the balusters out of their slots with a mallet.

Finding a match

Replacement balusters can be hard to find, but look around local architectural salvage yards before paying a wood turner to reproduce just one or two.

Plan ahead for best effect

Decoration and function

Mouldings are practical as well as decorative. Skirting boards save the base of walls from hard knocks. Dado rails are traditionally fixed at a height to protect walls from chair backs. Picture rails, fixed at or above the height of door frames, support heavy pictures and mirrors securely without the need for individual wall fixings. Choose each of these mouldings in a style that reflects the overall design of the room.

Fewer joins and less waste

Measure and list the length of every stretch of wall to which you are going to attach a moulding, then add about 50 mm (2 in) as a trim allowance for every corner cut required. Visit your timber merchant or DIY store and find out what lengths they have in stock; these usually start at 1.8 m and rise in increments of 300 mm (12 in). Then choose the mouldings you're going to use and work out a cutting order that involves as little waste as possible.

Architrave mouldings for door frames are often sold in pre-cut sets—two 2.1 m lengths for the sides of the opening and a 900 mm length for the top.

Marking the height

If the skirting board is level, cut a timber rod to match the height of a proposed dado rail. Then work around the room, using a spirit level to plumb the rod before marking its height on the wall. Join up the marks with a straightedge to make a fixing line.

Alternative to timber

Mouldings made from medium-density fibreboard (MDF) are an alternative to timber so long as you're planning to paint them. They are often sold primed, ready for the final coat to be applied. Don't use MDF mouldings in bathrooms or kitchens, however, because if they absorb moisture they will swell and distort. Remember to wear a dust mask when cutting or drilling MDF.

WOODEN CORNICE

PLASTER CORNICE

COVING

PICTURE RAIL

DADO RAIL

ARCHITRAVE

DOUBLE-SIDED SKIRTING

STANDARD SKIRTING

mouldings

85

mouldings Skilful ways at corners

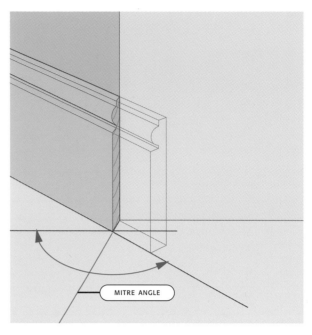

MITRE ANGLE

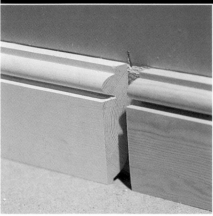

Draw angles on the floor

Mark the mitres where two skirting boards meet at an external corner by holding each length in turn against the wall so it overlaps the corner. Draw a line on the floor against the front edge of each board. Then hold one end of a ruler against the corner and draw a line from it through the point where the two lines on the floor intersect. This gives you the mitre angle (above).

Hold each board in place, mark its face where it crosses this mitre angle line and its back where it touches the corner of the wall. Extend the marks all round the boards and cut the mitres.

Inconspicuous joins

When you need to join two lengths of moulding along a wall, make a scarf joint by cutting the two ends at 45° angles. You can do this accurately using a jigsaw with an adjustable sole plate (top). Fix one length in place, then position and fix the other (above). Apply some woodworking adhesive to the cut ends and secure the joint with pins. Try to position it where it will not be seen–behind furniture, for example.

Guard against inaccuracy

If the floor slopes, do not match the height of a dado or picture rail to it. Either hire a laser level or mark the height of the moulding at one point only, then use the longest spirit level you can obtain to transfer the mark all around the room. Compensate for any slight inaccuracy in the level by turning it end over end as you go.

Plaster practice
Always saw fibrous plaster mouldings from the face side, so that any 'breaking out' occurs on the back. If the moulding has a hessian backing, cut through it with a sharp trimming knife. Mitre cut internal and external corners with a hardpoint saw, then drill clearance holes for the screws being used to secure the mouldings to the wall, otherwise they will crack the plaster when they are tightened. Seal the joints with plaster of Paris or a suitable filler, and sand smooth when dry.

Making mitres easy

A bench hook is a simple piece of equipment for holding small pieces of wood steady while you saw them. By making accurate 45° saw slots in the block screwed to its back edge, you can turn it into a mitre block that's ideal for cutting neat mitres on small panel mouldings and picture rails.

A deep mitre box is useful for cutting skirting boards. Make it up from offcuts, slightly deeper than the height of the skirting board. For accuracy, cut the 45° slots in each side of the box with a panel saw rather than a tenon saw. Stiffen the box by nailing or screwing a couple of battens across the top at each end.

Inside knowledge

The professional way to join mouldings at inside corners is to butt one length against the wall and scribe the second one over it. Use an offcut with an accurate 90° sawn end to trace the profile of the moulding onto the back of the length you want to scribe (left).

Reverse the blade in a coping saw to cut along the line (right). This enables it to cut on the pulling stroke, so that the face of the moulding is not spoiled by splintering. The straight section of the line can be squared onto the front of the board and cut with a tenon saw.

Ways of fixing

Wooden wedges for nails

Fix skirting board to brickwork by nailing it to wooden wedges, driven into every fourth vertical joint. Make the wedges by chopping opposing tapers on the ends of lengths of 75 x 25 mm timber, using a sharp carpenter's axe. Choose pieces of wood at least 400 mm long so your hand is well out of the way of the axe. Drive the wedges into the brick joints and saw off flush with the wall.

mouldings Ways of fixing

Too hard for masonry nails?

Masonry nails are the quickest way of fixing skirting boards, but try driving one into the wall first. They are easy to hammer into the lightweight blocks used to build the interior walls of most modern houses, but it can be hard or impossible to get them into old bricks. Make sure you wear goggles, because the nails can ricochet if they're not struck squarely with the hammer.

Backing blocks for cornices

Wooden cornicing is difficult to locate accurately. Rip a square-sectioned length of wood, say a 50 x 50 mm piece, diagonally to make triangular fillets. Cut short blocks off the fillets and fix these along the junction of the wall and ceiling. Hold the cornicing in place against the blocks and nail it to them.

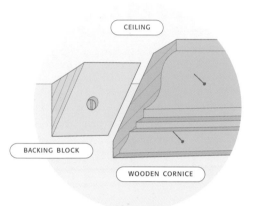

CEILING

BACKING BLOCK

WOODEN CORNICE

Nail architraves at the top

Secure the mitre joints on architraves around door and window frames by nailing them together. Drive the nails through the top piece, or head, where they won't be seen, rather than through the side pieces, or legs. It's a good idea to drill pilot holes for the nails, otherwise you're likely to split the wood when you hammer them down.

Use your weight

Press the bottom edge of new skirting board tight down to the floor before nailing it, by using a kneel board. This is simply a piece of floorboard or similar size timber, about 1.2 m (4 ft) long, propped on the top edge of the loose skirting board. Press down on it with one knee while fixing the skirting to the wall with nails or screws into wall plugs. On wooden floors that are normally covered, nail a small block into the floor against the end of the kneel board every time you move it along the wall. This traps the board so that it cannot slip off the skirting and leave you with a jarred knee.

A crafty quirk

Nail through the grooves and hollows of mouldings, especially if they're being varnished. Once the nail heads are punched in and filled over, they'll be almost invisible.

Mirror image

Before going to a timber merchant or architectural salvage yard for replacement moulding, it's a good idea to record its shape. The best tool for the job is a profile gauge, a comb-like tool composed of sliding 'needles'. Set the gauge by pressing it against the face of the moulding you want to duplicate.

Planning and care for a top-class job

Protect the decor
If a length of skirting board has to be replaced, first use a sharp trimming knife to cut through any wallpaper stuck to the top. Then find out how the board is fixed. Screws should be drilled out if they cannot be removed. Nailed boards should be eased away from the wall with a bolster chisel, until there is space to insert a nail bar, and then levered off the wall. Protect the decoration with a piece of thin ply.

Freedom of movement
Use a flexible decorator's filler to seal gaps between the tops of skirting boards and walls, and to disguise badly fitting joints in corners. The sealant is sold in cartridge form and can be painted over. It won't fall out when doors are slammed or crack because of the natural movement of the wood.

Architraving in order
When fitting architraving around a door frame, saw a 45° mitre cut on the top end of each architrave leg or upright and fix them on either side of the frame first. Then fit the head or top piece by holding it upside down across the tops of the legs, marking its length from them and cutting matching mitres.

Patching damaged skirting
The join between two pieces of skirting board butted together at 45° is less conspicuous than a square, 90° cut. If you need to patch in a piece of new skirting, tap some wedges in behind the board to ease it away from the wall slightly and create room for the saw blade. Guide the saw with a mitre block to make a 45° cut, and then use the piece you remove as a pattern when you cut the replacement to length.

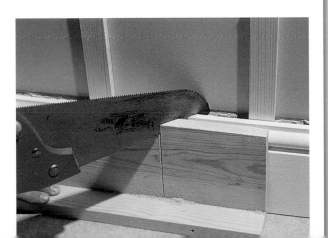

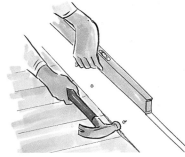

1 Cut board to length. Use a spirit level to ensure board is level. Fix temporarily to wall

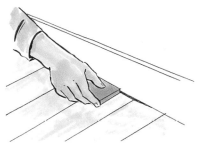

2 Cut a small block of wood slightly thicker than the widest gap between board and floor

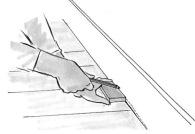

3 Use a block of wood and pencil to scribe profile of floor along skirting board

4 Remove board, saw along scribed line, then fix board permanently

mouldings

89

doors and windows

fitting Cures for jammed doors and windows

Wait for the swelling to go

When a door or window starts jamming in its frame with the onset of wet weather, it indicates that moisture is penetrating the paintwork, causing the wood to swell. Don't plane down the edges of the opening or you're likely to end up with too big a gap when the wood dries out. Instead, wait for a dry spell, then repaint the joinery.

Easy on the trigger

Speed up the drying process by playing heat from a hot air gun along the edges of a door or window that's swollen in its frame. The idea is to draw moisture out of the wood, so use the gun in short bursts, just warming the surface without scorching it. Take care not to crack the glass if you're working on a window.

Don't use force

Try not to force a jammed window or door open and shut repeatedly. If you do, there's a risk that the joints will be weakened and the putty loosened. You might even crack the glass.

Breaking a paint bond

Casements painted into their frames can sometimes be freed by running a trimming knife around the edge. Then release any catches and bolts before tapping the casement open from inside using a wood block and hammer.

Hold a door fast while you work

Make a clamp to hold a new door on its edge while you plane it to fit the frame. Saw a U-shaped notch in the end of a piece of 100 x 50 mm timber and fix it to the floorboards with a couple of screws. Then slide the door into the notch and jam it in place with a wooden wedge. Secure the wedge to the clamp with a length of string so it won't get lost.

No need to remove the door

You can plane the outer edge of a door if it is binding on the frame without having to take it off its hinges. To stop the door swinging as you work on it, tap in a pair of wedges beneath the door, one on top of the other (see top). Remove the lock or latch if there's a chance of the plane striking it. Plane off a little at a time, aiming for a 2 mm gap (about as thick as a 50p piece) between the door edge and the frame.

Hire an electric door trimmer (above) to shorten door bottoms so they'll clear a new fitted carpet or other floor covering. The trimmer takes off a thin sliver of wood, and it vacuums up the sawdust too.

1 Stand in front of doorway and 'walk' door up to frame. Get top of door and top of frame parallel with each other

2 Run a pencil around rebate on frame to mark door for planing. Allow an extra 2 mm all round to accept hinges

3 Plane door to fit. Check it in its frame, then sand off all sharp edges, cut recesses for hinges and hang door

fitting

fitting First aid for loose and broken joints

Metal reinforcements
Loose joints on windows and doors can be braced with metal corner plates (right). You can hide the plates by chopping out a shallow recess for them. Screw the plates in place, then paint them with a rust inhibitor before hiding them below a layer of wood filler. Once the filler has dried, sand it to blend with the surface of the wood and paint over it.

Dismantle to reassemble
Sometimes it is possible to dismantle a door or window if the joints are very loose. Carefully tap the uprights (called stiles) off the horizontals (called rails). If they don't come apart easily, look for nails or dowels pinning them together; drill out dowels and drive nails right through with a fine nail punch. Wear gloves, goggles and stout footwear if you are dealing with a window, because it is almost inevitable that the glass will break and drop out.

Test for squareness
Measure the frame diagonals (left) when cramping a repaired frame back together. The two measurements should be identical. Confirm that the frame is square by laying a try square on the corners; the two sides of the frame should match it exactly. If the frame is not square, slacken the sash cramps, angle them slightly, retighten and test again for squareness.

Pile on the paint
The bottom edge of an outside door should be painted to keep moisture out and prevent swelling. A strip of carpet is useful for doing the job without taking the door off its hinges. Slip a sheet of newspaper under the door. Then apply some paint to the pile side of the carpet, slide it under the door and rub it back and forth to coat the bare wood.

Pin the joint with a dowel
Wooden dowels can be used to reinforce loose corner joints. Drill holes for them through the faces of the stiles, so that they pass right through the joint. Make sure the drill doesn't cause splintering when it breaks through. Dowels with fluted sides provide a stronger bond for the glue than plain ones do.

Hinges with lift
Don't plane the bottom edge of a door that scrapes on the floor the wider it is opened. Otherwise, you'll end up with a wide, draughty gap when it is closed. Change the hinges for rising butts. The spiral on the knuckle of the hinge lifts the door as it opens. You will need to know how the door is 'handed' (see page 95) when you buy them.

hardware
Solutions to problems with hinges

Left hand or right hand?

Some items of door furniture, such as rising butt hinges, are 'handed'. In other words, they are made in left-handed and right-handed versions that are mirror images of each other. In order to buy the correct version for the job, imagine yourself standing inside the room, looking at the door. If it is hinged on the left and opens inward, you need a left-handed hinge. If it is hinged on the right, you need a right-handed one.

Aligning bolt and plate

If work on your door hinges means that a lock or latch bolt no longer engages cleanly in its striking plate, use shoe polish to reveal the distance by which it is overlapping the plate (right). Smear a little polish on the end of the bolt, then close the door and operate the lock to leave a mark on the plate. Use a file to enlarge the cut-out if the discrepancy is small (above); if it is more than about 1 mm, reposition the plate instead.

Stop doors binding

If a door binds in its frame as you close it, and the rebate into which it fits is formed by a planted stop (a strip of wood nailed to the frame), prise this off and refit it. Trap some card between door and stop to provide the necessary clearance. If the rebate is machined into the frame, reposition the door hinges with their knuckles projecting a little farther beyond the edge of the frame.

Avoid the joints

Solid panelled doors are assembled with either mortise-and-tenon or dowelled joints. You can avoid cutting into these when fitting door hinges by positioning the upper hinge about 150 mm (6 in) below the top edge of the door and the lower one 225 mm (9 in) up from the bottom. Follow the same principle when positioning hinges on a casement window.

hardware Solutions to problems with hinges

Fit a third hinge

Heavyweight hardwood front doors may need a third hinge, fitted midway between the top and bottom ones, to carry the extra weight and spread the load on the existing hinge screws.

Make sure that all three hinges are fitted with their knuckles precisely in line, otherwise the door won't open and close smoothly and the hinge screws will be forced out.

How to centre the screws

Use a countersink bit in a hand drill or power drill to mark the positions of the hinge screw holes. Then use these as a guide when drilling holes for the screws.

Add some packing

Use material of appropriate thickness—card or hardboard, for example—to pack out hinges which have been recessed too deeply. You can spot the problem by looking at the hinged edge from the opening side: there will be no space between the edge of the door (or window) and the edge of the frame.

Clear the frame

Fit parliament hinges if you want a door to open right back against the wall behind it. The T-shaped leaves ensure that the door clears the architrave or the sides of the reveal in which it is set. The hinges are sold with different depths of projection, or 'throw', so you need to measure the depth of the recess to calculate the size of hinge required.

When screws cause trouble

Providing a better grip

Try replacing loose hinge screws with longer ones of the same gauge. If you are working on a window, make sure the screws are not so long that their points can strike the edge of the glass and crack it as you drive them in.

Alternatively, remove the hinge and drill out the troublesome screw holes to accommodate lengths of dowel. Dip the dowels in woodworking adhesive, tap them into place, then cut off the excess with a chisel when the adhesive has dried. Drill pilot holes in the dowels for the new screws and refit the hinge.

Removing seized screws

Scrape paint from the slots in screw heads so the screwdriver can get a grip. If the screw won't budge, tighten it slightly if you can to free the threads. Next, try striking the screwdriver handle head-on with a hammer, heating the screw head with a soldering iron, or using an impact driver. This turns the screw slightly when hit with a hammer. As a last resort, drill out the screw.

Steel before brass

When fitting brass screws, drive holes with steel screws of the same length and gauge first. You will then be able to drive the softer brass screws without burring their heads. Rub some candle wax on the brass screw threads first.

Mend a split frame

A frame can split along the line of the hinge screws if the door or window it encloses blows open violently. Mend the split by squeezing woodworking adhesive into it, then forcing it shut with a G-cramp until the adhesive dries. Alternatively, drive screws through the face of the frame and through the split, countersinking the heads so that they can be concealed with filler.

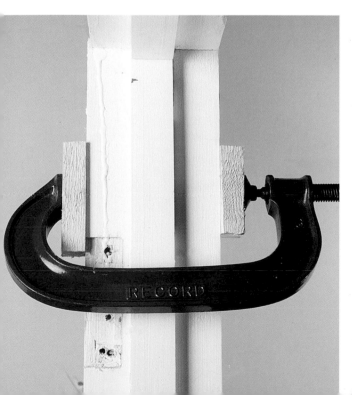

1 Open hinge to 90°. Hold knuckle against edge of door at hinge position and mark around the leaf of the hinge with a sharp trimming knife

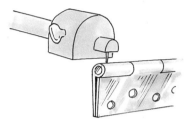

2 Set marking gauge to half total thickness of hinge and mark face of door with gauge

3 Use sharp chisel and mallet to chop out marked recess for hinge to gauged depth

4 Screw hinges to door. Then wedge door in open position and mark and cut recesses for hinges on frame

hardware

hardware Upgrading locks on external doors

LOCK BODY

DEADBOLT

CHUBB
5 LEVER

FACEPLATE

KEEP PLATE

Pick five levers

Look at the faceplate of the mortise lock fitted on your front door. If the information stamped on it says it has fewer than five levers, upgrade it straightaway to make it more burglar-proof. Most insurance companies now require 5-lever locks at least.

Avoid the joint

Fit a mortise lock about a third of the way up a door, below the middle rail or horizontal, if possible. Otherwise, you will have to cut into the joint securing the rail and stile (upright) together.

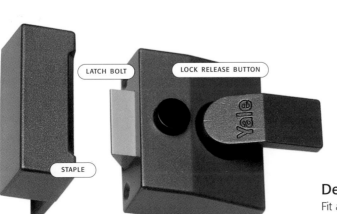

LATCH BOLT

LOCK RELEASE BUTTON

STAPLE

CYLINDER

ROSE

Dead secure

Fit a deadlocking cylinder nightlatch instead of a standard type if your front door is glazed. When locked from the outside, the indoor handle cannot be operated, so a burglar cannot get in by breaking the glass, reaching through and turning it as he can with a non-deadlocking type.

Better safe than sorry

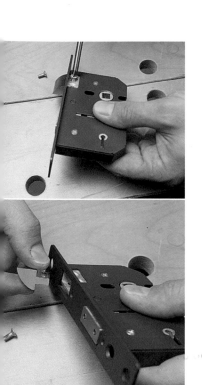

Who's there?

A door viewer, or peephole, is a valuable security device, but is of little use after darkness unless your doorstep is well lit. Keep the porch or hallway light switched on after dusk, or fit a sensor-activated light that will come on whenever someone approaches the door.

The strongest chain

The strongest door chains have a right-angled plate which fixes into the side of the rebate and turns round the frame edge. These are highly resistant to forcing. You can strengthen an existing fitting by exchanging the screws supplied with the chain for longer ones.

Making front doors more resistant to forcing

Matching the latch

A sashlock is a mortise lock plus a latch. When the door is unlocked, it allows you to open and close the door by operating the latch with a handle. The body of the lock is always fitted into the door edge with the handle at the top, and is made in both left-handed and right-handed versions (see page 95). If you can't obtain a correctly handed one, look for the type with a small cutaway in the casing. This allows you to reverse the latch by simply removing two screws (above). The alternatives are to take the body of the lock apart and reverse it yourself, to ask a locksmith to do it for you, or to buy one with a roller latch, which will work in a left-handed or right-handed situation.

Reinforcement for a cylinder latch

One way to give your front door extra security at relatively low cost and with very little DIY work is to fit reinforcements to the door, the frame, or both. Doors secured with a rim lock or cylinder nightatch are quite easily forced: a heavy blow drives the latch against the staple, which is held in place by just a couple of screws, shearing it away from the inside face of the frame and allowing an intruder to get in. The reinforcement (above) is designed to prevent this; it consists of a long steel bar shaped to fit tightly over the staple and is fixed all the way down the inside face of the frame with screws. (See also page 102.)

Sandwiched for strength

You can strengthen doors and frames around locks and hinges with so-called partnered reinforcements. These consist of two metal strips, joined together by bolts which pass right through the door or frame. For example, a mortise lock can be protected with a pair of strips bolted through the frame on either side of the keep plate, and by a further pair on the door, sandwiching the lock.

hardware

hardware Seven tips for fitting mortise locks

When to stop drilling

Drilling too deeply into the door stile can weaken the door and, if it's glazed, you could also crack the glass. To avoid this, wrap some tape round your drill bit so you can see when you've drilled holes to just the right depth—a fraction more than the length of the lock body. If your drill has a depth stop attachment, you can use that instead.

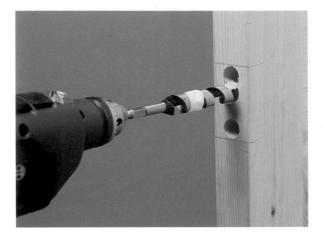

Avoiding an eyeful of dust

Resist the temptation to blow into the mortise to clear out loose shavings: you can easily end up with an eye full of splinters and wood dust. Pull out the waste with the drill bit or scrape it out with a narrow chisel.

Measure to fit

Look at the width of the door stile and the thickness of the door before buying a mortise lock for it. Lock bodies come in several different thicknesses and lengths. This is particularly important if you are buying a lock for a glazed door, which may have very narrow stiles.

Don't split your sides

Choose a drill that's just a fraction wider than the thickness of the lock body. If you create a wider mortise, you will weaken the door so much that it could split around the lock if forced.

Getting a firm grip

Turn the key to extend the bolt of the lock before you insert it in the mortise to test the fit. If it jams you can then grip the bolt with pliers and pull the lock body out again.

Measure up for a perfect fit

With the lock fitted, measure the distance between the bolt and the closing face of the door. Use this measurement to position the keep plate on the door frame so that the bolt just engages in the recess when the door is locked.

Mark the keyhole

When you have cut the mortise and the faceplate recess, hold the lock body against the face of the door so you can mark the position of the keyhole on it with a bradawl or pencil.

Improving window and door security

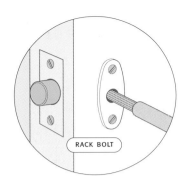

RACK BOLT

Awayday precautions

If you have sash windows without locks which you fear might be forced while you're away from home, drill two clearance holes through the top rail of the inner sash and drive long screws through them into the bottom rail of the outer sash. This will lock the two sashes securely together.

Open invitation

An intruder could quietly remove the panes of louvred windows by bending the metal clips that hold them in place. Prevent this by gluing the glass to the clips with an epoxy-resin adhesive.

Use longer fixings

Most window locks come with screws so short that they won't withstand forcing. Replace them with longer screws that will penetrate the wood as far as possible at the fixing point.

Replace worn parts

If the mechanism of a door lock is worn but the body is in good condition, you can replace just the worn component— a new cylinder in the case of a cylinder nightlatch, or new levers for a mortise lock. Take the lock to a locksmith to make sure that the new components will fit. You will also need new keys.

Fit concealed bolts

Fit rack bolts in pairs to external doors and to casement windows—one near the top corner and the other near the bottom. The bolt engages in a hole in the frame. They are more secure than surface-mounted locks, and are also much less obtrusive.

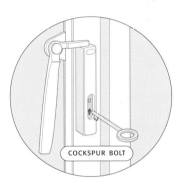

COCKSPUR BOLT

Block the handles

Screw a cockspur bolt to a metal-framed window to stop an intruder operating the handle after breaking the glass. The key locks the bolt in the up position for security, and lets it drop when you want to open the window. Avoid cracking the glass by drilling no deeper than necessary when making holes for the bolt's self-tapping screws.

Make external glazing beads secure

The best locks will not keep out a thief if all he has to do is prise away external glazing beads and then lift out the glass. You can secure wooden glazing beads to their frames with clutch-head security screws, which cannot be unscrewed. If you have double-glazed windows with external plastic glazing beads, ask your local glass merchant for advice. The usual method of securing these is to remove the beads and stick them back in place with special adhesive sealant.

hardware

hardware Improving window and door security

Push the button

Make sure wooden windows are always secure by fitting locks that don't need a key to lock them. With some types, you simply push a button in to secure the two parts of the lock together after closing the window. Other types lock together automatically as the parts meet. Both need a key to undo them.

PUSH-BUTTON LOCK

Lock the window stay

If you want security plus the option of leaving a window ajar for ventilation, and the window has a stay pierced with holes, replace the plain peg on which the stay normally fits with a casement stay lock. You can then secure the window in any position by attaching the screw-on lock to the threaded peg with the key, which is also used to unlock it.

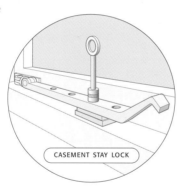

CASEMENT STAY LOCK

Bolt sliding sashes together

Fit dual screws—one at each side of the meeting rails—to secure sash windows. These consist of an internally threaded barrel that passes through the inner rail, and a bolt that passes through the barrel and screws into the outer rail.

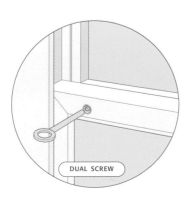

DUAL SCREW

Drill doors from both sides

If you have to drill through a door—to fit a cylinder nightlatch, a door viewer, a handle or a door knocker—take care not to burst through the wood and splinter its opposite face. Whether you are using a power drill and flat bit, or a hand brace and auger bit (above), drill until the tip of the bit just emerges through the opposite face of the door. Then withdraw the bit, insert the tip in the hole on the opposite face and finish drilling the hole from there.

Cramp on a scrap block

If you're drilling a hole close to the door edge–for a cylinder nightlatch, for example–you can use a G-cramp to hold a block of scrap wood tightly against the opposite face of the door as an alternative to drilling from both sides. Then you can drill right through the door and into the block without stopping and without causing any splintering. Use packing to protect the door face from the exposed cramp jaw.

Add locking bolts

Double up security on old aluminium-framed patio doors. If the only lock is part of the handle on the sliding door, fit surface-mounted patio door locks at the top and bottom of the door frame. These will stop intruders lifting the door off its track from outside the house. As you drill the holes in the doors to accept the bolts, make sure that they don't come too close to the edges of the sealed double glazing units.

More strength for hinges

Security hinges are an alternative to hinge bolts for outward-opening doors. When the door is closed, punched-out tabs on the hinge leaves interlock, preventing the door being lifted away from the frame even if the hinge pins are removed.

Secure the hinged edge too

Fit hinge bolts to prevent a front or back door from being forced, and to stop outward-opening french doors from being lifted out if their hinge pins have been removed. Two bolts are usually fitted, one near to each hinge. Insert the fixed bolt in the door edge and drill a hole in the frame to receive it. Make sure that the bolt is set centrally in the edge of the door, or it won't fit cleanly into the hole in the frame as the door closes.

1 Use power drill and flat wood bit, or brace and auger, to drill hole for bolt barrel

2 Insert bolt in its hole, then draw round faceplate and chisel out a shallow recess for it

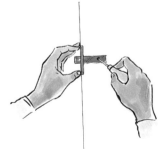

3 Hold bolt against face of frame and mark position of keyhole. Drill hole, fit bolt in place and test key operation

4 Fit keyhole cover plate. Operate bolt to mark position of receiver on frame, drill hole and fit receiver plate

hardware

glazing Fix a broken window

Emergency cover

Seal a cracked pane temporarily with transparent waterproof glazing tape, applied to the outside. If the pane is smashed, cover the whole window with heavy-gauge polythene secured by timber battens nailed round the frame.

If good security is vital, nail a sheet of plywood across the window frame until you can replace the glass.

Protection from cuts

Always wear thick leather shoes when removing a broken pane or cutting glass, in case a jagged piece falls on your foot. Protect your hands and eyes by wearing heavy gloves and safety spectacles or goggles.

Tape a cracked pane

If glass is cracked but intact, crisscross the pane with masking tape to lessen the risk of flying shards when you break it, then use a hacking knife to remove the putty. Break the pane from inside with a hammer and a block of wood. Lift out large shards first, then chip out and remove the smaller pieces.

The best glass for the job

Light and privacy

Choose patterned (obscured) glass where you need to let light in but at the same time retain your privacy–in bathroom windows and glazed front doors, for example.

Safe and secure

Use safety glass in doors and for any fixed panes prone to impact damage.

Toughened glass shatters into harmless granules if broken. It must be ordered to size because it can't be cut or drilled once it has been made.

Laminated glass, which can be cut in the usual way, is made of two layers of glass sandwiching a plastic interlayer. It cracks but doesn't fragment because the interlayer holds the pieces together. It also makes good security glazing.

Safety wired glass is often used in fire doors to reduce the rate of spread of fire. It should not be confused with ordinary wired glass, which has little security value.

TOUGHENED GLASS

LAMINATED GLASS

WIRED GLASS

Reduce glare and fading

Prevent soft furnishings, rugs and paintings in sunlit rooms from fading by installing laminated glass. The plastic interlayer filters out most of the sun's damaging ultraviolet rays.
Cut the heat build-up in a south-facing conservatory by using tinted or coated solar control glass (below).

Safety glass is essential

If you are carrying out improvements or alterations to your home that involve the installation of new glazed doors and windows, you must use safety glass in areas that are prone to impact damage to comply with Building Regulations. For full details of where it must be fitted, contact your local authority Building Control office or ask a glass merchant.

Allow for escape from fire

Include an opening casement big enough to act as a fire escape when choosing new windows, especially for upstairs rooms. Fixed double-glazed panes are very difficult to break in an emergency. Keep the keys to window locks to hand in each room and make sure everyone knows where they are.

Cover with safety film

You can make conventional glass in high-risk areas safer by covering it on the inside with a special strong self-adhesive plastic film which holds it together if broken.

glazing

glazing Keeping heat in and noise out

Choose extra efficiency

Fitting sealed double-glazed units in any window will reduce heat losses.
Cut these even more by specifying the use of low-emissivity glass in any new units you are ordering.
Its thin metallic surface coating helps to reflect heat back into the room. It also reflects away heat from the sun, reducing unwanted heat gain in the room without cutting the level of light it receives.

Watch the weight

Replacing existing glass with double glazing means doubling the weight of any opening casements. You may have to fit stronger hinges to carry the extra load if the casements sag and bind.
If you have sash windows, the sashes will be carefully counterbalanced by matching weights. Putting in double-glazing units will make the sashes difficult to open–and to keep open–unless you replace the weights with heavier ones.

Secondary choice

Fit secondary glazing for thermal insulation inside windows that are an irreplaceable part of the building's architecture, such as leaded lights or Thirties-style curved steel windows. It can be set close to the glass to leave a narrow internal sill.

Step into the frame

If existing window frames are sound but their glazing rebates are too shallow to accept standard square-edges units, you can overcome the problem by fitting so-called stepped units instead. With these, the outer layer of glass sits in the glazing rebate as a single pane does, while the body of the unit fits within the casement frame. Order them made to measure from a glass merchant.

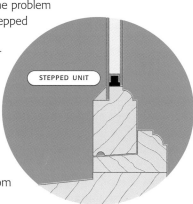

STEPPED UNIT

Roofing with plastic

Pick polycarbonate sheeting for roofing conservatories. It is light but strong, and current types neither discolour in sunlight nor become brittle with age. The triple-wall version has two layers of enclosed cells for insulation, so it keeps in heat more effectively than the original twin-walled product with its single layer of cells. It is even stronger and more rigid too.

Measure and cut with confidence

Soaking up the sound

Double-glazed units keep out traffic and aeroplane noise better than single glazing–but not much better. For effective sound insulation you need secondary glazing–an additional glass layer inside the existing glazing and up to 200 mm (8 in) away from it. Since the inner panes must be openable for ventilation, and as a means of escape, they are usually fitted into a sliding track mounted within the window opening.
For optimum performance, the secondary glazing should use glass of a different thickness from the existing glazing, and acoustic tiles should be stuck to the top, bottom and sides of the window opening between the two layers of glazing.

Measuring for new glass

When sizing old windows for new glass, measure the height and width of the openings at several points in case they're not exactly square. Then size the glass according to the smallest dimensions. Deduct a fitting and expansion allowance of 3 mm from the exact width and height of openings when you are cutting the glass yourself, but if you're ordering it, give the glass merchants the tight measurements and let them make the allowance.

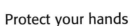

Protect your hands

Glass can break under its own weight, so always carry it on edge—but not tucked under your arm, which is dangerous. Wear leather work gloves, and to cushion your palms even more slit two short lengths of garden hose and slip them over the edge of the glass where you are going to grip it.

Making a paper template

If an opening is an unusual shape, taking accurate measurements can be difficult. To get round this problem, remove the old glass and tape a piece of paper over the outside of the frame. Then trace the edges of the rebate (or mark them onto the back of the paper from the inside). Remove the paper and cut along the marked lines to make an exact template for the replacement.

glazing

Listen for the sizzle

Before cutting glass, lay a blanket on a bench or table surface. Position the ruler to allow for the width of the cutter's shoulder, then score the glass with one smooth movement (top). Listen to the sound: if the cutter sizzles, you are applying the correct pressure. White flakes of glass mean you're pressing too hard, and a dull scraping sound shows that the cutter is blunt. **Fracture the glass** by lifting it and tapping the underside of the scored line with the cutter (centre). Then slip a pencil lengthways under the scored line at each end and press down gently on either side to snap the glass.

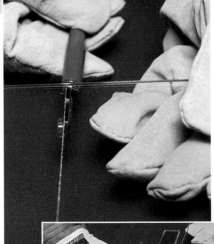

Taking a rubbing

To size a replacement piece of glass for a leaded window, carefully lever up the lead strips until they are sticking out at 90°. Then hold a piece of paper across the opening and take a rubbing of the lead strips. Flatten the lead strips with a small strip of hardwood, once the new piece of glass is sealed.

Nibble edges away

Glazier's pliers break off thin slivers of glass better than the notch on a glass cutter. Whichever tool you use, press down along the scored line, not up.

Clean with meths

Wipe a piece of glass with a clean rag dampened with methylated spirits just before you're ready to cut it. The meths gets rid of any greasy fingerprints and dust, and encourages the cutter to glide smoothly across the glass surface. Mark the cutting measurements onto the glass with a felt-tip pen, and wipe away any splinters of glass after cutting.

glazing Get the hang of using putty

Is the putty compatible?

Use linseed-oil putty on wooden frames and acrylic or universal putty for metal ones. Putty can cause laminated glass to discolour and the seals of double-glazed units to break down, so seek advice if you're fitting either of these.

Prime the rebate first

On wooden frames, apply wood primer to any bare wood in the rebate before fitting the glass. Otherwise the oil in the putty will be absorbed, causing it to dry too quickly and crack.

Seal against condensation

Press a bed of putty around the rebate before putting the glass in place. Push the pane firmly against the putty until it squeezes up and makes a continuous seal against condensation behind the glass. Then tap a couple of glazing sprigs into each of the four sides to hold the glass in place before puttying the outside.

Get a workable consistency

Dust your hands with talc to stop the putty sticking to them, then knead it on a sheet of absorbent paper to remove excess oil and get a smooth, even consistency. Don't work the putty on newspaper; the printer's ink will stain it black.

Be a smooth operator

Keep the blade of your putty knife clean and shiny to stop more putty sticking to it as you work. Dipping it in a container of clean water from time to time will also help.

Hold the glass securely

Tap in glazing sprigs (small headless nails) to hold the glass while the putty hardens, by sliding the head of your pin hammer flat against the glass. Fix sprigs every 200 mm (8 in) or so, and knock them well in so they won't catch your putty knife as you apply the putty.

Spring clips secure the glass in metal windows. If you need any replacements, take an existing clip along to your glass merchant for matching.

Finish with beads

You don't have to use putty. A simple alternative is to secure the glass with hardwood beads. Cut and mitre the beads individually, and number them so you know which goes where. Apply putty or glazing sealant to the inner faces of the beads before pressing them into place and securing them with nails or brass screws.

Practice makes perfect

Once you have pressed the putty into place, tilt the putty knife so its straight edge rests on the glass and the side of the blade is against the edge of the rebate. Press down firmly, then draw the knife along one edge in a continuous movement, not stopping until you reach a corner. The result will be a neatly bevelled bead of putty.

REPLACING A PANE OF GLASS

1 Remove broken pane and putty using hammer and old chisel or hacking knife

2 Press thin bed of putty all around rebate to seal back of glass to frame

3 Place new pane in rebate and press around edges to bed it firmly on putty

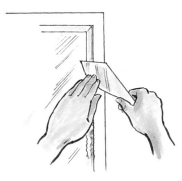

4 Tap in sprigs, apply putty and smooth off all round with putty knife

glazing

PULLEY

PARTING BEAD

SASH CORD

OUTER SASH

WEIGHT BOX

WEIGHT

INNER SASH

STAFF BEAD

sliding sashes
Restore to working order

Prise out the staff bead

You have to take the sashes out of the frame to replace broken cords. Start by prising out the staff bead at each side to release the inner sash. Use a wide chisel and begin at the centre of the bead to avoid damaging the corner mitres. If the beads split as you prise them out, keep the pieces. You can then use them as a pattern for cutting replacements.

Number the pieces and the corresponding frame edges if the old beads are intact and you intend to reuse them.

Don't drop the weights

If you cut an old sash cord, the weight will crash down inside its box at the side of the frame, taking the end of the cord with it. To avoid this, pull each sash down as far as it will go, and tie a length of string to each cord (below left). Then cut the cords (right) and lower the weights to the bottom of their boxes, letting the strings run over the pulleys. Lift the sash away from the frame. Leave the strings in position over the pulleys, so they can be used later to draw the new sash cords up inside the weight boxes and out over the pulleys.

Replace the parting beads

To release the outer sash, you have to remove the parting beads—narrow strips of wood at each side of the frame, which hold the two sashes apart. They are usually covered in paint and may have been nailed in place, so you will probably have to split them to get them out and then fit new parting beads. Use a narrow wood chisel or an old screwdriver to clean out the grooves in the frame into which they fit.

New cords all round
If one sash cord is broken, replace all four. The others will be worn, and this will save you having to repeat the repair in the near future. Look at the pulleys too. If they are old and caked with paint, unscrew them and prise them out so they can be replaced at the same time.

Finding the pockets

To get at the weights, locate the pocket covers—small removable panels in the sides of the frame near the bottom of each weight box. If layers of paint hide them, look for the saw lines which mark the edges of the pockets. Some covers are held in place with a screw, others with a nail that has to be prised out.

Label your weights

Although all sash weights look similar, the ones operating the outer sash may be a slightly different weight from those working the inner one. When you are replacing the cords, label the weights as you remove them so you know which ones belong to which sash.

STAGES IN
FITTING SASH CORDS

1 Prise off staff bead, lift out inner sash and cut through cords. Remove parting bead and free outer sash too

2 Measure and cut new cords, tie on string and weight, pass over pulleys and drop down to bottom of weight boxes

3 Tie each cord to its weight with a figure-of-eight knot and tuck into hole in weight. Melt cut ends of synthetic cord in flame of lighted match to prevent fraying

4 Nail sash cords into grooves. Replace outer sash in frame first, then inner one

sliding sashes

sliding sashes
Restore to working order

Stretch fibre cord

Polypropylene sash cord is the best type to use, because it doesn't rot or stretch. If you have to use traditional fibre sash cord, always stretch it before fitting it. If you don't, the weights will slowly stretch it until they touch the bottom of their boxes, and this will prevent the sashes from opening and closing properly.

Tie one end of the cord to a fixed object (a tree, for example), then pay out about 4 m (13 ft) of cord and pull on it with all your weight. When it won't stretch any more, untie the stretched length and cut it off. Repeat the process to stretch further lengths.

Guiding new cord into the box frame

If the old cords have dropped back into the weight boxes, tie some string to the end of the new cord. Then tie a screw, small enough to pass over the pulley, to the other end of the string. Push the screw over the pulley so it drops inside the weight box, pulling the string behind it. Reach into the pocket for the string and pull it to draw the cord over the pulley. Tie a loose knot in the other end of the cord so it can't pass the pulley while you are tying on the weights.

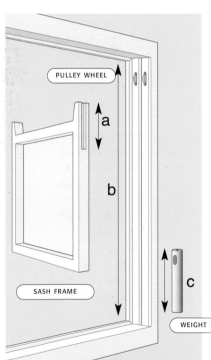

PULLEY WHEEL

a

b

SASH FRAME

c

WEIGHT

How much cord?

Measure the length of the groove which holds the cord in the side of the sash (a) and add 200 mm (8 in). Measure from the pulley wheel to the top of the sill (b) and subtract the length of the weight (c). Calculate a + 200 + b – c to find the cord length you need.

Remedies for rattles

Sashes rattle when they are a loose fit in the frame. If the inner sash is at fault, reposition the staff bead so it's closer to the face of the sash. Part-drive the fixing nails and test whether the rattle is cured by sliding the sash up and down a few times. Then drive them fully home.

Fit a fitch catch (right) if the outer sash is rattling. Its cam-shaped design draws the two sashes tightly together when they are closed. Another type—the Brighton catch—has a knurled knob on a threaded bolt and acts in a similar way.

Dual screws—a security device for sash windows—will also hold sashes firm and help to prevent rattles (see page 102).

Don't nail too high

If you nail the cord too close to the top of the sashes, it will bind on the pulleys and the sashes won't slide all the way up. Measure from the underside of the top of the frame to a point 38 mm (1½ in) below the pulley wheel. Position the top cord nails the same distance down the grooves in the sash sides.

Let a wedge take the strain

After tying the weights on, pull each one up until it stops against the back of its pulley. Then let it down by about 25 mm (1 in) and jam each cord in its pulley with a small wedge, while you nail the cords to the sashes. When you have finished, remove the wedges and let the sash close.

repairs Treating rotten woodwork

Checking the danger areas

Wet rot develops wherever rainwater gets trapped. Two of the commonest danger areas are the undersides of windowsills and the bottoms of exterior door frames. Joints open up as the wet wood swells, allowing water to soak into the vulnerable end grain. Then paint and varnish fail and rot soon takes hold.

Identifying dry rot

Dry rot rarely affects doors and windows; it needs poorly ventilated damp conditions, such as those found under a wooden ground floor. However, dry rot can spread into the hollow box frames on traditional sash windows if they are not well maintained. Many Victorian houses also still have vertically sliding shutters which extend into the underfloor space when they are not in use, and dry rot can get into these from the underfloor void.

Prospect for rotten wood

Poke suspect woodwork with a screwdriver to assess the extent of the rot. Remove blistered paint from sound wood so trapped moisture can escape and the wood can start to dry.

Let the wood dry out

After removing all the rotten timber, allow the newly-exposed surfaces to dry out thoroughly before splicing in a new piece of wood or using a filler. This process can take a week or two if the wood has absorbed a lot of moisture. However, you can speed it up with frequent short blasts from a hot-air gun. **Tape a piece of plastic sheet** over the wood to keep the rain off while it dries out, but don't make this airtight. Air needs to circulate freely underneath it.

Finding a replacement sill

Cutting out and replacing a wooden windowsill, or a section of one, is not a difficult job. Take a section of the original sill to your timber merchant, who will use it as a guide to help you select a matching replacement.

Preservation treatment

Always read the label on the tin before using any wood preservative, because some types can corrode metal fittings and affect glued joints in door and window frames, while others can kill nearby plants if splashed onto them. When applying preservative, rubber gloves, goggles and a face mask are the minimum essential safety wear. For complete protection, especially when you're putting preservative on with a spray gun rather than a brush, wear a disposable coverall with an elasticated hood and use a battery-powered respirator, both available from plant hire shops.

repairs

repairs Treating rotten woodwork

Using filler or adding new wood

The easiest way to replace small areas of timber destroyed by wet rot is with a proprietary wood repair system (see below). But when the damage is extensive, or the wood is varnished or stained and a repair with filler cannot easily be disguised, cut out the rot and patch in a new piece of wood.

Seal the gaps

To prevent rain getting in between a new door or window frame and the surrounding masonry, fill the gap between the two with a flexible frame sealant. This is available in white or brown to match painted and stained woodwork, and can be overpainted in another colour once it has formed a surface skin.

 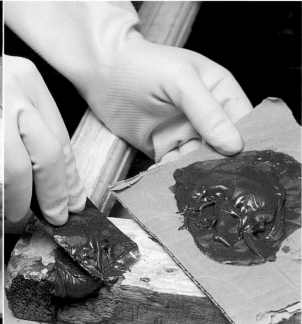

Two-stage repair

Patch small areas of rotten wood using a proprietary repair system consisting of liquid wood hardener and a specially formulated exterior wood filler.
After cutting away all the rot, put on rubber gloves and brush a generous coat of hardener onto the area to be filled, using an old paintbrush (left).

Spread the wood filler with the plastic spatula provided (right), overfilling the repair slightly so you can sand down the dried filler flush with the surrounding surface. Work quickly: the filler begins to harden after about 5 minutes at normal temperatures and even more quickly in warm weather.

Repairing door frames

The bottoms of exterior door frames often start to rot because moisture gets into the end grain of the uprights. Cut out the rotten wood, sawing upwards at an angle of 45°; this makes the repair stronger. If the bottom of the post is anchored to the door sill or the ground by a metal dowel, you will have to split the rotten wood away with a wood chisel.

Then cut off the dowel flush with the sill or the ground with a hacksaw, and glue and screw the new piece of wood in place, having primed and painted it first.

Keep rot at bay

You can help prevent rot from attacking repaired woodwork by drilling holes at roughly 50 mm (2 in) intervals in the surrounding wood, inserting preservative pellets and filling the holes. These pellets slowly release preservative into the wood, destroying any remaining rot spores and preventing future attacks.

Protective coating

Before fitting new doors and windows, paint those surfaces you won't be able to get at once the item is in place—the bottom edge of a door, for example.

1 Cut wedge-shaped piece out of sill, extending at least 50 mm (2 in) beyond rot

2 Mark outline of cut-out on replacement wood, then saw insert to shape and test for fit

3 Spread adhesive on mating surfaces and tap patch into place. Plane or sand patch flush with sill, then fill joints, prime and paint over it

repairs

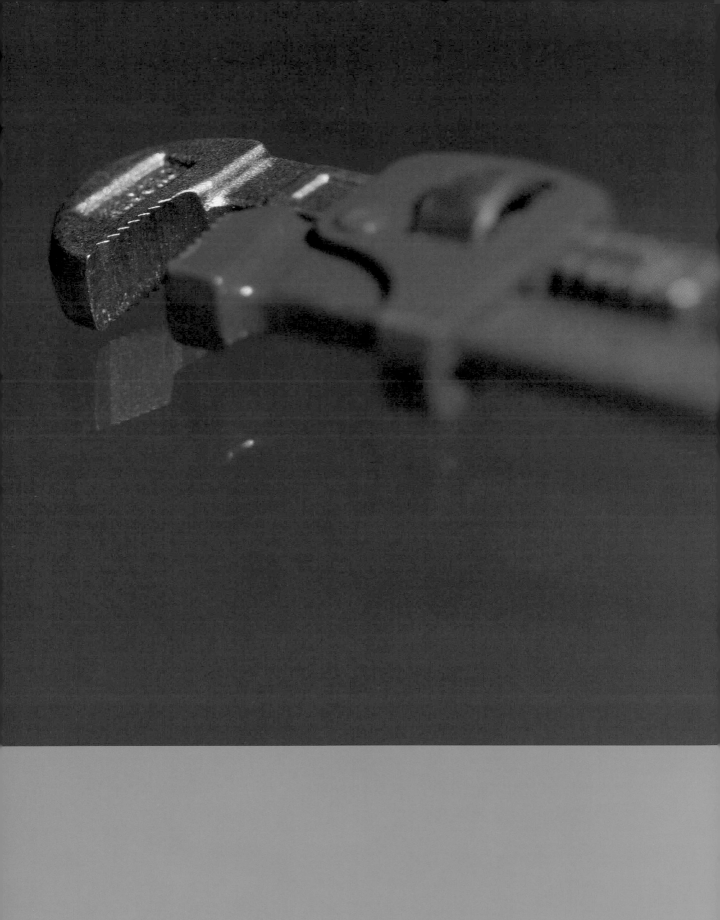

plumbing

DRAIN COCK

First find your stoptap

Even if you never intend doing any plumbing work, it's vital to know how to turn off the water supply in an emergency. The most important control is the indoor stoptap, which is fitted in the mains supply pipe close to where it enters the house. Make sure that everyone in the house knows where it is and how to turn it off.

Top priority

Older houses may not have had an indoor stoptap fitted, and still rely on an underground one fitted outdoors somewhere between the house and the road. If your system is like this, have an indoor stoptap fitted as soon as possible, even before you start updating the rest of the system.

Vital testing

A stoptap can seize up if not used for a while, and you will not be able to turn the water off in an emergency. To prevent this, turn the tap off and on again regularly to keep it moving freely and spray a little aerosol lubricant onto the tap spindle. Set the tap for normal operation by opening it fully, then closing it by a quarter turn.

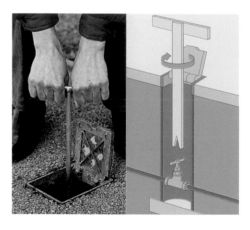

Check the tap type

Where there is no indoor stoptap, look for a small metal plate, close to the front gate, under which is the main outdoor stoptap, set in a deep hole. If this has a square-topped spindle, buy a special long-handled socket spanner from a plumbers' merchant so you can operate it. **If this stoptap has a T-bar handle,** you can improvise a spanner from scrap wood. Cut a piece long enough to reach the tap, and saw a V-shaped notch in one end to fit over the tap handle. Nail a second piece to the other end of the first to form a cross bar so you can turn the improvised spanner.

STOPTAP

Trace the pipe runs

If you have a cold-water storage cistern, look for on-off valves (called gatevalves) on the outlet pipes. One allows you to cut off the supply to the cold taps; the other controls the supply to the hot-water cylinder. Identify which is which by tracing the pipe runs if you can. If you can't, close each valve in turn then check which taps run dry. Label the valves accordingly.

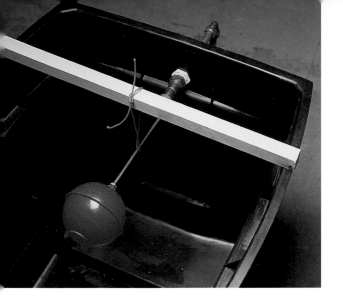

Coping without valves

If there are no gatevalves on the outlets from your cold-water storage cistern, or if the existing valves are jammed in the open position, lay a batten across the cistern and tie the arm of the float-operated valve to it. This will keep the valve closed while you empty the cistern by opening all the taps supplied from it. Once the cistern is empty, no water will flow from either your cold or hot taps.

If you need to drain a pipe in a hurry—because it's sprung a leak, for example—you may not have time to wait for the cistern to empty. In this case, push a carrot into the relevant outlet pipe and open the taps to drain the affected pipe.

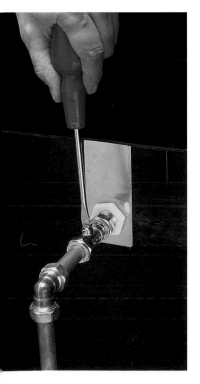

Look for local valves

Modern plumbing systems have small shut-off valves on individual supply pipes. These allow you to isolate a tap, a float-operated valve or a water-using appliance without having to turn off the mains supply or drain down cisterns. You operate them by inserting a screwdriver blade or a slim coin in the slot and rotating it by a quarter turn. The valve is open when the slot is in line with the pipe direction.

Water supplies

Safe to drink?

Unless the cold-water cistern is fairly new and well sealed, you should not drink water from taps supplied by it. Always take drinking water from the kitchen cold tap (or any other tap which you know is connected directly to the mains supply). If you have old lead pipes and live in a soft-water area, run the tap for a while in the morning to drain off water that has been standing in the pipes overnight, before filling a glass or kettle.

Replace a rusty cistern

Once the galvanising breaks down on an old galvanised water cistern, it will start to rust. If this happens to yours, have it replaced with a new plastic cistern, fitted with a 'Byelaw 30' kit —see page 135 for details. Flexible round polythene cisterns can be crushed for transit so they will fit through even a small loft hatch. The old cistern can be disconnected, moved to a corner of the loft and left there if you don't want the job of cutting it up and removing it from the roof space.

Locate the drain valves

To carry out certain plumbing jobs, you do not just have to turn off the water supply; you also have to empty the pipework of water. The plumbing and heating system will have several special fittings called drain valves, where you can attach a hose and open the fitting to allow the water to flow out.

On the plumbing system, one should be fitted just above the indoor stoptap (to drain the rising main) and another near the base of the hot-water cylinder.

On the central-heating system there may be several drain valves, fitted at the low points of the system (usually next to radiators and the boiler). Make sure that you know where all yours are.

Hot-water options

If you have an old-fashioned heating system relying on gravity circulation, it is not economical to use the boiler to heat your hot water in summer, when the central heating is not needed. It is better to use the electric immersion heater in the cylinder. Connecting it to an immersion heater timer will ensure that you always have hot water when you need it.

Obey safety rules

Call a qualified fitter

It's dangerous and illegal to work on any gas appliance or pipework unless you are competent to do so. Have all gas installation and servicing work in your home carried out by a qualified fitter who is listed on the Gas Safe Register (0800 408 5500 or www.gassaferegister.co.uk) covering the UK, Isle of Man and Guernsey. Gas Safe replaced CORGI in 2009/2010.

Detect deadly gas

Gas boilers and other gas appliances should be serviced every year. Never block up air vents, because an air supply is essential for complete combustion. When appliances are not working properly, they can emit deadly carbon monoxide gas. Carbon monoxide alarms are inexpensive and can be fitted near boilers, wall-mounted water heaters or gas fires. Choose one that complies with British Standard EN 5029.

Avoid the risk of scalding

If your heating system is fully pumped, there will be motorised valves on the circuit pipework to divert water to the hot cylinder or the radiators, depending on which needs heat the most. Keep the cylinder thermostat set at no higher than 60°C to avoid scalding water coming from the taps, and adjust the room temperature as required using the room thermostat.

Earth all metalwork

All the metal plumbing and heating fixtures in your house—the circuit pipework, the radiators and any metal baths—must for safety be cross-bonded to earth with special screw-on earth clamps. If you are in doubt about whether your system is properly bonded in this way, have it checked by a qualified electrician.

pipes Working with copper and plastic

Identifying the old

Houses built before the late 1940s may still have lead or steel pipework. Identify which is which by scraping the surface with a knife (lead is soft) and by examining the joints. Joints in lead pipe are smooth and bulbous; those in steel pipes have raised collars. Lead pipes should be replaced, especially if you live in a soft-water area. Ask your local water company for advice.

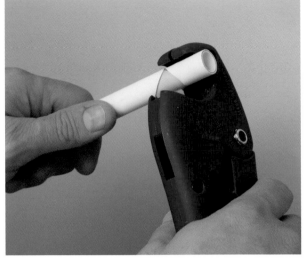

Cutting plastic pipe

Plastic plumbing pipe can be cut using a sharp trimming knife, but the best tool is a plastic pipe cutter – shaped rather like garden secateurs – which you should be able to buy at the same time as you buy the plastic pipe.

Cut waste pipe square

It's easier to cut plastic waste pipes squarely if you hold them in a mitre box. Use a full-size hacksaw—the frame of a junior one will foul on the box—and be sure to keep the blade vertical.

If you do not own a mitre box, wrap a piece of plain paper around the waste pipe and hold it firmly in place (with the sides lined up) to act as a guide when cutting.

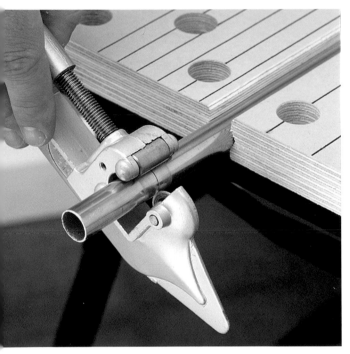

Cutting copper pipe

By far the best way to cut copper pipe is to use a pipe cutter. This has a hardened steel cutting wheel which you advance using the knurled knob as you rotate the cutter around the pipe. It leaves a perfectly square cut end with only a slight burr on the inside of the pipe. This can be removed with the V-shaped reamer on the tool (if fitted) or with a small half-round file.

Using a hacksaw produces a much poorer result, but may be necessary when you need to cut through pipes close to a wall (though there are circular pipe cutters available for doing this). A 'junior' hacksaw will be easier to use for cutting copper pipe than a full-size one. Clean up the ends of the pipe with a file.

pipes Making joints

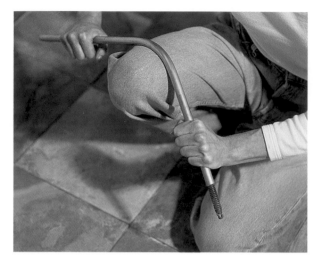

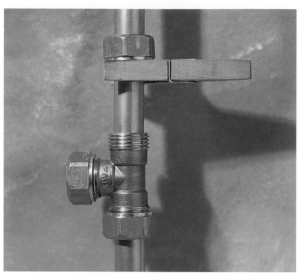

Springing into shape

When bending a pipe with a spring, overbend it slightly, then bend it back to the angle you want; this makes the spring easier to withdraw from the bent pipe. Tie a piece of string to the spring before bending a long pipe, so you can pull it out again when you have finished; with short pipes the spring will protrude from the end. Bending springs for pipes 12 mm or less in diameter are slid over the pipe, not put inside it.

Stop the drop

When you are inserting a compression tee into an existing vertical pipe run, cut the pipe at the connection point. Then thread the cap nuts and olives onto the pipe and use clothes pegs to stop them sliding down while you fit the cut pipe ends into the tee. Do up the lower cap nut first, then let the upper nut and olive drop down and tighten them too.

Imperial to metric

Copper pipe went metric in the 1970s, but older houses may still have pipework in imperial sizes. If you plan to connect into old pipe with soldered capillary fittings, you will need special adaptors for all pipes, whatever the size. **Metric compression fittings** connect 15 mm and 28 mm pipes directly to ½ in and 1 in pipes. However, to connect new 22 mm pipe to old ¾ in, you will have to replace one of the metric olives with a metric/imperial conversion olive.

Bending large pipes

Bending 22 mm or 28 mm pipe by hand is hard work. Consider hiring a pipe bending machine if you have a lot of bends to make in large-diameter copper pipe. Alternatively, you can make the pipe more flexible by heating the area of the bend with a blowlamp until the metal glows red. Allow the pipe to cool, then use a bending spring.

Pushing together

Copper and plastic supply and heating pipes can be joined with plastic fittings into which you simply push the pipe ends. The pipes are locked in place by steel-toothed rings inside the fitting, and can be freed by releasing a ring round the pipe opening. These fittings allow the pipe to rotate in the joint, which makes alignment of pipes easier. You'll need an earthing wire on copper pipe—see page 124.

Compression fittings for easy joints

For most DIY pipework, compression fittings assembled with a spanner are easier to use than soldered capillary fittings. As you tighten the fitting (one spanner on the fitting, one on the nut), a soft brass 'olive' fitted over the pipe is compressed to give a watertight seal. Compression fittings are more obtrusive (and more expensive) than capillary ones, but can be taken apart much more easily if required.

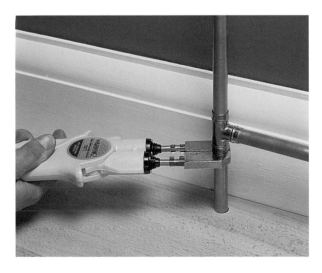

Clamping capillary fittings

You can make pipe joints with soldered capillary fittings in seconds using these cunning electric tongs. They work like a pair of soldering irons, clamping round the fitting and heating it up quickly and evenly. You change the clamp heads to suit the size of pipe you're soldering.

1 Dismantle old fitting, noting which way olives face. Slip nuts and olives over pipe ends

2 Push pipe into fitting until it meets the internal stop. Push up olive and then hand tighten first nut

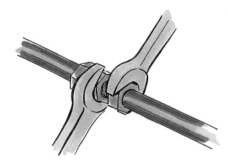

3 Repeat for other olive and nut. Then use a spanner to tighten each nut one full turn while holding fitting with a second spanner

pipes

pipes Connecting up

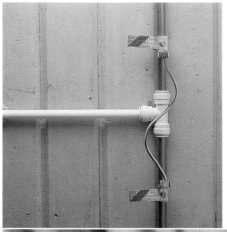

Bridge plastic fittings

If you use any plastic fittings on copper pipe runs, these will break the earth continuity (see page 124). It is vitally important to bridge every plastic fitting. Attach earth clamps to the pipes on either side of the fitting and link them with a short length of 4 mm² earth cable: unless all metal supply pipework is bonded to earth, there is a risk of severe electric shock if an electrical fault occurs and makes the pipe live.

Allow space for expansion

Plastic waste pipes expand as hot water runs through them, so you need to make an allowance for this. If you are using compression or push-fit fittings, make up each joint and then pull each pipe out of the fitting by about 3 mm (⅛ in). With rigid solvent-weld fittings, fit a flexible expansion coupling in the pipe run about every 2.4 m (8 ft).

Line up the joints

When making up a run of pipework with solvent-weld joints, assemble the run dry first of all and make sure the joints line up, especially elbows and tees. Make small pencil marks on both pipe and fitting at every joint to help you to align them correctly as you weld them together.

Easy assembly

Make compression and push-fit joints on waste pipe runs easier to assemble by using a file to chamfer the cut end of each pipe slightly, so it slips into the O-ring inside the fitting without snagging on it. Smear a little silicone grease on the end of the pipe so it slides into the fitting more easily.

Choosing plastic

Plastic (polybutylene or cross-linked polyethylene) water pipes can be used for both hot and cold supplies in the home–and also for central heating (but not the first 1m next to the boiler). Because they come in long rolls and are semi-flexible, they can be threaded through holes cut in floor joists and bent easily round corners–so fewer fittings are needed. They can be joined with plastic push-fit fittings or with normal compression fittings (using a metal support sleeve); the pipes need supports closer together than for copper pipe.

1 Assemble joint dry, and make register mark on both pipe and fitting if precise joint alignment is essential

2 Roughen end of pipe and inside of fitting with medium-grade abrasive paper

3 Brush solvent-weld cement onto pipe and into fitting, taking care not to get any on outside

4 Push pipe into fitting, give it a slight twist and align register marks. Then hold joint still for 30 seconds. Then leave for 24 hours before use

pipes

125

pipes Fixing leaks

Quick fix for a leaking fitting

A quick way of stopping a leak—without turning the water off—is to use LLFA (pronounced "alpha") tape. This self-amalgamating (or "compression") tape is simply wound under tension around the pipe and it immediately forms a watertight seal. It provides a permanent repair and will withstand considerable water pressure.

Wrap around

If a compression fitting still drips after you've tried tightening the nuts, dismantle it and start again. Turn off the water and drain the pipe. Then undo the nuts and slip the pipes out of the fitting. Wrap the brass olives with two turns of PTFE tape. Then reassemble the fitting and tighten the nuts.

Flux for flow

If you get a leak from a soldered joint, drain the pipe and use heat from your blowlamp or hot-air gun to dry it out thoroughly. Feed a little self-cleaning flux into the warmed joint. Then reheat the joint to melt the existing solder. The flux will help it to flow into the gaps and seal the joint properly.

Slip on a coupling

A 'slip' compression coupling has no internal stops and can be used to replace a short length (up to 90 mm) of damaged pipe. Cut out the damaged section and slide the coupling on to one cut end before bringing it back to join to the other.

Leave the nail in place

If you accidentally put a nail through a pipe while fixing floorboards, leave the nail where it is. It will form an almost perfect seal while you turn off the water and drain the pipework ready for repair.

Emergency clamp

Keep a pipe repair clamp (above) in your tool kit for emergencies. It can be fitted to a burst pipe in seconds with just a screwdriver. If you have a leak in a lead pipe and can't turn off the water, flatten the pipe upstream of the leak with a hammer to stem the flow of water. The whole pipe can then be replaced at a later date using copper or plastic.

Freeze a leaking pipe

A pipe-freezing kit lets you repair a leaking pipe without having to turn the water off and drain down the system. Flatten the pipe upstream of the damage to stop the flow, then freeze the pipe a little farther upstream. Make sure you have replacement pipe and fittings to hand. Cut out the damaged section downstream from the frozen zone and make the repair as quickly as you can.

Turn the nuts

When a compression fitting starts to leak, try tightening each nut very slightly. Don't tighten it by more than a quarter turn, because you might squash the olive inside and make the leak worse.

126

taps Getting at the works

INDICATOR DISC

RETAINING SCREW

HANDLE

SHROUD

SPINDLE

HEADGEAR

TAP WASHER

TAP TAIL

SPACER WASHER

HEADGEAR

TAP WASHER

TAP TAIL

Plug in first
Before starting to dismantle a tap, turn off its water supply and put the plug in the waste outlet. This will prevent any small parts you might drop from disappearing into the trap beneath the outlet.

Washers or discs?
Traditional taps have a mechanism that moves a rubber washer against or away from the water inlet to stop or start the flow. Many modern taps contain a pair of ceramic discs with holes through them, one of which rotates to control the flow. Turn the tap on fully to find out which type you have. A ceramic disc tap needs just a quarter turn, a traditional tap at least two turns.

Removing the handle
Some tap handles can be pulled off, but most have a small screw to retain them. Look for it on the side of a traditional (cross-top) tap handle. On a modern shrouded-head tap, it is usually beneath the hot/cold indicator disc. Gently prise this off to reveal the screw, which may also retain a small washer.

Reverse the washer
If you don't have a suitable replacement tap washer, remove the old one, turn it over and refit it. It will last a little longer, until you have a chance to get a new one of the correct size.

Soften the bite
When dismantling chrome or gold-plated taps, it's a good idea to wrap the jaws of your adjustable spanner with a few turns of PVC insulating tape to stop them damaging the plating.

Turn on the heat
Play a hot-air gun over a stuck tap shroud to warm it up. This should make the metal expand and break the grip of the threads. If it doesn't, squirt a little silicone lubricating fluid into the thread. You might need to repeat the heating and lubricating once or twice before the thread is freed. Don't try this on taps fitted to a plastic basin or bath, however, as the heat could damage it.

taps

taps Getting at the works

When the handle is stuck

If the cross-top handle won't come off an old fashioned shrouded tap, you might be able to remove it by using its shroud to push it off. Remove the screw securing the handle to the spindle and turn the tap on fully. Loosen the shroud and insert a thin spanner round the headgear nut. Then turn the tap handle to off; this action should jack the handle off the spindle.

Keep some spares

Tap washers are very cheap, so you can afford to keep a supply in your tool kit. They are still made in just two imperial sizes—½ in and ¾ in. The larger size fits bath taps, the smaller size everything else.

Fitting a new washer

Try a domed washer

If the seating (the water inlet inside the tap against which the washer closes) is worn, a standard washer may not make a watertight seal against it. Try fitting a domed washer instead. This sits inside the seating and effectively changes the sealing point. The only drawback is that it takes several more turns than usual to open the tap fully for a fast flow rate.

Dissolve scale

The most common cause of jammed headgear nuts in hard-water areas is limescale. Once you have removed the headgear, soak the threaded parts in vinegar, lemon juice or a proprietary scale remover to dissolve the scale. Smear some silicone grease on them to lubricate and protect them before you reassemble the tap.

Bed in an insert

If a domed washer doesn't do the trick, the seating is probably badly corroded. Buy a nylon insert to push into the tap seating and give the washer a new surface to seal against. If you cannot bed the insert all the way into the seating by hand, replace the headgear and turn the tap on and off a few times (before turning the water back on). This will push the insert evenly into place.

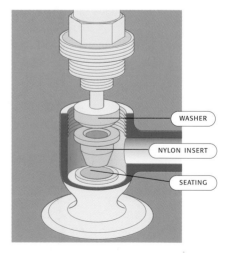

WASHER

NYLON INSERT

SEATING

Stop weeping

When water oozes up from round the spindle of a tap, the packing gland round it is faulty. You don't have to turn the water off to fix this. Tighten the small hexagonal gland nut on the top of the headgear by half a turn. If the leak persists, remove the gland nut and pack in some PTFE tape pulled into a string. Replace the nut and test the tap.

Protect the pipework and ceramic ware

Remove the brass headgear from the tap body by turning it anticlockwise with a spanner. As you do so, brace the tap with a piece of wood so that it cannot rotate, otherwise the connection between the tap and the pipework may be damaged. Allowing the tap to rotate could also result in a cracked ceramic basin.

Replacing O-rings

Take it with you

The diverter on a shower mixer tap will drip if the O-rings and washers inside are worn. To replace them, you will have to remove the diverter by turning off both taps then raising the diverter knob and undoing the headgear nut with a spanner. Take the complete unit with you to a plumbers' merchant so you can be sure of obtaining the correct replacement O-rings and washers.

Ringing the changes

Modern taps have O-rings instead of a packing gland. Remove the headgear, hold it securely in one hand and turn the spindle clockwise to unscrew and remove the washer unit. Prise off the old O-ring with a small screwdriver and fit a new one after smearing it with a little silicone grease.

Spouting off

Swivel-spout mixers use one or two O-rings to seal the join between spout and tap body. If they are worn, water will ooze out between the two. To remove the spout, locate and remove the grub screw behind it if there is one. Otherwise turn the spout so it's parallel with the tap body and pull it sharply upwards. Remove the worn O-ring(s) and fit same-size replacement(s), applying a little silicone grease first.

taps Changeover time

Swapping supplies

Baths, basins and sinks usually have the hot tap on the left and the cold tap on the right. If yours are the other way round and you find this confusing, undo the tap connectors and cut back the supply pipes by 150 mm (6 in) or so. Attach a flexible pipe and tap connector to each pipe, then link each connector to the correct tap. Swap over the hot and cold indicators on the tap handles.

Measure the two tails

Look at the two inlet pipes on a monobloc basin or sink mixer tap before fitting it. If they're 10 mm or 12 mm in diameter, you'll need reducing adaptors to connect them to the hot and cold supplies. But if the pipes increase in size to 15 mm, then standard 15 mm straight couplings will do the job.

HOT TAP

COLD TAP

Check the spacing

When replacing a two-hole mixer tap on an old sink, you may find that the distance between the holes doesn't match the standard separation to which modern mixer taps are made. If this is the case, ask your plumbers' merchant for mixer taps with cranked swivel tails which can cope with a range of non-standard hole separations.

Made for mains

Most imported taps are designed to operate at mains pressure, so do not fit them where the cold water comes from a storage cistern or the hot water from a hot water cylinder. Water will merely trickle from them.

COLD SUPPLY PIPE

HOT SUPPLY PIPE

Off with the old

Replacing old taps means disconnecting the supply pipework from the tap tails, which can be difficult (see page 140). For a start, you have to work in a confined space, and the tap connector may be corroded. Apply some penetrating oil to the tap connector nuts, leave it for a while to soak into the threads, then use a crow's-foot spanner (also called a basin wrench) to undo the nuts.

Pick a longer spout

If you are choosing a sink mixer tap to serve a sink with two bowls, pick one with a spout that projects by 230 mm rather than the standard 180 mm to make it easier to fill a kettle or pan.

Bridging the gap

Check the length of the tap tails on any new taps you buy. Modern taps have tails around 10 mm (⅜ in) shorter than older types, so you will need adaptors called tap extenders to bridge the gap between them and the existing pipes.

Match the taps to the pressure

British bath and shower mixer taps and valves are designed to use hot and cold water at low pressure. If your bathroom has mains-fed cold water, ask your supplier for taps that can cope with the pressure difference between hot and cold.

Plan for the future

Turning the water off so you can fit new taps often involves finding gatevalves in the loft or draining down the cold-water cistern. Take this opportunity to install an in-line isolating or shut-off valve on each supply pipe. Thereafter replacing the washers and any other work on the taps will only involve closing these valves.

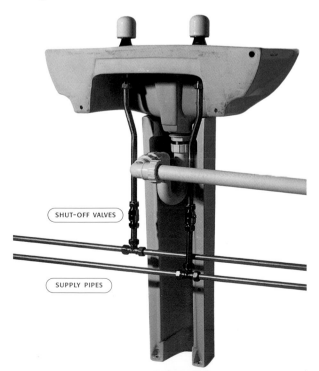

SHUT-OFF VALVES

SUPPLY PIPES

STAGES IN
REPLACING A TAP

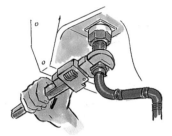

1 Turn off water supply to tap. Then undo nut on tap connector that links supply pipe to tap tail

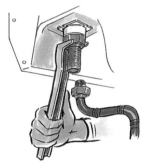

2 Use a basin wrench to undo backnut on the tap tail

3 Lift out old tap and clean away any sealant round the hole. Then put in the new tap, complete with its gasket

4 Secure the new tap with its backnut and reconnect supply pipe. Use a tap extender if the new tap tail is too short

taps

taps Fixing ceramic disc taps

Dripping discs

Ceramic disc taps were designed to end the need for tap washers, but they can still drip and they cost a lot more to put right. Before buying a new cartridge, remove the existing one—a job that's similar to taking the headgear out of a conventional tap—and fit a thicker O-ring on the base of the cartridge. This pushes the discs together and may stop the drip.

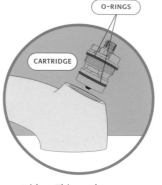

O-RINGS

CARTRIDGE

Changing cartridges

If fitting a thicker O-ring doesn't stop the drip, you have no alternative but to replace the entire cartridge. To get the right spare you need to know the make of tap, which may be stamped on the indicator disc. If it isn't and you have no other way of identifying the manufacturer, remove the cartridge, and take it with you to a plumbers' merchant in the hope of finding a matching spare. Note that cartridges are either left-handed or right-handed, so make sure that your replacement turns on in the same direction as the original.

Water in the garden

Ensure one-way flow

By law, a tap serving a hosepipe must be fitted with a double-check valve to stop back-siphonage (caused by loss of mains pressure) contaminating the mains water supply. You can either fit a tap with an integral check valve (as below), or fit a separate valve in the pipework after the new stoptap.

TEE

NEW STOPTAP

ELBOW

OUTDOOR TAP

INDOOR STOPTAP

BACKPLATE ELBOW

DRAIN SCREW

Prepare for winter

The check valve in a tap with an integral valve (right) can be damaged by frost. At the beginning of winter, turn off the water supply from inside the house. Then open the drain screw under the tap so any water left inside can run out.

Snappy connections

To save having to unscrew the hose every time you want to fill a watering can, fit a quick-release hose union and tap connector. This allows you to pull off and push on the hose in a second.

ballvalves Choosing the right type

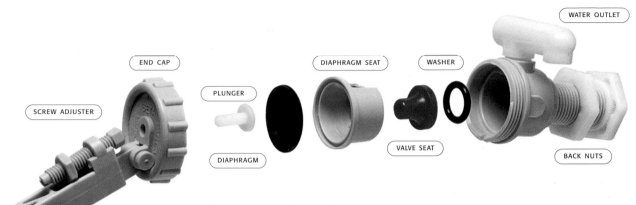

SCREW ADJUSTER · END CAP · PLUNGER · DIAPHRAGM · DIAPHRAGM SEAT · VALVE SEAT · WASHER · WATER OUTLET · BACK NUTS · FLOAT ARM

Diaphragms or pistons?

It's well worth examining the ballvalves in your loft cisterns before anything goes wrong with them, so you know which type you have. Newer homes will have diaphragm ballvalves (above), while older homes will probably still have piston-operated ones (below). Diaphragm ballvalves are usually made of plastic, while piston-operated ones are brass.

END CAP · PISTON · VALVE BODY · WASHER · BACK NUTS · VALVE SEAT · UNION NUT · WATER OUTLET · SPLIT PIN · FLOAT ARM

New pistons for old

In hard-water areas, piston-operated ballvalves can grind to a halt because of a build-up of scale inside them. You can dismantle them and clean them out, but it's better to replace an old-style ballvalve with a new diaphragm type, which is more reliable and less likely to scale up and seize.

On the quiet

As an alternative to a diaphragm ballvalve, a WC cistern can be fitted with an equilibrium ballvalve (often known as a "quiet" ballvalve), which can cope with a range of water pressures and has the additional advantage of virtually silent filling.

Beware the big freeze

In cold weather, water escaping down an overflow pipe can freeze, eventually blocking it. If no water is being drawn off, the storage cistern can then overflow inside the house and cause a major flood. If this happens, adjust or replace the ballvalve to stop the water overflowing. It is a good idea to turn off the water supply before winter holidays in case a fault occurs while you're away.

overflows
Problems with ballvalves

A regular press

The smaller of the two water cisterns in the loft is the header tank for the central heating system. It 'tops up' the system if there are any slight leaks—but because this happens rarely, the ballvalve can get stuck in the closed position and evaporation can run the tank dry. To avoid this happening, check the valve's operation regularly by pressing the float arm down. The tank should only be around one-third full when the water is cold (it rises as the water heats and expands).

Don't make a splash

The ballvalve in the cold-water storage cistern opens and shuts many times a day. If it's a piston-operated type, this heavy wear can cause the washer to perish. Fitting a replacement is easy, but don't try to do the job while leaning over the cistern; you are bound to drop and lose a vital component. After turning the water off, remove the whole ballvalve and take it to a work surface where you can replace the washer.

Curing cistern drips

A damp patch on the floor below a WC cistern fitted with a bottom-entry ballvalve is probably due to a failed sealing washer where the pipe passes through the base of the cistern. To cure the problem, empty the cistern and disconnect the ballvalve. Fit a new sealing washer between the inner back nut and the cistern and re-make the connection.

Early warning
Go outside and check the WC cistern overflow pipe from time to time. If the cistern is persistently overflowing, even very slightly, the water dripping from the pipe can trickle down the house wall and cause unsightly stains. At worst, it can lead to damp penetrating the wall to the inside.

It's in the bag

A metal float can corrode and develop pinhole leaks. As the float fills with water, it sinks lower and lower and no longer closes the valve properly, so the cistern overflows. Until you can fit a new float, unscrew the old one and empty out the water (by drilling a larger hole in it if necessary), then tie a plastic freezer bag tightly over it to stop the leak temporarily.

Pressure counts

Before fitting a new ballvalve in a WC cistern to cure an overflow, check where the cold-water supply comes from so you can fit the correct valve seat inside the new valve. You need a narrow seat for a high-pressure mains supply, and a wider one for a low-pressure supply run from a storage cistern.

Free to move

Because space is limited inside the WC cistern, the float arm may catch on the siphon mechanism, resulting in a jammed valve and overflow. If this happens, bend the arm of a metal valve so it is free to move, or rotate a plastic valve slightly so it clears an obstruction. Or fit a new equilibrium valve (see page 133) which takes up less space.

Clean the tubes

Baths and sinks often have flexible plastic pipes that link the overflow to the waste outlet. These must be clear of any obstructions to work properly. Check yours from time to time to see if they can cope with the flow when both taps are left running and the plug is in. If they can't, dismantle them and flush them through with hot soapy water.

Line up the banjo

When reassembling bath and sink waste and overflow connections, make sure that the hole inside the plastic collar (known as the banjo) at the bottom end of the flexible overflow hose is lined up with the slot in the waste outlet.

Storage cistern tips

Keeping it clean

New water cisterns are sold with a Byelaw 30 kit (Byelaw 60 in Scotland) to protect the water inside. This is mostly illustrated above and includes:

- A lid incorporating a screened breather
- An insulating jacket (not shown)
- A grommet to fit round the safety open vent pipe where it passes through the lid
- An overflow pipe connector with a filter (to prevent insects crawling up the pipe) and a dip tube (to keep draughts out)
- A supporting plate for the ballvalve.

You must fit this kit when putting in a new cistern—but you may be able to add it to an existing cistern, too.

1 Turn off water supply to valve and unscrew large end cap on body of valve

2 Withdraw float arm and plunger from body of valve and place to one side

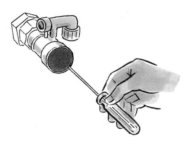

3 Use slim screwdriver blade to prise old diaphragm out of valve body

4 Clean any dirt from valve. Fit new diaphragm the right way round, reassemble valve and restore water supply

overflows

blockages Clearing a waste pipe

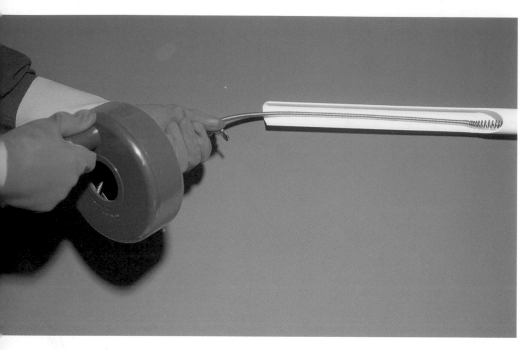

Try a plumber's snake

For blockages which cannot be cleared with a plunger, it is worth trying a device called a spiral cleaner or plumber's snake. You can buy one or hire one. Disconnect the blocked pipe from its trap and feed the end of the wire into it. Then turn the handle to rotate the spiral. This drives the cutting head into the blockage and breaks it up.

Take the plunger

For clearing blocked waste pipes, a simple plunger is hard to beat. As you plunge it up and down it pushes and pulls the blockage apart, rather than compacting it. **For a plunger to work,** its cup must be covered with water, and the overflow inlet must be sealed. Holding a wet cloth over it is the best method.

Start from the outlet

Waste pipes joined with compression or push-fit connectors are easily taken apart when there is a blockage. Start dismantling the pipe at the outlet end and work your way along the pipe. When you reach the blocked section, put a bucket under the end of the pipe and dislodge the obstruction with a length of stiff wire.

Reassemble with care

Once you have cleared a blockage, you have to reconnect the various components you dismantled. Check that all the sealing rings are correctly positioned inside screw-up fittings, or the joints will leak. Replace any rings that are worn or have been stretched out of shape, and apply a little silicone lubricating grease to the sealing rings inside push-fit connectors.

Chemical soup

Avoid using strong chemicals—especially caustic soda—when you are trying to clear sink blockages. If they don't work, you'll still have the blockage, plus a sink and trap full of unpleasant and possibly dangerous liquid to deal with.

Warmth and water

If you have poured hot fat down the kitchen sink and it has blocked the trap, try warming the bend of the trap gently with a hair dryer. This should soften the fat plug enough for you to disperse it. Once the waste is on the move, run the hot tap for a minute or two to make sure that all traces of fat are flushed well out of the system.

Hose it out

If a blockage can't be shifted from the sink end, and the waste pipe discharges into an outside gully, push a garden hose up the pipe from outside. This might do the trick by itself, but if you need to turn on the garden tap, use only enough pressure to move the blockage. Otherwise, the contents of the pipe could be sprayed out of the plughole and all over the kitchen.

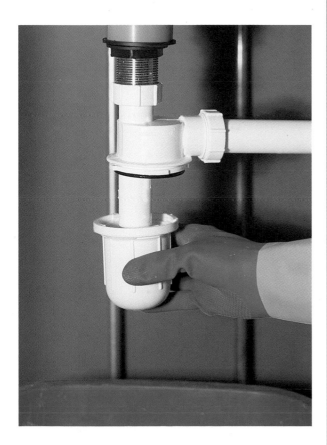

Open the bottle trap

If you cannot clear a blocked waste pipe from either end, the next step is to take the trap apart. Modern plastic traps are easy to dismantle without tools.

Put the plug in the plughole and a bowl or bucket beneath the trap first. Then unscrew the base of a round bottle trap or undo the coupling nuts on a pipe trap. Remove any blockage from the trap, rinse it out and reassemble it.

1 Screw two or three lengths of drain rod together and fit plunger disc to one end

2 Feed rods into drain, adding more as needed. Rotate rods clockwise or they will unscrew and be lost in the drain

3 If plunger will not shift the blockage, withdraw rods and fit corkscrew head to pull the obstruction out

4 Once blockage is cleared, fill bath with cold water. Then pull out plug so water gushes out and sluices drain clean

blockages

137

blockages Unblocking a WC

Make do and mend

If you don't have a proper WC plunger to deal with a blockage, improvise by wrapping a plastic bag round a mop head. Tie the bag to the handle of the mop so it can't work free. **If you have a set of drain rods** and a rubber plunger disc, fit this to one of the rods to make a WC plunger.

Snake with a hook

You will need a plumber's snake with a hook attachment to clear the blockage caused by an item such as a disposable nappy. Feed the snake into the trap until you feel it has reached the blockage, then rotate it and push it forward gently so it grabs the object. Withdraw it slowly from the trap.

Heat treatment

Try clearing a partly blocked WC by pouring a bucket of hot water down it. If it seems to be draining more quickly after one bucket, follow up immediately with two or three more.

Problems outdoors

Clearing debris from a gully

Water spilling out of a garden gully usually indicates a blocked trap below ground level. Remove the gully grating and scoop out the debris by hand, wearing heavy-duty PVC gloves. Then flush the gully through with water to clear any remaining debris and discourage another blockage from forming.

Rodding out a soil stack

Soil stacks rarely get blocked–but if they do, you can rod them out. Plastic soil stacks usually have small access 'doors' on them, which you can unscrew (stand well back!) and then insert drain rods fitted with a plunger. If you have an old cast iron soil pipe, you may have to get a long ladder so you can insert drain rods from the top–not an easy job. Flush through with water to clean after removing blockage.

Removing a drain cover

Often the hardest part of unblocking a drain is getting the metal cover off the underground inspection chamber. Lever the edge up with a spade or brick bolster. If it won't budge, tap around the edges with a hammer to break the rust seal. If the grab bars are intact, tie a loop of rope through each one. Pass a length of wood through the loops and lever off the cover.

new fittings Out with the old…

Beef up your wrench

Undoing old tap connectors from tap tails can be hard work, as corrosion often locks the nuts on their threads. To get more leverage on the nuts, clamp an adjustable spanner onto your basin wrench. It's also a good idea to spray some penetrating oil onto the locked nut first.

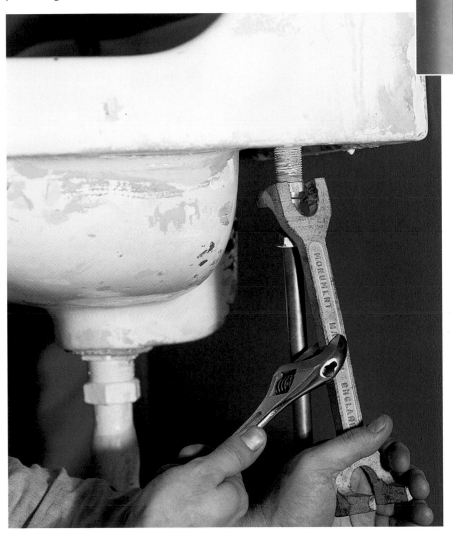

Strap gives more grip

Disconnect the waste pipe by unscrewing the connector linking the trap to the waste outlet. You should be able to undo this by hand, but if it will not move try loosening it with a Boa Constrictor strap wrench. This works in the same way as the smaller versions designed for opening screw-top jars.

Seal sink slots

If you are fitting an inset sink or basin in a worktop, seal the cut edge of the chipboard with diluted PVA sealer first. Otherwise moisture may be able to seep in, causing the chipboard to swell and lift the laminated surface.

Watch the earth

Look out for earth bonding wires as you plan the removal of old plumbing fittings. They are covered in green-and-yellow PVC insulation and connected to special metal clamps or tags on the pipes. Undo these and set them aside for reconnection later. If there are no earth wires, call in a qualified electrician to check your whole plumbing system for electrical safety.

Prepare to mop up

Before starting to remove an old plumbing fitting, double-check that you have turned off its hot and cold water supplies. Even so, the pipes will still contain some water, so have old towels or other absorbent material handy to mop up the spills as you disconnect or cut through the pipes.

new fittings
Out with the old...

...and in with the new

Remove an untidy collar

Old pipe collars behind toilet pans are unsightly, and are no longer necessary thanks to modern push-fit connectors. Cut off a cast-iron collar with a hacksaw or chain cutter where it passes through the wall, and break off an earthenware one where it goes into the floor. Provided you strike from the inside outwards, the collar will break off cleanly at floor level. The new push-fit connector will fit inside the pipe and should cover the exposed end neatly.

The right connector

If you are replacing a toilet pan, choose the correct type of connector to match the existing soil pipe. You need a straight connector if the pipe passes through the wall immediately behind the pan, and a right-angled one otherwise.

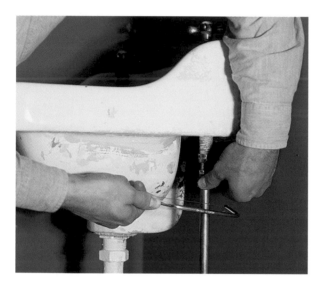

Cut the connection

If tap connectors refuse to budge when you're trying to remove an old fitting, just cut through the pipes with a hacksaw or pipe cutter. You can replace the pipework when you install the new fitting. This also gives you the chance to fit a new tap connector and an in-line isolating valve to each pipe, which will make future tap repairs a simple job.

Demolition job

If you need to remove an old cast-iron bath, and it isn't a valuable Victorian roll-top type worth saving and selling, break it with a sledgehammer to make it easier to move. Wear safety goggles, ear defenders and strong gloves, and drape the bath with an old blanket to contain flying debris. Smash holes through the inside corners of the bath first, then punch more holes across the base and up the sides until you have pieces you can lift away easily.

Skip the mortar

Don't bed a new WC pan on mortar, which can shrink and crack the pan. Instead, secure it to the floor with woodscrews, fitted with rubber washers to protect the china. Alternatively screw nylon pan fixings to the floor, place the pan over them, trim the threads to length and fit and tighten the nuts.

Slowing down the flush

Modern WC pans are made for use with low-level cisterns. You can use a high-level cistern if you particularly want one, but you might need to fit a flow restrictor in the pan inlet to reduce the speed of the flush. Without it, the water can splash over the edge of the pan.

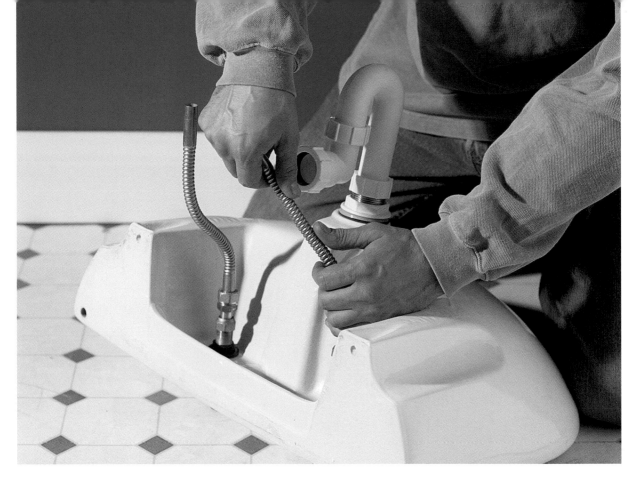

Pedestal planning

When installing a new pedestal washbasin, first turn the basin upside down on the floor. Fit the trap and the tap connectors, then bend the two flexible supply pipes so they will fit neatly out of sight behind the pedestal once the basin is installed.

Before you begin

Attach everything you can to a new plumbing fitting before you start work to install it–space will be limited once it is in place. Tighten the back nuts of taps well so that the bodies of the taps do not rotate when they are turned on and off, and fit sealing washers supplied when securing the waste outlet. Check that flexible overflow pipes are correctly linked to their waste outlets.

First fittings

To save having to make connections once a sink, basin or bath is in place, try to fit the taps, flexible tap connectors, waste outlet and overflow (if necessary) whilst you can still get at them easily.

Support when cutting out

When making the cut-out for an inset sink or basin, it is best if the worktop or counter top is in place so that it is well supported. With a kitchen sink, in particular, you will be left with narrow strips front and back and the worktop could break if you then try to move it.

Left or right?

Some sinks with drainers can be fitted either way round, with the drainer on the left or on the right. These sinks will have two tap holes (or two sets of tap holes) and you may need to move a blanking plug from one hole to the other.

Improve access to tap connectors

Whether you're working on a sink, a basin or a bath, tap connectors are always difficult to get at. To make life easier next time around, replace the old tap connectors with new push-fit ones which screw onto the tap tails by hand, rather than needing a basin wrench. They contain an integral rubber sealing washer to ensure a watertight joint.

baths Attaching the fittings

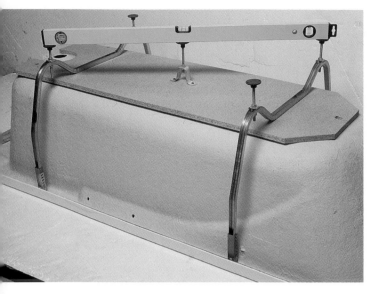

A level footing
A plastic bath usually comes with a supporting frame. Turn the bath upside down to fit it and use a spirit level to get the adjustable feet approximately level, so that you have only fine levelling adjustments to make once the bath is in position.

Choose thick plastic
Don't choose a plastic bath on style and colour alone. Check the thickness of the material from which it is moulded; it must be 4 mm at least, and preferably nearer to 6 mm. A bath thinner than 4 mm will distort in use.

No leak, no strain
Bath mixer taps come with a rubber or plastic gasket. Fit this between the tap body and the bath to stop water seeping beneath the tap.
On a plastic bath, fit a metal reinforcing plate between the back nuts and the underside of the bath rim to prevent any strain on the plastic.

Line up the overflow
Baths come with an all-in-one hose and connector for the overflow. One end is fitted to the overflow opening near the rim of the bath. The other, called the banjo because of its shape, fits round the waste outlet. Align the hose inlet with the waste outlet slot carefully.

Tails you win
Once a bath is in place against the wall, it is almost impossible to reach up and attach the tap connectors to the tap tails. It's best to fit a length of flexible pipe (above) or braided hose to each tap tail and cut down the existing supply pipes to nearer floor level. Then there's plenty of room to reconnect the pipes using compression fittings. These will be easier to undo than soldered fittings when the bath is next replaced.

Applying a waterproof seal

Mind the gap
Fill a plastic bath with water before applying any seal to the join between bath and wall. This will widen the gap between the edge of the bath and the splashback to its maximum, and help to prevent the seal from pulling away with use at a later date.

Silicone is best
You can use any type of non-setting sealant to waterproof the join between bath and wall, but silicone is best. It comes in clear, white and several popular sanitaryware colours. Look for one containing a fungicide that will stop black mould growing on its surface.

A neat finish
As an alternative to using masking tape (top right), you can buy a special applicator tool for applying silicone sealant. This will give a much neater finish than you can ever achieve by hand.

Getting it taped

To get a neat bead of sealant around a bath, stick parallel strips of masking tape to the base of the wall and to the bath rim. Then fill the gap with sealant and smooth its surface with a moistened finger or the back of a small plastic teaspoon. Pull the tape off once the sealant has formed a skin.

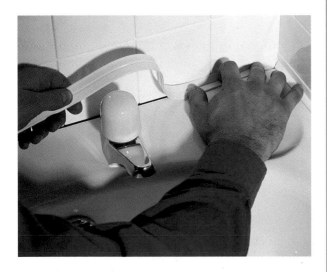

Stick on plastic strips

Use self-adhesive plastic sealing strips around the bath if the gap is wider than about 6 mm (¼ in), or varies in width from place to place. Silicone sealant will simply keep disappearing into the void. Clean the wall and bath surfaces scrupulously, first with strong household detergent and then with methylated spirits. Then cut the seals to length, peel off the release paper and bed them in place with firm hand pressure.

STAGES IN
BOXING IN A BATH

1 Screw two 50 x 25 mm sawn timber battens to floor directly beneath bath rim

2 Clamp matching battens beneath bath rim. Then fit 50 x 50 mm posts about every 400 mm, and at corners

3 Cut front and end panels to size. Coated hardboard is lightweight, but use 9 mm waterproof plywood if you want to apply tiles

4 Attach all the panels with decorative mirror screws or pairs of magnetic catches so you can remove them easily for access to the plumbing

baths

143

baths Remedies for surface damage

Read the label
If you plan to use a branded limescale remover to get rid of a build-up of hard limescale around the bath taps or the plughole, read the manufacturer's instructions carefully before you buy. Many of these chemicals are unsuitable for plastic baths, and some may also damage enamel.

Disguise scratches and chips
If a plastic bath has become scratched, rub the surface lightly with metal polish wadding. The colour goes right through the plastic, so you will not mark it. Deeper scratches and chips in the plastic can be filled with a bath repair kit, available from plumbers' merchants and DIY stores.

Restore the shine
Treat an old metal bath that's lost its shine with a car body restorer. Then put a shine on the surface with a high-glaze liquid car body polish. A lambswool polishing bonnet fitted to a mains electric drill does the best job; cordless drills don't spin fast enough to polish the surface properly.

Renew old sealant
To replace existing silicone sealant, cut away the bulk of the strip with a sharp trimming knife and then use special silicone sealant remover to take off the last traces. Wipe the cleaned surface with a cloth soaked in methylated spirits before you apply new sealant.

Rust buster
If a chipped steel bath has developed rust spots, remove them with a car body rust remover. Then paint the bare metal surface with a rust inhibitor and fill in the chips with fine car body filler. Smooth the repair with very fine wet-and-dry abrasive paper (used wet) before disguising it with enamel paint.

Enamel restorer
Remove stains from the enamel surface of a cast-iron or pressed-steel bath by rubbing the surface hard with a device called a bath rubber, which is available direct from bath manufacturers or from plumbers' merchants. Use enamel paint touch-up kits to conceal minor scratches, but be sure to clean the bath thoroughly before applying the paint.

WCs Curing flush problems

A straightforward job to handle

If you have to pump the handle to make the WC flush, and the water level in the cistern is up to the 'full' mark on its inside wall, the plastic flap valve inside the siphon unit needs renewing. The replacement part is inexpensive and the job requires little skill, although it can take time—so do it yourself rather than calling out a plumber.

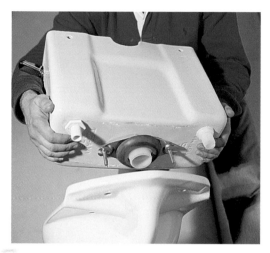

Siphon sequence

Unless your close-coupled toilet is fairly new and contains a two-part siphon unit (right), you will have to take the cistern off its pan to replace the flap valve. Cut off the water supply, flush the cistern and bale it out. Then disconnect the supply and overflow pipes. Next, undo the screws holding the cistern to the wall, and remove the wing nuts below the rear edge of the pan. Now lift off the cistern, remove the doughnut seal round the siphon outlet and undo the back nut to release the siphon unit.

Time to improvise

You probably won't have a spanner big enough to grip the siphon back nut. If this is the case, measure the size of the nut and use this measurement to make a matching cut-out in a plywood offcut and use it as a makeshift spanner.

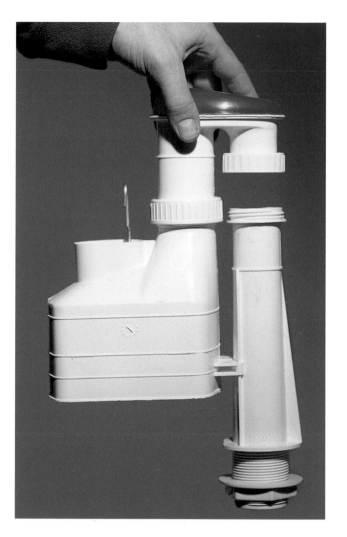

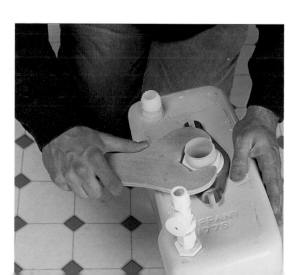

Easier next time

The flap valve in the siphon unit can last years or may fail in months. To make future replacement easier, fit a two-part siphon unit in place of the existing one. You will then be able to change the flap valve in future without having to go to the trouble of removing the cistern or even turning off the water. You just undo the coupling nuts and slide the siphon unit up so you can get at the flap valve from below.

toilets

WCs Curing flush problems

Raise the water level

When a WC won't flush, check that the water level in the cistern is up to the 'full' mark. If it is too low, adjust the angle of the float arm. How you do this depends on the type of valve you have.

With a plastic valve (below), you alter the angle of the arm by turning its adjustment screw with a screwdriver.

With a brass valve, you may have to bend the float arm up a little, or loosen the securing nut on a movable float and slide the fixing up the arm slightly.

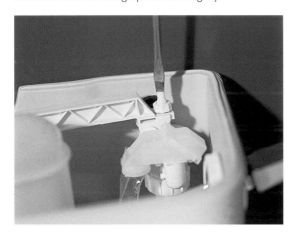

A broken arm

The flush lever arm in a cistern links the end of the flushing lever with the wire link that lifts the siphon lift rod. If the arm is plastic, it can snap. However, a universal replacement is available from plumbers' merchants. It fits most makes of cistern, although you may have to shorten it with a junior hacksaw to stop it catching on the siphon unit.

Perpetual running water

WCs with cisterns that are supplied by mains-pressure water can suffer from continuous flushing. It happens because water enters the cistern through the inlet valve at the same speed as it leaves through the siphon, so preventing air from entering the siphon and breaking the flow. The problem can be cured either by replacing the low-pressure seating inside the inlet valve with a high-pressure one, or installing an in-line isolating valve on the supply pipework and using it to reduce the water pressure.

Reconnect the link

If you cannot flush the WC because the handle is hanging limply, check the connection inside the cistern between the flush lever arm and the siphon lift rod. This S-shaped or C-shaped wire link may have become unhooked. Simply reconnect it to restore the flush action. To do this you may have to slip a finger beneath the siphon unit and push the plate inside up so that the top of the lift rod is exposed.

A smoother action

The flush action of a WC cistern should be smooth. If it starts to feel stiff, check whether the flush lever arm has worked loose on its spindle—it should be held in place by a small grub screw. If the arm has moved along the spindle, it will no longer raise the siphon lift rod vertically. Reposition the arm on the spindle and tighten the screw to ensure a straight lift.

Get rid of scale

Remove an unsightly build-up of limescale from WC pans using a paste made from citric acid powder and water. Lower the level in the trap by using a mop or brush to push some water round the bend, then leave it blocking the pan. Brush the paste onto the ring of limescale and leave it overnight. Repeat as necessary. The paste also works well on scale beneath the rim of the pan.

Remedies for leaks

Replacing the doughnut

Leaks from beneath a close-coupled cistern are a sure sign that the sealing washer between the cistern and the pan (called a doughnut) has perished. To replace it, start by removing the cistern, following the same sequence of operations as if you were replacing the flap valve (see right). Then pull the old washer off and fit a new one, seating it evenly over the siphon retaining nut. If the leak has rusted the mild-steel plate that retains the two cistern fixing bolts, remove the rust with wire wool before reassembling everything.

Tighten the nut

Water running down the outside of the flush pipe when a separate cistern is flushed is due to a leaking seal. Try gently tightening the nut that joins the flush pipe and cistern.

If this doesn't work, turn off the water supply to the cistern and bail out the water. Then undo the nut and slide it down the pipe to reveal the damaged rubber washer inside it. Remove this and wrap at least ten turns of PTFE tape around the top of the pipe. Replace and tighten the nut.

Fit a flexible cone

The flush pipe from a separate cistern is connected to the back of the pan with a rubber connector. If this perishes and starts to leak, replace it with a universal flush cone. You can turn the cone inside out like a sock to fit either 32 mm (1¼ in) high-level pipes or 38 mm (1½ in) low-level ones. The cone won't work with metal flush pipes.

1 Turn off water to a separate cistern, flush it and bail out. Disconnect flush pipe and undo siphon back nut

2 Disconnect supply and overflow to close-coupled cistern and undo pan fixings. Lift pan off and undo siphon back nut

3 Undo wire link from top of siphon lift rod and lift siphon unit out of cistern. Slide out lifting plate and rod

4 Pull off worn flap valve and fit replacement, cut to same size first if necessary. Then reassemble everything

toilets

147

showers Picking the right hardware

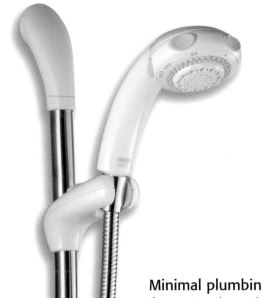

Worth the raise?

Lifting the cold-water cistern in the loft will increase the flow rate to a shower, but the job is worth considering only if you have to replace an old cistern anyway or are carrying out a loft conversion. Otherwise fit a shower pump.

A safe temperature

To guard against the danger of scalding, fit an antiscald device to manual showers. This small device is normally fitted between the shower head and its hose and will shut down the flow almost immediately if it exceeds a certain temperature – because of cold water supply failure, for example. An essential safety feature for young children and the elderly.

Minimal plumbing

If you want a shower that needs the bare minimum of installation work, fit a bath/shower mixer tap in place of your existing bath taps and take your shower standing in the bath. Thermostatic types are more expensive than conventional mixers, but they do prevent unexpected water temperature fluctuations. You will get a reasonably powerful shower provided your cold-water storage cistern is at least 1 m above the level of the shower rose. If not, add a pump to the system to boost flow rates.

Check the seals

When an over-bath shower is fitted, make sure the seal between the bath and any wall tiles is completely watertight. Much more water will splash onto the tiles when you shower than when you bathe, and this will quickly find any gaps. A neglected leak could rot the floor beneath the bath, or bring down the ceiling in the room below.

An electrical alternative

Install an electric shower (above left) if you have no storage cistern. This takes cold water via a single supply pipe direct from the incoming mains. The most powerful units are now rated at more than 10 kW, so you should call in a qualified electrician to provide the new power circuit and controls, unless you are fully competent at doing your own wiring work. You can install the shower unit over a bath, but it is more commonly fitted in a separate shower cubicle.

Allow for access

Once a shower tray is installed, the trap and waste pipe will probably be fairly inaccessible. Unfortunately, blockages are common, caused mainly by people washing their hair in the shower. Make sure the waste pipe run includes a rodding eye so you can clear it easily if it blocks. Better still, fit a top-access trap (above). This can be unblocked simply by removing the grid.

Pressure booster

Fit an integral low-voltage single-impeller pump and mixing valve (below) to boost the flow rate of a sluggish shower that is fed from the cold cistern and hot cylinder. The pump can be installed on the wall of the shower cubicle or over the bath.

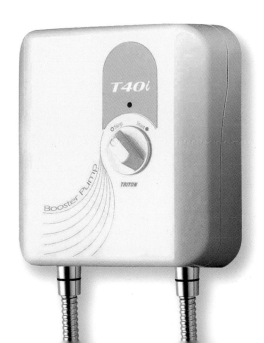

1 Set shower tray in place and level it, adjusting feet if these are fitted. Secure tray to floor with brackets

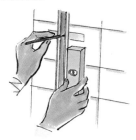

2 Mark positions of all fixings that secure cubicle uprights to walls. Then drill holes and screw them into place

3 Connect top frame rails with corner block and add cubicle wall panels, following maker's instructions carefully

4 When assembly is complete, seal joints between cubicle, bathroom walls and shower tray with silicone sealant

showers

149

showers Picking the right hardware

T is for thermostat
The most popular shower arrangement is a wall-mounted shower mixer valve fitted in a separate shower cubicle. Pick a thermostatically-controlled mixer, and you can 'tee' its water supplies directly off the existing hot and cold pipes in the bathroom. The thermostat will prevent fluctuations from occurring in the shower water temperature if hot or cold water is drawn off anywhere else in the house.

The long way round
A manual mixer is cheaper to buy than one with a thermostat, but its cold supply must be taken directly from the cold-water storage cistern. This ensures that the flow rate to the shower can't be reduced by cold water being drawn off elsewhere in the house. If that happened, the shower temperature could suddenly reach scalding point.

Keeping the water flowing freely

Have a clear head
To descale a clogged up shower head, unscrew it from its hose and immerse it in a container of lemon juice, vinegar or proprietary descaler. This will soften the limescale and, when you replace the head and turn the shower on, it will wash away. Keep the descaler and re-use it every few weeks. When it no longer makes the limescale fizz, the acidity has been neutralised and you need fresh descaler.

Clean the filters
If the flow rate of your shower starts to slow noticeably and you have already descaled the shower head, clean the shower pump filters—located within the hot and cold pump inlet connections. Accumulated debris will restrict the flow unless it is cleaned out every year or so.

More power

If you want a real drenching in a shower, or the tingling sensation of needle jets or the calming effect of aerated 'champagne' water flow, a power shower is for you. This has a pump which increases the flow rate of both the hot and cold supplies to the shower—these supplies must be separate feeds from the cold water cistern and hot water cylinder, and not be direct from the mains. Fitting a power shower almost certainly means employing a professional plumber and electrician.

There are two types of power shower. In the first, a twin-impeller pump is fitted in the airing cupboard or under the bath and the hot and cold water pipes are taken to this first before passing on to a shower mixer valve. In the second, the pump and mixer valve are combined in a single 'box-on-the-wall' integral unit.

A power shower can be fitted over the bath, but it will need a good screen to prevent water splashing on to the floor and it is usually better to fit one in a separate enclosure with a well-fitting door.

Prime position

The easiest place to fit a washing machine is in the kitchen, close to the supply and waste pipes which serve the sink.

Connection choices

The arrangement shown on page 153 shows the hot and cold supplies taken from tees on the pipes supplying the kitchen sink and leading to washing machine stopvalves where the washing machine supply hoses can be connected (a dishwasher normally needs only a cold supply). The waste water hose from the washing machine is shown connected to the 'spigot' of a washing machine trap which can be fitted under the kitchen sink in place of the normal trap—unless this is above the level of the washing machine drum or incorporates an anti-flood loop as shown, you will have to fit a non-return valve to prevent waste water back-siphonage.

There are alternative ways of connecting both the supply pipes and the waste hose and these are described on this page and the next. Check your machine's instructions to see which methods are allowed. One solution for the waste hose not shown is to fit a separate standpipe, from which the waste pipe is led to the drains and into which the washing machine waste hose is hooked. The top of the standpipe needs to be higher than the level of the washing machine drum.

A longer reach

When you have to site a washing machine or dishwasher farther from its supply pipes than the existing hoses can reach, use longer hoses, available from plumbers' merchants. Check the machine handbook for the maximum permitted length you can fit.

To a tee

If your machine is close to the sink hot and cold supply pipes, you may be able to use washing machine tees (as shown right) in place of the compression tees shown on page 153. Each washing machine hose can then be connected directly to its own tee, which incorporates a stoptap to turn the water off when required.

Choose connectors carefully

Before using self-cutting supply connectors (below left), check the appliance manual to make sure they are suitable. Since they cut only a small hole in the main supply pipe, the flow rate to the machine may be insufficient, especially with supplies that are not at mains pressure. If so, use tee fittings instead to provide a larger bore.

Clamp and go

Self-cutting supply connectors provide a quick and easy way to link your washing machine or dishwasher to existing hot and cold supply pipes but they are not suitable for all appliances, so check the user manual first. Clamp the two-part base around the existing pipe, then screw in the tap to pierce it and make the connection. Screw the hose directly onto the threaded outlet of the tap.

appliances

appliances Providing a water supply

Soap solution
If the plastic connector nuts bind on the threaded plastic spigots at the back of the washing machine as you tighten them, smear a little soap on the threads before making the connection. This will make the hoses easier to undo later.

Fit a slip-tee connector
You may not have enough play on the pipes to be able to spring the cut ends into a standard compression tee fitting, so fit a slip-tee connector, which has no internal stops and can slide freely onto one end of the pipe and then back over the other. Mark the position of the ends of the tee on the pipe, without the cap nuts attached, before fitting so you know when it is centred on the cut.

Washer backup
Don't tighten a leaking supply hose connector with a spanner: you'll crack the plastic. Instead, turn off the washing machine tap, disconnect the hose and add a second sealing washer. Reattach the hose, which shouldn't leak even when the nut is just hand tight.

Getting rid of waste water

Easy link from waste to hose
If there's an existing 38 mm diameter waste pipe behind or close to the position of your washing machine or dishwasher, you may be able to use a self-cutting plastic waste connector to link into its outlet hose; check with your machine's instructions. The connector works in the same way as a self-cutting supply connector, and incorporates a non-return valve. Attach the hose to the connector outlet with a hose clip so it cannot be pulled off.

Soil-pipe connections
You can connect a new waste pipe into a soil pipe if it is near the machine. First cut a hole in the soil pipe with a hole saw. Then stick a boss connector in the hole with solvent-weld cement and fit the strap around the soil pipe. Finally, push the waste pipe into the boss. Connect the machine outlet hose to a standpipe fitted with a 75 mm deep trap.

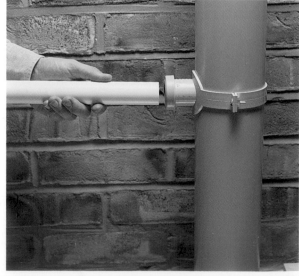

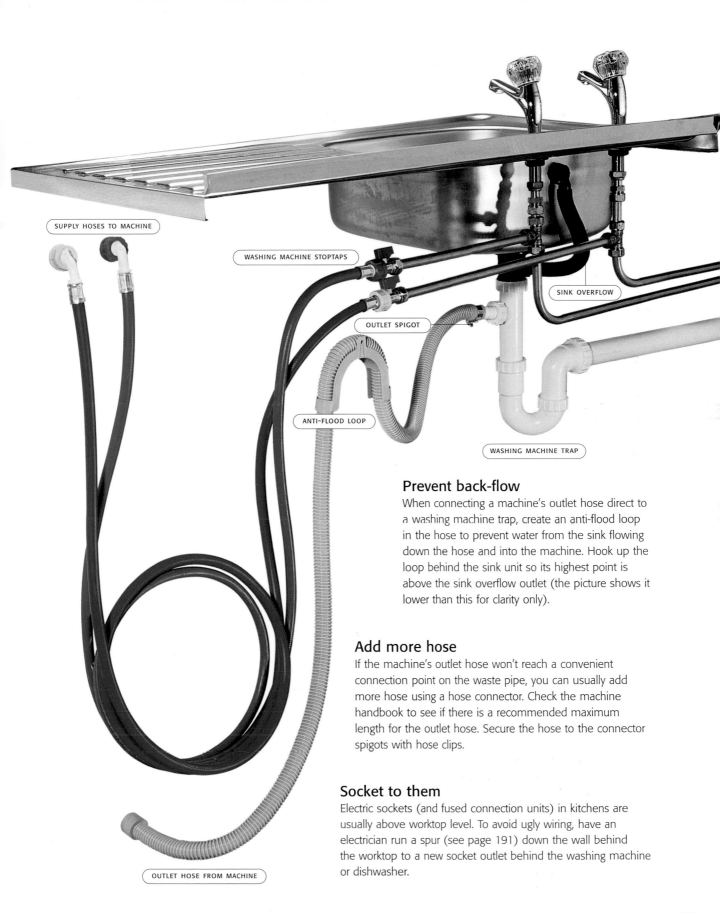

SUPPLY HOSES TO MACHINE

WASHING MACHINE STOPTAPS

SINK OVERFLOW

OUTLET SPIGOT

ANTI-FLOOD LOOP

WASHING MACHINE TRAP

OUTLET HOSE FROM MACHINE

Prevent back-flow

When connecting a machine's outlet hose direct to a washing machine trap, create an anti-flood loop in the hose to prevent water from the sink flowing down the hose and into the machine. Hook up the loop behind the sink unit so its highest point is above the sink overflow outlet (the picture shows it lower than this for clarity only).

Add more hose

If the machine's outlet hose won't reach a convenient connection point on the waste pipe, you can usually add more hose using a hose connector. Check the machine handbook to see if there is a recommended maximum length for the outlet hose. Secure the hose to the connector spigots with hose clips.

Socket to them

Electric sockets (and fused connection units) in kitchens are usually above worktop level. To avoid ugly wiring, have an electrician run a spur (see page 191) down the wall behind the worktop to a new socket outlet behind the washing machine or dishwasher.

boilers
A new generation

Energy saving

Modern boilers are very much more efficient than older boilers – and, since your boiler accounts for around 60 per cent of your energy bill, it makes sense to have the most efficient type of boiler that you can.

Replacing an old boiler with a modern condensing boiler (plus a proper set of controls – programmer and thermostats–if necessary) could save you a considerable amount of money each year as well as reducing your home carbon dioxide emissions.

Condensing boilers

Unless it is physically impossible to fit them, condensing boilers have been a legal requirement for replacement gas boilers since 2005 (2007 for oil-fired boilers).

They differ from the 'conventional' boilers they replace in that they have a much larger heat exchanger which extracts more heat from the exhaust gases. This cooling of the exhaust gases produces water (hence the name condensing) that needs to be piped away to the outside.

Open-vented or sealed?

A condensing boiler can be fitted in place of an existing boiler which is part of an 'open-vented' system with a feed-and-expansion cistern in the loft. Or it can be fitted in a 'sealed' system, where an expansion vessel is fitted and any necessary topping-up of the water in the system is done by connecting a filling loop to the rising main until the pressure gauge on the boiler registers the correct figure. Condensing boilers which have the sealed system expansion vessel and circulating pump built-in to the boiler casing are known as 'system' boilers.

Keeping it balanced

Virtually all condensing and combination boilers are fitted with a balanced flue–a two-part (often concentric) duct passing through the house wall or through the roof above, which allows fresh air in for combustion and allows the flue gases to pass to the outside.

In combination

The alternative to a normal condensing boiler is a combination condensing boiler which can directly heat the domestic hot water as it is needed, as well as running the central heating system. Since the water supply to the domestic hot water side of the boiler comes directly from the mains, you do not need a hot water cylinder or a cold water cistern in the loft, provided the cold water system can also be supplied from the mains. Combination boilers have higher heat outputs and they are designed to operate with a sealed central heating system (see left), having the expansion vessel, pump and control valves all built in to the boiler casing.

Who fits?

It is illegal to fit a gas (or LPG) boiler yourself–all gas work must be carried out by a Gas Safe registered installer–see page 120. For oil-fired boilers you should use an installer who is registered with OFTEC (Oil Firing Technical Association 0845 6585 0080, www.oftec.co.uk).

radiators Cures for valves with problems

Dry repair for a faulty Belmont valve

You can repair leaking valves with the name Belmont on them without having to drain the system. Remove the valve handle and then undo the gland nut by turning it clockwise; it has a left-hand thread. Remove the nut quickly so the spring-loaded plunger inside the valve snaps up and cuts off the water flow. Remove the spindle (right) and the O-rings; they will be either red or green, depending on how old the valve model is, and should be replaced with new ones of the same colour. Finally reassemble the valve.

Clear the jam

Thermostatic radiator valves (TRVs) can jam in the closed position, especially if they are not used regularly. To free the internal mechanism, try tapping the valve body (not the top sensor head) gently with a mallet or hammer. If this fails to free it, pull off the sensor head (left). Then grip the exposed end of the valve activator pin with pliers and move it up and down gently. Don't wiggle the pin from side to side; it may bend or even break.

No need to dismantle the leaking joint

Leaks can occur between the valve tail (the short pipe to which the valve is connected) and the threaded inlet to the radiator itself. This can often be cured with a smear of silicone leak sealant. Run the radiator hot to dry out the leak, then apply the sealant. The leaking water will start it setting immediately, but you should leave the heat on for at least 2 hours to get a total seal.

Check the obvious

A single cold radiator may simply have been turned off at the hand-operated valve (called the handwheel valve and fitted with a fluted handle). Check that the valve is open fully. If a TRV has been fitted instead, turn it to a higher temperature setting so the valve opens.

radiators Cures for valves with problems

Repack the gland

Radiator valves, especially cheaper ones, often weep round the spindles. Before replacing the valve, it is worth trying to repack the gland to cure the problem. Turn the valve off, remove the plastic handle and undo the small gland nut at the base of the spindle. Wrap some PTFE tape around the spindle and then push it down into the gap between spindle and valve with a small screwdriver. Add a little silicone grease round the spindle, then replace the nut and handle.

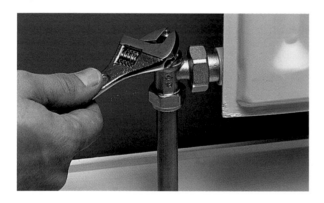

Isolate first

Before you can clear a blocked air vent or carry out any other repair work on a radiator, you need to isolate it from the rest of the central heating system to stop water pouring out of it. First turn the handwheel valve off in a clockwise direction. Then remove the plastic cover from the lockshield valve and use pliers or a small spanner to turn the spindle clockwise as far as it will go. Note how many turns this takes, so that when the repair work is done you can reopen it by the same number of turns and leave the system properly balanced.

Different solutions for cold radiators

Brass vent keys are best

Radiators that feel cold at the top and warm at the bottom need bleeding to remove air from the system. Because air rises, upstairs radiators are more often affected than ground floor ones. Keep a radiator bleed key in your tool box—brass keys are stronger than aluminium ones—to open the air vent found at one top corner of every radiator. You may need a screwdriver instead of a key to bleed some modern radiators.

Only some radiators are cold

If radiators are cold upstairs but hot downstairs, check the water level in the feed-and-expansion cisten—it should be a third full when the system is cold. If either the upstairs or downstairs radiators are cold and the system has zoned heating, suspect a faulty motorised valve (see page 161).

Blocked with sludge

A radiator with a cool patch at the bottom and a warm top and ends is probably full of black sludge produced by corrosion within the system, a problem that needs curing by the addition of a corrosion inhibitor (see page 158). To clear the blockage, isolate and remove the radiator, take it outdoors and flush it through with water from a garden hose.

Suspect a broken pump

Cold radiators downstairs, lukewarm ones upstairs, but plenty of hot water in the taps, are signs of pump failure. If the hot taps are running cold as well, check the timer settings on the programmer and then make sure the boiler pilot light is on.

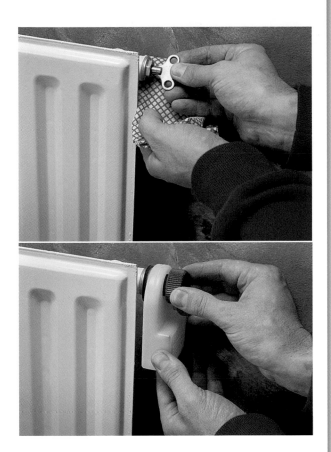

Gently does it

Open a radiator air vent by at most half a turn anticlockwise. Undo it further, and you might drop and lose the tiny needle that seals the vent. Hold a cloth under the vent (top) or use a combined bleed screw and container (above) to catch the water. Close the vent when water starts to spurt out.

Water shortage

If no water emerges from a radiator when you open the air vent, the hole may be blocked, or the system may be short of water. Try bleeding another radiator on the same floor. If this has water in it, you can return to the original radiator and set about unblocking the hole. If no water comes out of the second radiator, check that there is water in the feed-and-expansion cistern. Refill it if it has run dry by pressing down the arm of the float valve.

Clean as a new pin

To unblock an air vent, turn off both radiator valves. Then open the vent with the key; remove the small needle and put it in a safe place. Use a thin piece of stiff wire to clear the hole in the body of the vent by pushing any obstruction back into the radiator. Replace the needle and reopen the radiator valves. Water should now flow out through the vent.

1 Close valves at each end. Lift or protect flooring and put a container under one of the coupling nuts to catch water

2 Brace valve body so you don't bend supply pipe. Undo coupling nut and let water run out of radiator

3 Open air vent to speed up flow of water. When it stops, undo coupling nuts fully on both valves

4 Lift radiator off wall brackets and empty out any remaining water. Stuff tissue paper or cloth into the outlets to stop drips before taking it aside

radiators

radiators Draining the system

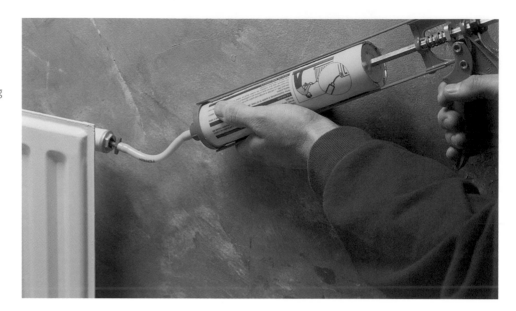

Keep it healthy
Keep a sealed heating system healthy by adding a chemical corrosion inhibitor to the water. As there is no feed-and-expansion cistern, you have to pump it in from a special cartridge through a radiator air vent.

Flush out the pipes
You can add special flushing agents to your heating system to loosen debris from the circuit pipework and radiators. Turn off the water supply to the feed-and-expansion cistern. Then drain off about 20 litres of water through a hose attached to the drain valve at the lowest point on the system. Pour in the cleansing agent (normally a whole bottle) and turn the water back on so the tank refills to the original level. Run the heating with the cleanser in for about a week. Then drain the system completely and refill it with clean water.

Allowing the water out
Letting air into the system helps water to run out of it. Locate the drain valve at the bottom of the system, and run a hose from it to an outside gully. Open the drain valve and then open the air vents on each of the radiators in turn, working from the top of the system downwards (see page 119).

Shut off the water
Before repairing your radiators and central-heating pipework, you will need to drain the heating system. If it is an open system (with a header tank in the loft), first turn off the boiler. Then shut off the water supply to the heating circuit by turning off the stoptap on the supply pipe to the tank. If there is no stoptap, tie up the arm of the float valve to a length of wood laid across the tank so the valve can't let in water.

Fill from the bottom up
To re-fill the system, close the drain valve and all the air vents. Then allow water back into the feed-and-expansion tank so the system fills up again from there. Bleed the system, opening the lowest air vents first until water flows out, and working upwards until you reach the top of the system. **Clean the heating system pipework** thoroughly by emptying and filling the system two or three times. Include corrosion inhibitor for the final fill, turn the boiler back on and let the pump circulate the heated water around the system. Bleed the radiators for a few days to release any air.

Fitting a replacement

An exact match
The most common reason for replacing a steel panel radiator is because it has sprung a leak caused by corrosion eating it away from inside. If possible, buy a replacement that is the same model and size as the one it's replacing, so it will fit on the existing brackets and will connect up to the existing pipework without the need for time-consuming adjustments. Measure the old radiator, paying special attention to the position and separation of the bracket hooks, and use this information to track down a suitable replacement.

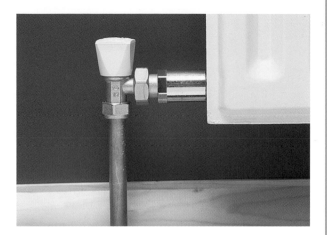

Imperial to metric

Metric radiators are often a little shorter than their imperial-sized equivalents, so the valve connections will not meet. Fit valve tail extenders to one or both ends of the new radiator to make up the gap and avoid having to modify the circuit pipework.

Double the output

Choose a new convector radiator with fins on the back to replace a standard panel radiator of the same size, and you will virtually double the heat output. However, the fins attract dust and fluff and can be difficult to keep clean. Make a simple dust buster by fixing a wad of washing-up sponge or any old rag to a straightened-out wire coat hanger.

1 Wind PTFE tape around valve tail. Screw in until hand tight, then a further 1½ turns

2 Fit new olive on circuit pipe and sit valve body on top. Connect coupling nut on valve tail to valve body by hand

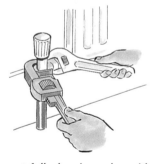

3 Tighten nut fully, bracing valve with second spanner to stop it bending circuit pipe

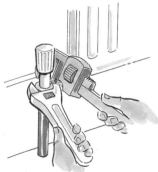

4 Push up new olive on circuit pipe to meet valve inlet. Slide cap nut up inlet and tighten with spanner, again bracing valve body

radiators

radiators
A new valve

VALVE COVER

Check out the parts

A new valve should come with a new valve tail, an olive (compression ring) and a coupling nut. You will need a special hexagonal radiator valve key for removing the old valve tail and screwing the new one into the radiator.

COUPLING NUT

VALVE TAIL

VALVE BODY

OLIVE

CAP NUT

Shop with care

If a faulty handwheel or lockshield valve resists all attempts at repair, you will have to replace it (see panel on page 161). Remove the old valve and take it with you when you shop for a replacement, so you can choose one of the same style that will align with both the circuit pipework and the radiator connection.

Removing an olive

You may be able to remove the olive left squashed onto the circuit pipe when you take off the old valve by sawing carefully through it with a junior hacksaw. To avoid nicking the pipe underneath (which could cause a leak), stop the cut just before you are all the way through and twist the blade of a screwdriver in the cut to break the olive.

Hidden connection

An alternative approach to dealing with the old olive is to cut off the existing circuit pipe just above floorboard level, and then to join on a new section of pipe to reach up to the new valve inlet. Use a capillary fitting so the join to the existing pipework is inconspicuous. Dry the existing pipe first by playing the flame of your blowlamp over it.

Spotting the flow

Fit a new thermostatic radiator valve (TRV) on the flow (inlet) side of a radiator. Before draining the system to fit the new valve, switch the heating on and feel the two circuit pipes that supply the radiator; the one that gets hot first is the flow pipe.

Automatic balance

Fit the body of a new TRV as you would a standard handwheel or lockshield valve. Then fit the sensor onto the valve body. The new valve will balance the flow rate into the radiator automatically, so the existing manual valve on the other end of the radiator becomes redundant, whether it is a handwheel or lockshield type. Leave it fully open.

Taking off the old valve

To remove an old radiator valve, you must first drain the heating system (see page 119). Then place some absorbent material such as an old towel beneath the valve to catch any drips. Undo the coupling nut linking the valve to the radiator, then the cap nut connecting it to the circuit pipework, and lift off the valve body. Before you can fit the new valve, remove the old valve tail from the radiator with a hexagonal radiator valve key (below) or a spanner on some types of radiator. You will also have to remove the old olive from the pipe (left).

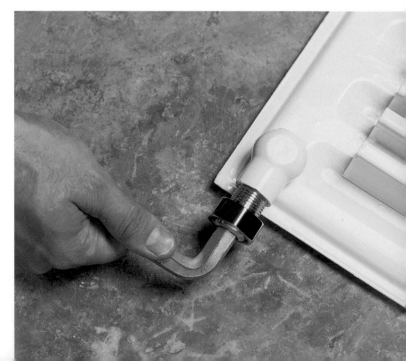

heating controls Misbehaving valves

Flushing through

If a motorised valve appears to be jamming, turn off the power and remove the actuator. Then try turning the spindle with a pair of pliers. If the spindle feels stiff, the valve either needs cleaning or replacing. Drain the heating system, undo the connections to the circuit pipework and remove the valve. Take it to the sink, flush it through with water to remove any debris from the mechanism, then reconnect it. If it still jams, fit a replacement valve body.

Replace the actuator

You do not normally have to replace a motorised valve if the motor has burnt out. On some models you replace the actuator–the top part of the valve. On others you remove this and replace just the motor unit within it. Turn off the electricity supply to the control system. Then undo the screws attaching the actuator. Disconnect the wires, reconnect them to the terminals on the replacement actuator or motor and reattach it to the valve.

Avoid a flat battery

Most modern programmers have a battery that ensures you will not lose all the settings if the electricity supply is turned off or is interrupted by a power failure. Replace this every year so you are never caught out with a flat battery.

Match up the sizes

Motorised valves come in 22 mm and 28 mm sizes; ensure you buy one to match your pipe diameter. Note the length of the valve too, and try to buy a replacement the same size so you do not have to modify the pipework in order to install it.

Manual operation

Many motorised valves have a manual lever you can operate to open the valve if it has jammed or the motor has burnt out. Slide the lever as far as it will go and then engage it in the J-shaped 'parking space' to keep the valve open. The heating and hot-water temperatures will now be controlled by just the boiler thermostat, so turn this down to a setting of 2 or 3 to avoid overheating.

heating controls Programmer problems

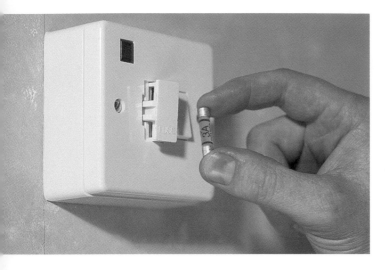

New for old

If the programmer doesn't work even after you have checked that it has a power supply, try fitting a new one (see far right). So long as the unit is a relatively recent one with an 'industry-standard' backplate, you will be able to remove the old faceplate and fit the new one to it without having to do any complicated rewiring.

Check the fuse first

If the system stops working, check the electricity supply to its controls. The fuse may have blown, leaving you with no display on a digital programmer and no response when thermostats are reset.

Turn off the socket outlet or fused connection unit (FCU) supplying the wiring junction box, and fit a new 3-amp fuse in the plug or fuseholder.

Get modern

When replacing an old electro-mechanical programmer, look at the range of electronic programmers available. These have features such as separate programming for weekdays and weekends (or separate programming for each day), manual override, separate 'channels' for heating and hot water and up to three on/off periods each day. They can be a bit of a fiddle to set initially, but can then be largely forgotten.

Checking thermostats

Ignore the thermometer

Don't expect the temperature setting on the room thermostat and the temperature recorded by a thermometer sited elsewhere in the room to agree precisely. The thermostat can only sense the air temperature close to it. Adjust it until you get the room temperature you want, and make a note of the thermostat setting required to achieve it.

Change the range

A typical room thermostat is calibrated to operate between about 10°C (50°F) and 30°C (86°F), but you can change the operating temperature range if you wish. On the model right, you pull off the control knob and reposition the two wire pointers in the numbered notches on its reverse; one represents the 'off' temperature setting, the other the 'on' one.

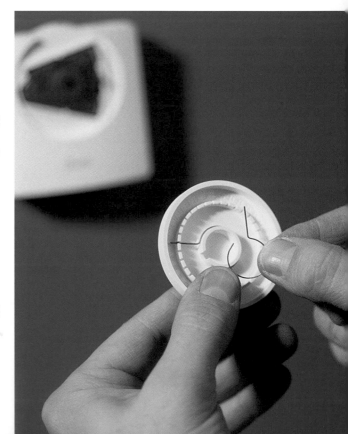

Make sure it's working

Check that the room thermostat is reacting to temperature changes by holding a switched-on table lamp underneath it for a few seconds. If all is well, the thermostat should turn the heating off as it is warmed by the heat from the lamp, and then back on after a few minutes as it cools down.

Continuity counts

If the water overheats or doesn't heat up at all, check whether the cylinder thermostat has failed. Turn off the electricity supply to the controls and remove the thermostat cover. Use a circuit tester to make sure there is continuity between the common terminal marked C and the terminal marked 1. Then turn the knob to the maximum setting and see if there is continuity between C and 2. If there isn't, fit a new thermostat.

The optimum position

The cylinder thermostat should be securely strapped to the cylinder about a third of the way up the side, and must be in contact with the bare copper if it is to work properly. If it is too high, cut away part of the foam insulation on the cylinder and move it. Fit a cylinder jacket so that the thermostat is exposed between the sections.

Swapping the valves

For more precise control of individual room temperatures than can be provided by a room thermostat, fit thermostatic radiator valves (TRVs) in place of standard on/off valves. To ensure that water can circulate freely through the heating circuit even if all the TRVs are closed, retain manual valves on at least one radiator.

1 Turn power off. Then undo screws securing programmer faceplate and remove it from its wallplate

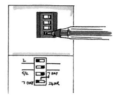

2 Set microswitches on back of new programmer to give required functions and on/off times (as per its instructions)

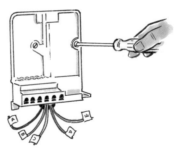

3 If new programmer will not fit on old wallplate, label and then disconnect cable cores. Remove and discard old plate

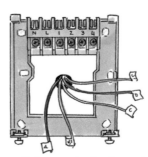

4 Fit new wallplate and wire it up following your labels and maker's instructions. Push on new faceplate. Restore power

heating controls

163

noisy plumbing
Problems arising with pipework

Knock out water hammer
Turn down the water pressure slightly at the indoor stoptap to reduce banging noises in supply pipes to cold taps and ballvalves. When these turn off, the sudden stop in the water flow can set up shock waves in the pipework, which are the cause of the hammering noise.

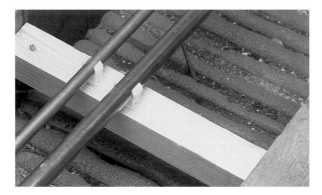

Stop vibration
Pipes running parallel with the joists under suspended timber floors need firm support to stop them vibrating. Copper pipe 15 mm in diameter should rest on a support batten or be clipped to the joists every 1.2 m on horizontal runs and every 1.8 m on vertical ones. For 22 mm pipe, increase the spacings to 1.8 m and 2.4 m respectively.

Cushions for creaks
Hot-water and central-heating pipes are often run in notches cut in the floor joists. If they are a tight fit, they will creak as they expand and the noise will be amplified in the underfloor void.
Lift boards to expose suspect pipes, and widen tight notches by cutting out a little more wood with a sharp wood chisel. Then cushion the pipes in the notches by surrounding them with pipe lagging.

Under arrest
Fit a water-hammer arrestor on the supply pipework if reducing the mains pressure fails to cure banging noises in the pipes. This device contains a small air-filled bellows or piston which absorbs the shock waves causing the noise.

Cough remedy
A spluttering kitchen sink hot tap is caused by a partial airlock in the pipe run from the hot cylinder. To cure the problem, attach a short length of garden hose between the hot and cold taps. Then turn on first the hot tap, then the cold one. The higher pressure in the cold tap, which is supplied directly from the rising main, will blow the airlock back up the hot pipe so it can escape into the cylinder.

Gurgling away
A sink, bath or basin that empties with a gurgle has a problem waste pipe. It's either too long or it doesn't have sufficient fall. In each case the waste pipe runs full until the sink, bath or basin is empty, when air is drawn into the pipe and causes the noise. The only solution to an over-long pipe is to replace it with pipe of a larger diameter. You may be able to increase the fall on the waste pipe by fitting a shallower trap so the pipe starts at a higher level.

Plastic fantastic

You can cut down on the amount of noise transmitted along copper pipework by cutting out a section and inserting one or two plastic push-fit fittings into the run. You can even replace sections of copper pipework with plastic pipe if the noise persists. Remember to fit wire earth–see page 124.

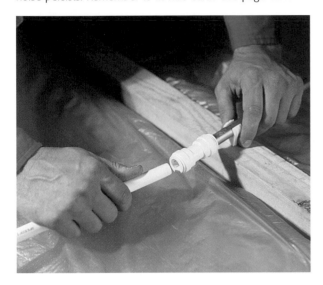

Trouble at the tank

Fit a bigger float

Drawing water from the cold-water storage cistern can set the arm of the ballvalve bouncing up and down as water rushes into the tank. This in turn causes the valve to open and close rapidly, sending a tell-tale chugging sound through the supply pipework. Try curing the problem by replacing the existing float with a bigger one.

Silence noisy valves

Worn components inside old brass ballvalves can cause a variety of high-pitched sounds in the supply pipework. If you have a noisy old valve controlling your storage cistern, replace it with a modern plastic one. This will have a spray inlet, which helps to reduce the sound of water splashing into the cistern as it refills.

Hush-hush opportunity

Replace a noisy old-fashioned brass ballvalve in a WC cistern with an almost-silent plastic equilibrium one, such as a Torbeck valve. At the same time, fit an in-line isolating valve on the supply pipe to the cistern. You can then shut off the water easily when any maintenance work is needed on the ballvalve or siphon unit in the future.

Dampen the bounce

Another way to stop ballvalve bounce is to fit a float damper. This can be a small plastic flower or yoghurt pot hung from the arm on a length of stiff wire. The extra drag created by the submerged pot stops the float bobbing up and down.

Brace the tank wall

Fit a tank bracing plate between the tank wall and the backnut on the threaded tail of the ballvalve. This plate is designed to stop the wall of the tank flexing and causing vibration in the supply pipe as the valve operates. A plate should be fitted on every new plastic tank, but it is often omitted. You can buy one from any plumbers' merchant.

noisy plumbing
Noises in heating systems

Check the thermostat
Banging noises in the pipes may be due to overheating. To find the cause of the fault, start by checking if the boiler thermostat is working. Turn the boiler off but leave the pump running to help to cool the system down. Then turn the boiler on and turn up the thermostat. If you do not hear a click, turn everything off again and call a heating engineer.

Cure a water shortage
A common cause of overheating and pipe noise in the heating system is a shortage of water. This is usually caused by losses from evaporation not being replaced by the header tank in the loft. Check your tank, and operate the ballvalve to refill the tank to about a third full if it has run dry. Service or replace the ballvalve if it is stiff to operate, to ensure that in future it tops the tank up when necessary.

Stop pipes humming
A humming sound in the heating system pipework usually comes from the pump, and is often caused by the pump speed being set too high. Try turning down the speed control knob on the pump body by one setting. If this fails to cut the noise and also makes the radiators take longer to heat up, call in a heating engineer for some expert advice. He may suggest relocating the pump.

Banish boiler blues
Loud banging noises or sounds like a kettle boiling coming from a boiler indicate the presence of corrosion in the heating system and possible scale build up within the boiler's heat exchanger. Both can be removed by cleaning the central heating system as described on page 158 and further corrosion prevented by adding a corrosion inhibitor.

Air in the system
Vent the radiators if a sound like rushing water travelling around the heating system pipework occurs whenever the pump switches itself on. This is a sure sign that there is air or gas in the system. Air is most commonly sucked in via the system's open vent pipe because of poor system design, and you will need expert advice to cure the problem. Hydrogen gas is created by corrosion which can be prevented by adding a chemical corrosion inhibitor at the feed-and-expansion tank.

insulation Keeping the pipes warm

Spiral wrapping
Where you can't easily fit split-sleeve foam insulation, such as around a gatevalve, wrap the pipe and fitting in self-adhesive foam wrap, making generous overlaps of about one-third of the width of the wrap. Take care to cover the pipe well at bends— these are the vulnerable areas most likely to freeze. Take the wrap around any valves or stoptaps as you meet them, leaving only the handle exposed.

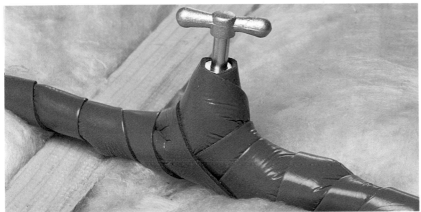

A thicker coat
Replace old insulation on vulnerable pipes with new split-sleeve insulation. In recent years, the manufacturers have increased its wall thickness so it can cope with lower temperatures for longer.

Tailored to fit
Shape a length of insulation to encase a pipe with a gentler bend, such as a vent pipe, by making a series of wedge-shaped nicks in it. The insulation will then fit snugly round the curve. Again tape the joints to keep them closed.

Foam alone
Polyurethane foam filler, which comes in aerosol form, is ideal for insulating pipes in inaccessible places such as where they pass through walls. Squirt the foam into the gap, leave it to expand and set hard, then trim off any excess with a sharp knife. **It is also good for insulating** outside pipes and garden taps, since it sticks well to the metal. This stops rainwater penetrating the insulation and freezing the pipe inside. Make a weatherproof box to fit round the tap and pipework from exterior-grade plywood, then fill the box with foam. Trim excess foam away from the tap handle with a knife and fit a wooden cover to the box.

Cut neat joints
Make 45° cuts in split-sleeve pipe insulation with scissors or a sharp bread knife so you can form neat joins at elbows and tees. Use PVC electrical insulating tape to keep the joints tightly closed and avoid a freeze-up.

insulation

167

insulation How to keep the heat in

Add an extra layer
Where plumbing pipes run across the loft floor, double up their protection against frost by insulating them in the usual way (see page 167) and then placing the loft insulation over them. Keep electricity cables above the insulation wherever possible, so they can't overheat.

Remember the hatch
Tape a piece of insulation blanket to the upper side of the loft hatch and fit self-adhesive foam draught-proofing around the edges of the hatch opening, to prevent valuable heat from the room below escaping into the roof space.

Meet the standard
Add another layer of insulation blanket in your loft if what you have is less than 100 mm thick. The current Building Regulations require a minimum of 270 mm of loft insulation in new houses, so adding an extra 170 mm blanket on top of 100 mm already there will bring your property up to present-day standards. **Because glass fibre can irritate the skin,** buy insulation blanket that's wrapped in a thin layer of plastic to make it more pleasant to handle (above).

Allow breathing space
Keep loft insulation blanket away from the eaves by fitting proprietary plastic ventilator trays between the joists and rafters. If the eaves ventilation is blocked, warm moist air rising from the house will condense within the cold loft space and settle as moisture on the roof timbers. This condensation can cause the wood to rot, saturate the insulation and spoil the plaster and decoration on the ceilings in upstairs rooms.

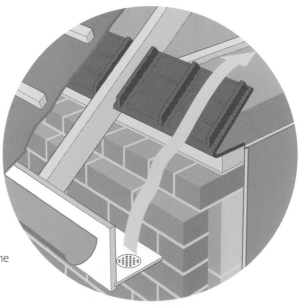

Keep cisterns warm

Don't insulate the loft floor under the cold-water storage cistern; a little warm air from the room below should be allowed to rise around the base of the cistern, helping to prevent it from freezing in very cold weather. Instead, make as tight a seal as possible between the loft floor insulation and the insulation around the cistern itself, so that heat is trapped below the cistern rather than being lost into the roof space.

Fast and loose

If the space between your joists varies, as it may in older homes, or if your loft is an awkward shape, insulation blanket may not fit very well. Get round the problem by laying loose-fill material instead. You can use vermiculite granules (above) or loose mineral wool, both of which can be pushed into hard-to-reach parts of the roof space with a broom. Plastic ventilator trays will stop the granules being lost down a cavity wall if it is open at the top.

Blowing in the wind

Vermiculite granules laid as insulation in a well-ventilated loft will almost certainly be blown into heaps by draughts. You can prevent this by laying the granules level with the tops of the joists and then covering them with sheets of building paper, stapled over the joists. Don't use polythene; it will trap water vapour and cause condensation.

Warming the loft

Insulate the underside of the roof slope if you want a warm loft (to use as a playroom, for example). You need to maintain a ventilation gap immediately below the roof covering to prevent any risk of condensation, so use insulation 50 mm thick and don't push it against the underside of the slates or tiles. Slabs of mineral wool are stiff enough to wedge between the rafters and stay in place without support, but widths of expanded polystyrene must be secured by garden netting stapled in place even if they are already cut to size.

Line the roof slope with hardboard or plasterboard if you want to conceal the insulation and achieve a neater look.

insulation

169

17th Edition changes

The Wiring Regulations (BS7671) is not the easiest of documents to read, but the three most important changes introduced by the 17th Edition are:

1. New cable that you bury or conceal in walls at a depth of less than 50mm (which effectively means all new cable in walls) must either be stringently mechanically protected (for example by earthed metal conduit) or be protected by an RCD.

2. All new socket outlets (not just those that might be used to supply equipment outdoors) must be RCD protected – either by an RCD in the socket itself or by having an RCD in the circuit to which it has been added.

3. All new wiring for bathrooms (including that for lighting and for a new electric shower) must be protected by an RCD (as must all changes to existing bathroom wiring).

In order to meet these requirements, you may need to have RCD protection added to one or more circuits in your home. See page 174 for how this can be done. See below for a consumer unit designed to meet the 17th Edition.

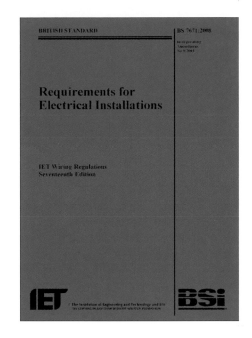

17th Edition consumer unit

If you already have a 'split' consumer unit with miniature circuit breakers (MCBs–see photograph and description on page 174), it should be possible to have the non-RCD protected circuits upgraded by replacing each non-protected MCB with an RCBO (combined MCB and RCD), but if you have any kind of fuse box with rewirable or cartridge fuses, you'll need a new consumer unit like the one featured below. This is known as a 17th Edition consumer unit and it contains two RCDs, with the circuits divided between them.

This is done so that no room is left without light should one of the RCDs trip–so that in a living room, for example, the lights would be protected by one RCD and the socket outlets (with table lamps) by the other. In this example, the right-hand RCD protects four circuits and the left-hand one five.

Non-RCD circuit

You are allowed to have a non-protected circuit feeding a single socket outlet–provided the wiring is surface run and the socket outlet is labelled. You might need such a dedicated socket outlet for a freezer–so that the contents of the freezer are not ruined if an RCD should trip whilst you are away on holiday. In the consumer unit shown here, the MCB on the extreme left (next to the ON/OFF switch) is for a non-protected circuit.

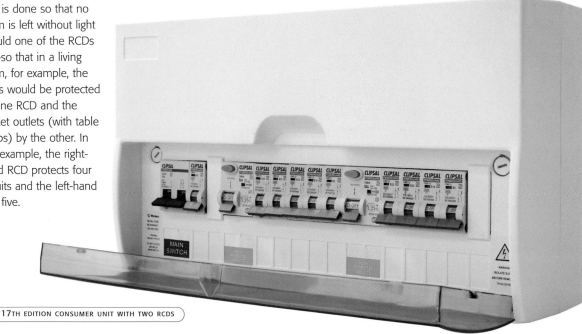

17TH EDITION CONSUMER UNIT WITH TWO RCDS

systems
Investigating your power supply

Be a detective

Before you can fix faults or make any changes to the wiring system, you need to know where the main fuse board is, what circuits it supplies, which lights and appliances are on which circuits, what sort of electrical protection the system offers and how everything is wired up. In short, you have to be an electrical detective. What you discover will be invaluable when you come to work on your wiring, and is crucial for your safety. The first thing to do is to find out where to turn the house's power supply on and off.

Switching off

Before doing any work on the wiring, make sure the power is off. If the system has MCBs, and you intend to work on a single circuit, just switch off the relevant MCB (above). If the dead circuit is a lighting one and you need light, plug a lamp into a socket. Run an extension lead to a separately supplied socket if you've switched off a power circuit and lead need to use power tools.

No more fuses

Many homes that have not been recently rewired will still have the kind of fuse box shown in the left-hand column opposite. You will most likely find this under the stairs–or in the garage if you have one. Some older installations may even have separate fuse boxes for each circuit and some may have a mixture of old and new. If any of these apply, ask an electrician to replace the fuse box or fuse boxes with a completely new 17th Edition consumer unit, such as the one shown on page 173, which will provide you with the RCD protection you need. Do not carry out any wiring work until this has been done.

Upgrade a split consumer unit

In homes built or rewired since the 1960s, you are likely to find the kind of 'split' consumer unit shown below. This has some circuits (in this case, the five on the right) protected by the central RCD with the remaining circuits (in this case, the four next to the main ON/OFF switch on the left) left unprotected. Typically, socket outlet circuits and shower circuits would be RCD protected and lighting circuits would not be. This kind of consumer unit can usually be upgraded to provide RCD protection on all circuits by replacing the non-protected MCBs with RCBOs–a job best left to an electrician. Individual RCBOs are not cheap. If you need to replace more than four, they could cost more than a new 17th Edition consumer unit–but fitting this is more time-consuming and requires the mains electricity supply to be disconnected.

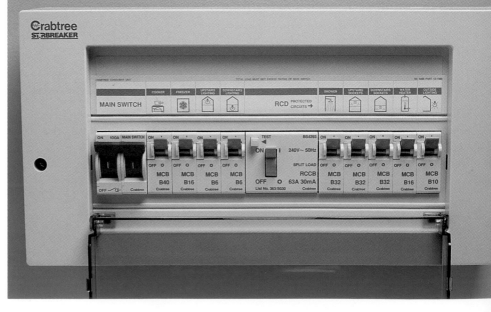

Preventing shocks and fires

As well as MCBs, modern consumer units also contain one or more residual current devices (RCDs). An RCD is a safety feature that detects the current imbalance caused if you touch something that's live and current starts to flow to earth through your body. It cuts off the current in a fraction of a second–fast enough to prevent the shock from stopping your heart beating. It also detects current leaks resulting from problems such as faulty insulation, which can cause electrical fires to start, and again shuts off the power. If you have any RCDs, check regularly that they are working properly by pressing the TEST button on each one to trip it off. Re-set afterwards.

Pocket for safety's sake

If you have circuit fuses, turn off the power at the main on/off switch before starting work. Then remove the fuse for the circuit you will be working on. Keep it in your pocket so no one else can replace it until you have finished.

Counting circuits

A typical modern home may have two or three lighting circuits, two or three circuits supplying socket outlets into which portable appliances are plugged, plus circuits to individual appliances that use a lot of current–a cooker, an immersion heater or an electric shower, for example. Each circuit will have its own circuit fuse or MCB in the consumer unit. Check your unit so you know how many different circuits you have, and stick a label inside the lid so you can see at a glance which fuse or MCB controls which circuit.

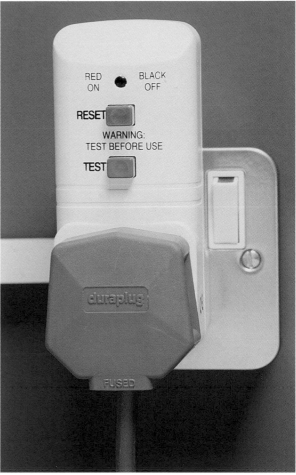

Stay safe outside

Even if your socket outlet circuit has an RCD to protect it, it is still a good idea to plug garden power tools, such as lawnmowers and hedge trimmers, into a special socket outlet or adaptor containing a high-sensitivity RCD (above). This will give you even greater protection against the risk of shock if you cut through an extension lead and touch a live conductor.

Don't blow a fuse

Fuses exist to protect circuits from overloading. If you try to draw more current from a circuit than it's intended to supply, the cable may overheat and cause a fire. The fuse is a weak link, designed to melt and cut off the current if overloading occurs. Take care when plugging in a number of appliances containing heating elements all at once: they are the big current consumers.

In modern installations the fuse's job is done by a miniature circuit breaker (MCB). This switches the current off if it detects an overload, and cannot be switched back on until all of the offending appliances have been turned off or disconnected.

systems Investigating your power supply

Which light, which circuit?
A 5-amp fuse or 6-amp MCB rating means that the circuit is supplying fixed lights. If you have more than one such circuit, it is helpful to know which one supplies which rooms. The way to find out depends on whether you have fuses or MCBs. Either turn off the main switch and remove one of the fuses, or simply switch off one of the MCBs. Then, with the power on, turn on all the fixed ceiling and wall lights in the house, and make a note of which ones are lit and which are not.

Check socket allocation
To find out which socket outlets are on which power circuit, follow the same procedure as for the light circuits, but with the 30-amp fuses removed or 32-amp MCBs switched off. Don't expect all the sockets in a room to be on the same circuit; electricians often wire up outlets that are physically remote from one circuit—at the end of a long room, for example—as spurs from adjacent circuits. It is important to know this, as you might otherwise start work on an outlet you think is isolated but which is live.

Keeping spares
If your system is fitted with rewirable fuses, buy a couple of spare wired-up fuseholders—one rated at 5 amps and one at 30 amps—and keep them next to the consumer unit. You will then be able to replace a blown fuse as soon as the fault has been rectified, and rewire the fuse later at your leisure.

Health checks for plugs
Your plugs should look like the one on the left below, not the one on the right. Once a year, set aside a couple of hours to give the plugs on all your appliances a quick health check.

Open each one up and check that all the terminal screws are tight and are gripping their flex cores securely, with no stray wires visible. Hold the plug and tug the flex to check that the cord grip is working. Replace any plug that has a cracked casing. Finally, check that the plug contains the correct fuse for the appliance—a 3-amp one (colour-coded red) if the wattage is below 700 watts and a 13-amp one (brown) otherwise.

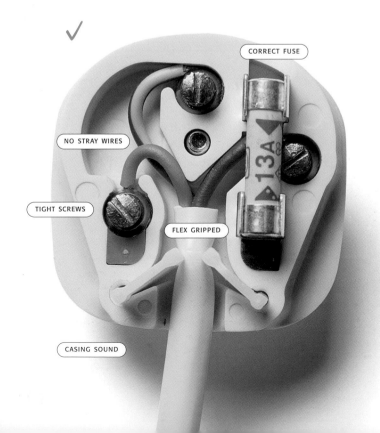

✓

CORRECT FUSE

NO STRAY WIRES

TIGHT SCREWS

FLEX GRIPPED

CASING SOUND

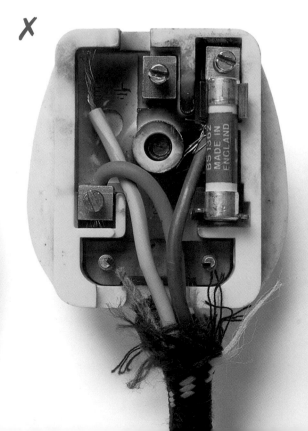

✗

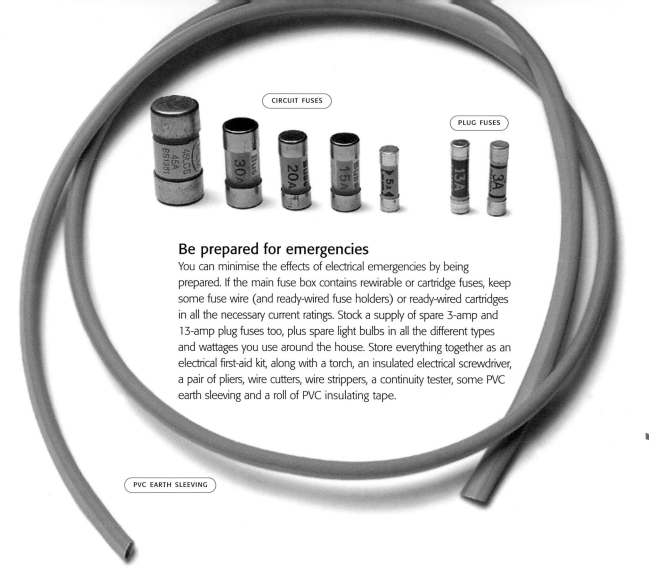

Be prepared for emergencies

You can minimise the effects of electrical emergencies by being prepared. If the main fuse box contains rewirable or cartridge fuses, keep some fuse wire (and ready-wired fuse holders) or ready-wired cartridges in all the necessary current ratings. Stock a supply of spare 3-amp and 13-amp plug fuses too, plus spare light bulbs in all the different types and wattages you use around the house. Store everything together as an electrical first-aid kit, along with a torch, an insulated electrical screwdriver, a pair of pliers, wire cutters, wire strippers, a continuity tester, some PVC earth sleeving and a roll of PVC insulating tape.

PVC EARTH SLEEVING

systems

faultfinding Tracing problems

No lights?

Suspect a blown light bulb first, and fit a replacement of the correct type and wattage. If mains lights still don't work, inspect the consumer unit to see if the lighting circuit fuse has blown or its miniature circuit breaker (MCB) has switched itself off.

If plug-in lights do not work, check first whether the plug fuse has blown or whether there is a loose flex connection inside the plug or the light. Then check whether the power circuit fuse has blown or whether the circuit MCB has cut off the supply.

No power?

Unplug the appliance and plug in another. If this works, the first appliance is at fault. If it does not, then there is probably a fault in the circuit. If the faulty appliance feels hot or is smoking, take it to a service engineer for repairs. Otherwise check the plug and flex for loose or broken connections.

Circuit down?

When nothing on a circuit works, turn off the lights or unplug the appliances that run from it. Then check the consumer unit to see if the circuit fuse has blown or the MCB has switched off. Replace the fuse or switch the MCB back on. If it blows or trips immediately, there is a fault in the circuit wiring and you need to call an electrician to find it. Otherwise, switch on lights or plug in appliances one by one to identify which is causing the problem. Check, too, that you are not overloading the circuit.

faultfinding Tracing problems

Watch the watts

When replacing a bulb in a light fitting, check inside the lampshade for a label indicating the maximum bulb wattage the manufacturer recommends. Do not exceed this, or you risk damaging the shade or the fitting. This only applies to incandescent (tungsten filament) bulbs—it's not a problem with compact fluorescent lamps (CFLs).

Look for the fuse rating

Make sure that every appliance has the correct fuse in its plug, by checking its wattage (power consumption). For light fittings this is on the bulb; appliances have it printed somewhere on their outer casing. Fit a 3-amp fuse if the wattage is less than 700 watts and a 13-amp fuse for higher wattages.

Easy tripping

Some lighting circuit MCBs can trip off when a tungsten filament light bulb fails. The problem is caused by pieces of rupturing element wire causing a short circuit inside the bulb. This is not a problem with modern energy saving lamps–compact fluorescent lamps (CFLs) or light-emitting diodes (LEDs)–which will eventually replace all tungsten filament light bulbs.

A safe grip

If a tungsten filament light bulb is smashed, turn the power to its circuit off at the mains. Then use pliers to grip the stump of the bulb and remove it from its lampholder. Wear safety goggles in case any of the broken glass falls out. Replace the bulb with an energy-saving type (see left).

Total power failure

If the whole house has no power, check first whether there is a local power failure. If there is, report it to your electricity supply company. If yours is the only house without power and there is a residual current device (RCD) in the consumer unit, this may have tripped off. Try resetting it; if you cannot, the fault is still present. In this case, run through the appliance and circuit checks on page 177, or call an electrician. Lastly, your main service fuse may have blown. If it has, call your supply company and ask for an engineer to come and replace it.

Using testers

Look for the light

One useful job for a continuity tester is checking whether flex and cable cores are unbroken, since you cannot inspect them visually. Just touch the probe to one end of each core and attach the clip (or second probe) to the other; if the core is sound the indicator lights up. **If you have a multimeter,** use it as an ohmmeter to measure the resistance of the circuit or core (a reading shows there is a continuous current path).

Plug in and test

A socket-outlet tester will show whether outlets have been wired up correctly. Plug it into the outlet you want to test, switch the power supply on and see which combination of the three indicator lights is lit.

Indispensable item

There is one piece of equipment every DIY electrician needs—a continuity tester. It allows you to identify breaks in any electrical circuit, and to test components such as switches and fuses.

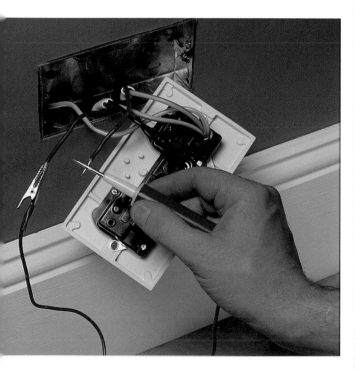

Circuit continuity

Don't attempt any testing on live electric circuits. But you can use a continuity tester after you have turned the electricity off—here, testing a socket to see if it is part of a ring circuit (and so suitable for connecting a spur, see page 191) or not (so not suitable for a spur).

❶ **Cable core colours have changed – see page 172.**

1 Turn mains switch off and remove fuse-holder for blown circuit from its socket

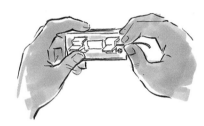

2 With rewirable fuses, loosen terminal screws and remove remains of burnt-out wire

3 Feed new wire through tube or across bridge of fuseholder and connect it to the terminals. Trim off excess wire

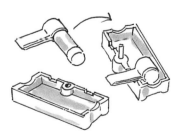

4 With cartridge fuses, take out old fuse and fit new one. Some fit into clips; others are held by the fuseholder pins

faultfinding

flex Make safe and secure connections

Getting inside appliances

To fit a new flex to an appliance, you need to be able to get inside it so that you can reach the terminals to which the flex is connected. If you cannot see immediately how to open the appliance casing, or if screws with unfamiliar head types have been used to fix it together, don't try to go any further. Have the flex replaced by an electrical repair shop.

Dispose of plugs safely

Discard a moulded-on plug if you have to replace the flex to which it is connected; you can't re-use it because the plug casing is designed not to be opened. Hammer one of the plug pins to bend it out of line, so the plug cannot be inserted in a socket outlet by an inquisitive child; the cut ends of the flex would be live in this situation.

Yearly inspection

Flex—short for flexible cord—links appliances and portable light fittings to the mains supply. If the outer sheath gets damaged, you could get a shock. So inspect all your flexes once a year for wear and tear. When you find flex that's been damaged, make it safe temporarily with PVC insulating tape, and replace the whole flex as soon as possible.

Use the right size

Flex is sized by the cross-sectional area of the conductors. Use 0.75 mm^2 flex for lights and small appliances up to 1.4 kW, the 1 mm^2 size for appliances rated up to 2.3 kW and 1.5 mm^2 flex for more powerful appliances. If you are buying flex for a pendant light with a heavy lampshade, use 1 mm^2 flex; it's stronger than the 0.75 mm^2 size.

Earthed or not

Most appliances are fitted with flex containing three cores—live and neutral to carry the current in and out, plus an earth core that takes current away safely in the event of a fault. Only use two-core flex with no earth core on light fittings with no metallic parts, and also on double-insulated appliances such as power tools. The latter have a double-square symbol on the outer casing to show that they are double-insulated.

Resistant to heat

PVC-sheathed flex can withstand heat well enough for everyday use. However, you should use special heat-resistant flex of the appropriate current rating—usually the 1.5 mm² size—to wire up immersion heaters (above), water heaters and things like toasted sandwich makers that get hot.

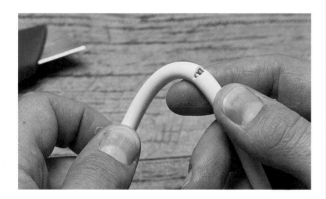

Nick and split

Before connecting new flex to a plug or appliance, you need to remove some of the PVC outer sheath and also the insulation on the individual cores to expose the conductors inside. Fold the flex at the point where you want to cut the sheath, and 'nick' it with a sharp knife. The tension will open up a split. Fold the flex the other way and repeat the process to extend the cut all round the sheath. This method avoids any risk of your knife cutting into the core insulation.

Tidy up loose ends

Fabric-covered non-kink flex, used mainly on irons, has an outer layer of braided fabric over a flexible rubber sheath. After nicking and cutting these away as for PVC flex, wrap the end of the flex in PVC tape to stop the cut fabric from unravelling in use.

1 Strip outer sheath from flex, lay flex over open plug and lead each core to its terminal. Cut each core to length

2 Remove the insulation from each core with wire strippers, then twist strands of wire together neatly

3 With pillar terminals, loosen screw, insert core in hole and tighten down screw again. Check that core is secure

4 With stud terminals, remove nut and its captive washer. Wind core clockwise round stud and screw down nut

flex

flex Make safe and secure connections

Leave the earth long

After removing the outer sheath, you need to cut the individual flex cores to length so they can comfortably reach their terminals inside a plug, or at an appliance terminal block. Always cut the earth core a little overlong, so that if the flex is tugged and the cord grip fails to work, this core will be the last to be pulled away from its terminal.

Eliminate guesswork

Use wire strippers to remove the core insulation. Depending on the type of tool you have, either set the separation of its jaws to match the core diameter, or select the right aperture in the tool's body. Then grip the core to cut through just the insulation, and slide the severed portion off the conductors. If you cut through any of the conductors as you do this, cut off the rest and start again.

Connect and extend

If an appliance needs a longer flex, you can add an extra section using a one-piece flex connector. Connect like cores to like within the connector, and ensure that the sheath on each section of flex is securely held in its cord grip.
Use a two-piece connector if you need to disconnect the extension for storage or use with another appliance. The part with the pins must always be fitted on the flex to the appliance.

Heat softens insulation

You can remove the insulation from flex cores without any risk of cutting the conductors by using heat to soften the plastic. Simply light a match or use a cigarette lighter and gently warm the core at the point where you want to remove the insulation. Then strip the insulation with pliers before it can harden again.

Remember remember
To remind you of which flex core goes where inside a plug, use this simple reminder. Looking down on the open plug with the flex inlet at the bottom, the core with the BRown insulation goes to the Bottom Right terminal and the core with the BLue insulation goes to the Bottom Left terminal. If the flex also contains an earth core, this goes to the top terminal.

Using extension leads

Extension leads are long lengths of flex with a plug at one end and a socket outlet at the other. Always unwind them fully before using them, even though you may not need all the length. This prevents the coiled-up flex from overheating. Check the extension lead's current rating if you intend to use it with a fire or heater; many leads are rated at only 5 amps and will overheat if used to supply the higher current these appliances take.

Taking the strain with a cord grip

The flex sheath should extend inside a plug or appliance and should be held by a cord grip so that a tug on the flex does not put any strain on the flex cores or pull them away from their terminals. If any flex cores are visible outside the plug or appliance, unplug it. Remake the connections after shortening the cores a little, and ensure that the flex sheath is securely held in the cord grip. Press the sheath between pairs of nylon jaws (left) or screw down the crossbar onto it (right).

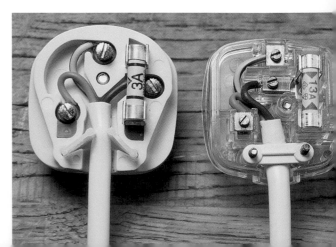

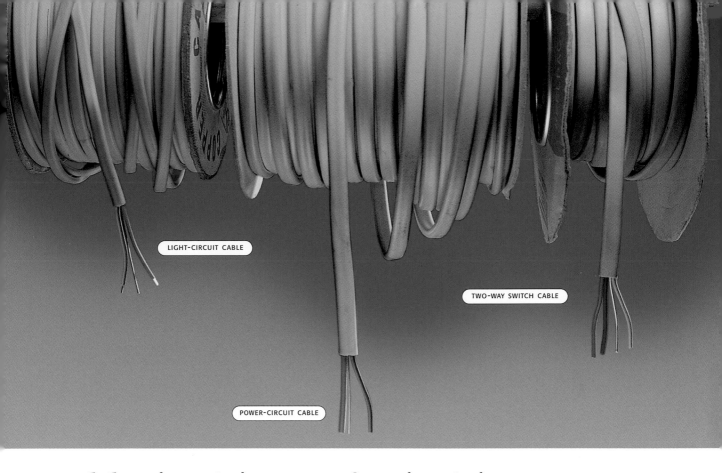

LIGHT-CIRCUIT CABLE

TWO-WAY SWITCH CABLE

POWER-CIRCUIT CABLE

cable The right type for the job

Sizing things up

All the concealed wiring in the home is made up of cable. Like flex, cable is sized by the cross-sectional area of its conductors. The 1 mm² size is used for lighting circuits and the 2.5 mm² size for circuits supplying socket outlets. Heavy current users such as electric cookers and showers are usually supplied by 6 mm² or 10 mm² cables.

Identifying the cores

Cable contains live and neutral cores (insulated in brown and blue PVC respectively) to carry the current, and a third core (the earth), which provides a continuous path throughout the wiring system along which current can flow to earth in the event of an electrical fault. Never disconnect it or cut it away.

For two-way switches

One special cable has three insulated cores, plus an earth core. Use it solely for wiring up two-way switches. The cores are colour-coded brown, black and grey for identification purposes only; all may be live at one time or another, depending on which switch is on.

Buying in bulk

If you have a lot of wiring to do, buy 1 mm² and 2.5 mm² cable by the reel. Each reel contains 50 m or 100 m of cable, giving you a unit price far lower than buying by the metre.

Avoid kinks

If you are using cable off a reel, mount it on a makeshift axle. Then you can rotate it and pull off lengths of cable without it curling into an awkward spiral, as it will if you lay the reel flat.

❗ Cable core colours have changed – see page 172.

Safety sleeve for the earth

The earth core in cable is a bare copper conductor. Whenever it is exposed inside a mounting box, to make a connection to a wiring accessory, it must be covered with a piece of slip-on green-and-yellow PVC sleeving of the right size. Cut this to length to leave about 10 mm ⅜ in) of earth core exposed. Fold the end of the bare core over the sleeving to retain it until you are ready to connect it to an earth terminal.

cable
Routes to take

Avoiding disruption

When a house is built, circuit cables are concealed under timber floors, above ceilings, beneath wall plaster and inside stud walls. Hiding new cables once a house is complete means disturbing wall and floor decorations, so run them on the surface as a temporary measure, either secured with clips or in stick-on plastic mini-trunking. You can conceal them properly next time you decorate.

Running wiring on the surface is also a way of meeting the requirements of the 17th Edition of the Wiring Regulations (see page 173). If you conceal new wiring in walls, the circuit must now be RCD protected – even if the wiring is run (as it should be) in one of the 'permitted cable routes':

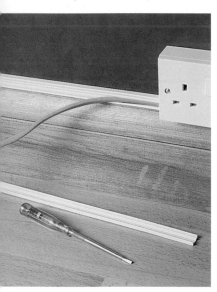

- vertically or horizontally from the socket, switch or other accessory;
- horizontally in a zone 150mm (6in) from the top of the wall;
- vertically in a zone 150mm (6in) from the internal corner of a room where two walls meet.

See page 174 for the ways of adding RCD protection to an unprotected circuit.

Beware of insulation

In lofts, make sure cables are kept above any insulation that's laid on the loft floor. If you are adding loft insulation (page 168), fit the new insulation under the existing cables, not over or around them.

Keep tiles intact

If you need to run cable to a new wiring accessory that will be mounted on a solid wall that is already tiled, you can avoid disrupting the tiling by cutting a chase for the cable in the plaster on the other side of the wall. Drill a hole through the wall from the tiled side first so you know where the chase is to terminate.

Out of harm's way

Clip surface-mounted cables next to mouldings such as skirting boards and door architraves. These will give them some protection from accidental knocks. The clips are easy to remove if you later decide to conceal the cable permanently in the wall.

Inside the box

Sockets and switches are installed in metal or plastic mounting boxes, either fixed on the surface or recessed in the wall. Strip enough sheath from the incoming cable to allow each core to reach its terminal easily, but make sure that the sheath itself terminates inside the box, not outside it.

Installing in stud walls

The horizontal braces, or noggings, inside stud walls (see page 73) prevent cable from being dropped down the full height of the wall once it has been covered with plasterboard. To keep disruption to a minimum, feed cables up the wall from below to supply new socket outlets (see right). For light switches, drop cable down the wall – if you do meet a nogging, remove a square of plasterboard and cut a slot in the nogging to run the cable. Replace the plasterboard square and make good.

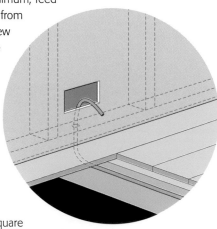

Under the floor

If you have timber floor boards, it is possible to extend circuits by running new cables beneath them. This is easiest to do in upstairs rooms with a plasterboard ceiling below, and where the new cable is to run parallel to the joists. Lift a section of floorboard at each side of the room and slide the cable through the 'tunnel'. On ground floors, lift boards at intervals across the room so you can pass the cable along from one opening to the next, and clip it to the sides of the joists as you do so.

Crossing the joists

When a new cable runs at 90° to the line of the floor joists, lift a couple of adjacent floorboards—or maybe just one—across the room. Then you can drill a hole through the centre of each joist and feed the cable through. When you replace the floorboards, fix them with screws rather than nails to make them easier to lift if you need access to the cable. Write 'cable under' on the boards if they are covered by carpet, to remind you of what lies underneath.

1 Mark cable sheath at point where you want to cut. Then split sheath lengthways with a sharp trimming knife

2 Peel back split sheath and cut off excess neatly to expose required length of cores

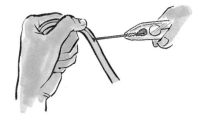

3 Alternatively, grip bare earth core with a pair of pliers and pull backwards along cable to split sheath

4 Remove about 10 mm (⅜ in) of insulation from live and neutral cores with wire strippers, set to suit core size

cable

185

fittings Replacing switches and socket outlets

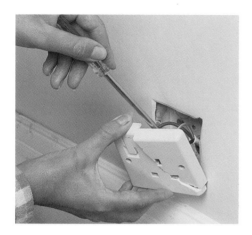

Make a sketch
It is generally obvious which cable cores go to which terminal. However, if you are in any doubt, make a sketch of the existing wiring arrangement before you disconnect anything. Then you can mimic this as you connect up the new faceplate. If you are confused by what you reveal, ask an electrician to make the changeover for you.

Spray to unlock
If you want to replace a ceiling rose or a pendant lampholder, you may not be able to undo the covers because heat has locked the threads. To free them, turn the power off and spray some aerosol lubricant such as WD-40 onto them. Leave it to penetrate for a few minutes before trying to undo them. If this doesn't work, you will have to break it—see page 192.

Off with the old
New wiring accessories in place of dirty, damaged or simply old-fashioned ones add a finishing touch to a redecorated room. It is best to remove the old fittings before you start to paint or hang wallpaper. Turn the power off at the fusebox or consumer unit first. Then undo the screws holding old faceplates to their mounting boxes and ease them away from the wall. Loosen the terminal screws so you can disconnect the cables and free the faceplates.

Danger signals from old rubber
What you find when you turn off the power and open up old-fashioned wiring accessories tells you a lot about your wiring system. The circuit cables should be insulated and sheathed in PVC plastic. If you find old rubber insulation, do not disturb it. The cables are highly dangerous and the system needs rewiring without delay by a professional electrician.

Save the screws
Keep the old faceplate fixing screws; the ones supplied with the new wiring accessory will have metric threads, and these won't mesh properly with the old imperial threads inside the lugs of an old mounting box. If the new faceplate is thicker than the old one, you may need longer screws to fit it.

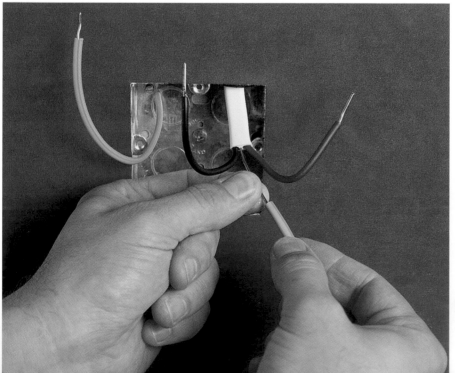

Sleeve all the earths
You may find one or more bare earth cores within the mounting box when you open up an existing faceplate. If you do, disconnect them from the earth terminals and slip a length of green-and-yellow PVC earth sleeving over each core, then reconnect them to the terminals. You must also use earth sleeving on the earth cores of any new cables you add to your wiring system. See page 188 for earthing metal boxes.

❶ **Cable core colours have changed – see page 172.**

Name each switch

Many kitchens have switches above the worktop that control appliances fitted underneath. To make it clear which switch controls which appliance, replace existing plain switches with new ones that have the appliance name engraved on them.

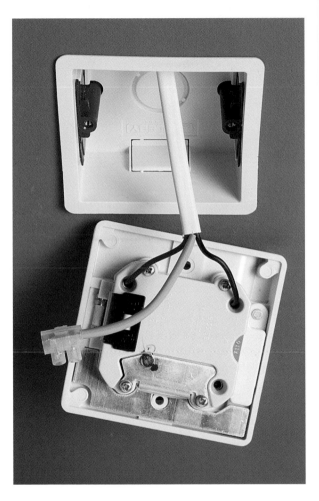

Controlling brightness

Consider replacing existing light switches with dimmer switches, which allow you to control the light level in the room. When choosing one, make sure it is suitable for the lamp (bulb) it will be controlling. Check too that it will fit on the existing switch mounting box; some dimmers need a deeper box.

Safety insulation

If a plastic faceplate is broken and the live parts are exposed, make it safe at once by covering the hole with PVC insulating tape. Tape over the switch in the off position, too, so that you can't use it until you replace the faceplate.

1 Mark out cable route and, if necessary, position of new flush mounting box to which it will run

2 Use a sharp bolster chisel and club hammer to chop out chase and recess for box. Cut plaster back to solid masonry

3 Drill down behind skirting board with long masonry drill bit, to clear cable route down to floor level

4 Fit box in recess. Fix oval PVC conduit in chase with galvanised nails. Feed in new cable

17th Edition rules See page 173 for details of the new rules for burying cable in walls.

fittings

fittings Replacing switches and socket outlets

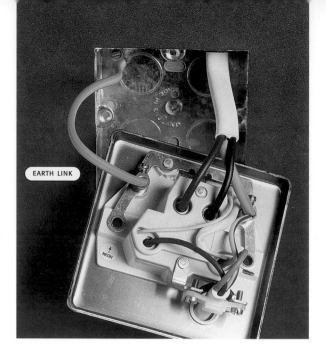

EARTH LINK

NEON

Playing by the rules

You do not need approval under Building Regulations Part P for replacing existing socket outlets or switches – even if they are in a kitchen or bathroom.

You will, however, need approval from your local authority building control department if you intend to extend a socket-outlet circuit (see below and Adding a spur on page 191) or to extend a lighting circuit (see page 192) AND the changes are in either the kitchen or bathroom. See pages 172 for more details. Completely new circuits always require approval, wherever they are.

If you are extending any socket-outlet or lighting circuit and the work will involve running new cable buried in or concealed in walls, the whole circuit will have to be RCD protected to meet the Wiring Regulations – see pages 174 and 184 for more details.

Cut the seal

An old faceplate may be stuck to the wall with paint or wallpaper. Turn off the power and run a trimming knife around the line where the two meet to break the seal. Then the decorations won't be damaged as the faceplate is removed.

Flying to earth

All accessories (sockets, switches and fused connection units) in metal boxes need a 'flying earth link' – a spare piece of earth wire (cut from spare cable) - connected to the terminal on the box. This prevents the fixing screws becoming live in the event of a loose wire.

With plastic sockets and fused connection units, this is taken from the earth socket on the accessory; with plastic light switches, the cable earth core goes straight to the earth terminal in the box. Plastic accessories on plastic mounting boxes (surface mounting or dry-lining boxes) do not need this flying earth.

Metallic accessories must always be earthed, even if they are in plastic boxes. With sockets and fused connection units, the normal earth terminal will do this; metallic light switches are fitted with an extra earth terminal to earth the faceplate.

Extending existing socket outlet circuits

Floor area limit

NEW OUTLETS

NEW CABLE

NEW CABLE

DISCARDED CABLE

You can extend an existing ring circuit to provide extra socket outlets—in a new home extension, for example—so long as the total floor area of the rooms to be supplied by the extended circuit does not exceed 100 m². Disconnect the circuit wiring at two socket outlets next to each other on the ring, and discard the cable that connected them. Then run 2.5 mm² cable from the first existing outlet on to the new outlets in turn. Finally run cable back to the second existing outlet to complete the extended ring.

Convert a radial

You can achieve the same effect if you have a radial power circuit. Convert it into a ring circuit by running 2.5 mm² cable from the last socket outlet on the existing circuit back to the consumer unit via a number of new socket outlets. At the consumer unit, connect the live core of the new cable to the existing radial circuit fuse or MCB, and the neutral and earth cores to their terminal blocks inside the unit. If the circuit fuse or MCB was rated at 20 amps, replace it with one rated at 30 amps.

extra sockets More places to plug in

Doubling up

With the power turned off, all existing single socket outlets can be converted to doubles, without any need to alter the circuit wiring. Surface-mounted sockets are easiest – just replace the single plastic box with a double one. Sockets in dry-lining boxes are also easy (simply enlarge the hole in the plasterboard), but flush-mounted sockets in solid walls are hard work, unless you use a pattress – see page 190.

❶ **Cable core colours have changed – see page 172.**

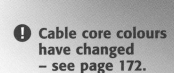

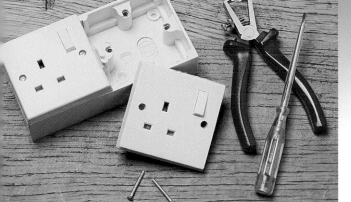

Save your singles

Don't throw away the single socket outlets you have replaced with double or triple ones, they can be re-used. Buy some dual boxes, which are designed to accept two single outlets side by side. Install these as you would any other surface-mounted or flush mounted box. Then wire the main circuit cables into the terminals of one of the outlets, and wire the second outlet as a spur from the first.

extra sockets More places to plug in

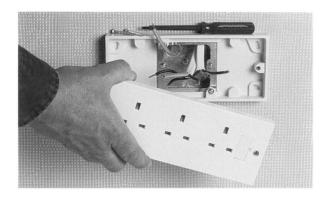

Clever conversion

There is a clever alternative to the standard mounting box which you can use if you are converting flush single outlets to surface-mounted doubles (or triples). It is called a pattress, and is designed to be screwed to the lugs of the existing box rather than to the wall. Save the old faceplate fixing screws for use in attaching the pattress.

Multiple outlets

You need more socket outlets for home entertainment and computer equipment than for any other type of appliance. The individual components take relatively little power, so you can safely plug them into multi-way adaptors. Each adaptor needs only one single socket outlet for its power supply.

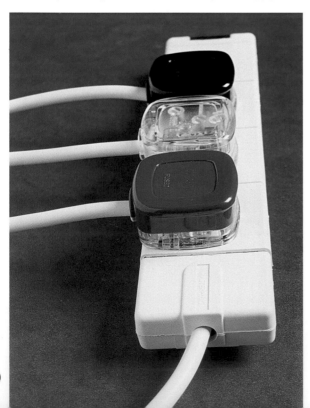

Adjust until level

Always try to fix socket outlets so they are level. Metal flush-mounting boxes have one adjustable fixing lug, which can be moved up or down as the faceplate fixing screws are tightened, allowing you to get the faceplate level even if the box is not. Plastic surface-mounting boxes have slotted fixing holes, allowing you to get the box level on the wall.

Check the cables

If you open an existing socket outlet and find circuit cables insulated with hard rubber, rather than soft PVC, do not attempt to carry out any wiring work. Call in a professional electrician to check whether the system is safe to use and, if it is not, have it fully rewired at the earliest opportunity.

Firm, safe contacts

Plug pins may become a loose fit in the slots of an old socket outlet. This indicates that the metal contacts inside are worn, and this can lead to sparking, overheating and the risk of an electrical fire. Replace the old socket.

Clip in a box

Use a drylining box if you are fitting a new socket outlet on a stud partition wall. Hold the box in place and draw round it. Then drill a hole and cut out the plasterboard with a padsaw and push the box into the recess. Its push out lugs will grip the back of the board securely when you tighten the screw. Feed in the cable and connect it to the faceplate.

How many sockets?

The recommended number of double socket outlets for a modern home is:

Living room & kitchen	6 to 10 in each room
Dining room	3
Bedroom	4 to 6
Study/home office	6
Hall	2
Landing/stairs & loft	1 each
Garage & utility room	2 in each room

Regard these figures as a minimum: far better to have too many socket outlets than too few to avoid the use of adaptors and to avoid having trailing flexes. Adding sockets is disruptive, so better to get it all done at once.

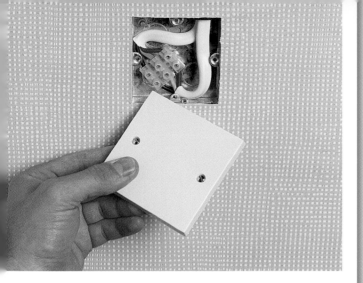

Reposition an awkward socket

A socket outlet on a spur in an inaccessible position—behind heavy furniture, for example—can be used as a junction box, allowing you to re-site the outlet somewhere more convenient. Disconnect the existing faceplate, connect the circuit cable cores to strip connectors and wire in the spur cable which is to run to the new socket position. Fit a blanking-off plate to the junction box and use the old faceplate for the new socket.

Spurred into action

Down to earth

A spur is like a small branch line running off the main ring circuit, feeding just one single or double socket outlet. There are two types of spur: fused and unfused.

A fused spur is connected to a fused connection unit and leads to a socket outlet or a flex outlet plate and is something you use for connecting equipment like cooker hoods, extractor fans, heated towel rails and appliances (such as washing machines) situated under work surfaces. With a fused spur, you can use smaller (1.5mm²) cable for the cable between the fused connection unit (FCU) and socket as this will be protected by the 13A fuse in the FCU. If a switched fused connection unit is used for equipment in a bathroom, it must be positioned more than 3m from the bath (probably outside the bathroom itself).

Unfused spurs are connected to an existing socket outlet (or a junction box inserted in the ring) and simply go to one single or double socket outlet. The big advantage of using (unfused) spurs to provide extra sockets compared with extending the ring is that far less wiring is involved—especially if you can fit the new socket close to an existing one (the other side of an internal wall is favourite).

**❶ Cable core colours have changed
– see page 172.**

see page 172.

1 With power off, locate an outlet with two cables and connect in a new cable. Run this cable to new outlet position

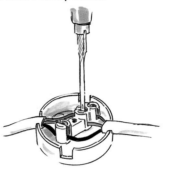

2 Alternatively, find circuit cable under floor, turn power off and cut it. Reconnect ends in three-terminal junction box

3 Connect new cable cores to same three terminals, linking cores like to like, and run cable to new outlet position

4 At new outlet position, fit mounting box, feed in spur cable and connect it up. Add flying earth link to metal box (not shown)

extra sockets

191

lighting Extending existing circuits

Count the cables before extending a circuit

If you want to add extra light fittings to existing circuits, you first need to find out how the system is wired up so you can decide how to extend it. Switch off the power to the circuit you are likely to be working on, then unscrew the cover of one of the ceiling roses. If just one cable is present, this tells you that your system has been wired using junction boxes. If you find two or three cables, as pictured, you have loop-in wiring–the commonest system in modern homes.

! **Cable core colours have changed – see page 172.**

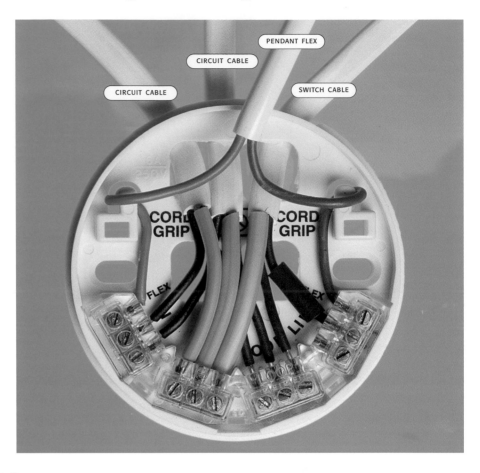

How many light points?

When planning to extend a circuit, first count up how many separate lighting points it supplies. Lighting designers rate each point at a nominal 100 watts, so a circuit that is protected by a 5-amp fuse or 6-amp MCB (miniature circuit breaker) can in theory supply up to 1150 watts (5 amps x 230 volts), or 12 lighting points. With the demise of high-wattage tungsten filament light bulbs–and their replacement by low-wattage compact fluorescent lamps (CFLs) and Light Emitting Diodes (LEDs), this restriction no longer applies, but it is still best to have at least two lighting circuits for the average home.

Dealing with stuck roses

You may find that you can't undo the cover of a ceiling rose because it has become encrusted with paint. Turn the power off first, then try to free it by running a knife blade around the edge. If this fails, you have no option but to crack the cover with a sharp hammer blow to get it off. Disconnect and discard the old baseplate and fit a complete new rose.

Both cores are live in switches

Most light switches are wired up with ordinary two-core-and-earth cable, so the black (or blue) core (properly called the switch return core) is in fact live whenever the switch is on. Every exposed black (or blue) core in a switch cable should be wrapped in some red (or brown) PVC tape or covered with a slip-on length of red (or brown) PVC sleeving to warn of this.

Spur from a junction box

If you are adding a light and you have junction-box wiring, locate the box that's nearest to where you want to install the new light fitting. With the power off, unscrew the box cover and identify which terminal is which.

If you want the existing switch to control the new light, wire in the spur cable using the switch return, neutral and earth terminals in the box. Fit the cable sheath into one of the cut-outs in the side of the box base, and replace the cover. Run the spur cable from the box to the new light position.

SPUR CABLE

CIRCUIT CABLE

CIRCUIT CABLE

Cut into the circuit

To add a spur to an independent light and switch, locate the circuit cable. With the power off, cut it and reconnect the ends in a three-terminal junction box. Then wire in the spur cable (above) and run it on to the new light position, where its new switch can be wired in.

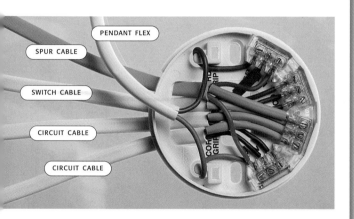

PENDANT FLEX

SPUR CABLE

SWITCH CABLE

CIRCUIT CABLE

CIRCUIT CABLE

Take a spur from a rose

If you have loop-in roses rather than junction boxes, you can connect your spur at one of them. With the power off, unscrew the rose cover and feed the spur cable in from above, through the rose baseplate. Break out an extra central section of the baseplate if necessary, using a screwdriver blade. To add another light that will be controlled by the existing switch, connect the new cable cores to the 'pendant' terminals (above) and replace the rose cover. For an independent light, wire it to the through terminals instead (below).

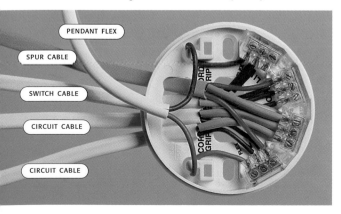

PENDANT FLEX

SPUR CABLE

SWITCH CABLE

CIRCUIT CABLE

CIRCUIT CABLE

1 Mark outline of conduit box (page 194) on ceiling, drill a hole within waste area to admit padsaw blade and cut out the hole

2 Cut batten to fit exactly between joists, then drill a hole in it to accept conduit box spigot and screw box to batten

3 Screw scrap blocks to each end of batten, then position it between joists so lip of box is flush with ceiling below

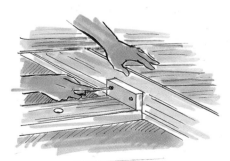

4 Screw scrap blocks to joists to secure batten in place, ready for cables to be run in

lighting

lighting Installing new lights

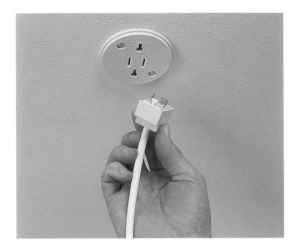

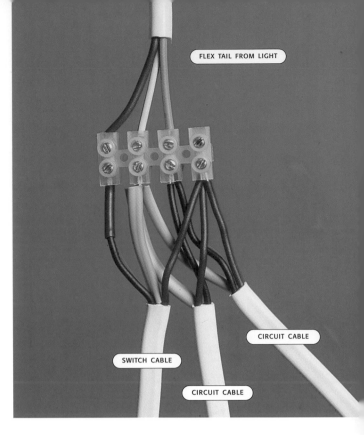

FLEX TAIL FROM LIGHT

SWITCH CABLE

CIRCUIT CABLE

CIRCUIT CABLE

Plug-in pendants
If you are installing new pendant lights, consider fitting the plug-in versions, called luminaire supporting couplers (LSCs), instead of conventional roses. These allow the pendant flex and the lampholder to be unplugged and removed in seconds for cleaning or maintenance, or when decorating.

Knock out a knockout
Modern ceiling roses are designed so they can be screwed to the underside of a ceiling joist with the cable entry point offset to one side. This means that the cables can be run down the side of the joist, through a hole in the ceiling and straight into the rose. Break out the thin plastic sections (called knockouts) from the rose baseplate before fixing it in place.

How many strip connectors are needed?
If you are installing a new light fitting over a conduit box (below), use small insulated strip connectors to link the flex tail from the light fitting to the circuit cables. You need three to link the flex to a single cable run to the conduit box from a junction box, and four (above) if the switch cable is looped in at the lighting point.

All-in-one refit
Old ceiling roses, lampholders and pendant flexes eventually become discoloured. Replace them quickly and easily using pre-wired pendant sets. All you have to do is to disconnect and discard the old rose and then fit the new one, complete with a new pendant flex and lampholder, in its place.

Space for connections
Many light fittings fit flush with the ceiling surface, and unless they have a terminal block within a hollow baseplate, you have to make an enclosure above the ceiling to contain the wiring connections. This is usually a round conduit box. To install it you need to cut a hole in the ceiling and fix a supporting batten between the adjacent joists, to which the box can then be screwed (see page 193).

Mounting the fitting
Ceiling light fittings have holes in their baseplates so you can screw them in place. If the holes are at the same 51 mm centres as the screwed lugs on the conduit box, you can screw the baseplate to them using 3.5 mm diameter (M3.5) machine screws. Otherwise, use ordinary woodscrews long enough to pass through the ceiling and into the batten fitted above.

lighting Fitting wall lights

Useful when decorating

Most wall lights are designed to be installed in a similar way to close-mounted ceiling lights. Their baseplates also fit over (and conceal) an enclosure, but in this case it's recessed into the wall surface. Some modern wall lights have a special plug within their baseplates, which engages in a matching socket in the wall. This device, called a luminaire supporting coupler (or LSC for short), allows you to remove and replace the fittings in seconds without having to do any wiring work—a bonus when you want to clean the fittings or redecorate the room.

Convenient connections

When fitting new wall lights, think about the most convenient source of power. As far as those in upstairs rooms are concerned, it is generally easiest to connect into the upstairs lighting circuit, which is accessible in the loft. Downstairs, it may be easier to use a spur from the socket outlet circuit (page 191). This will avoid the need to lift carpets and move built-in furniture in upstairs rooms to gain access to the downstairs lighting circuit under the upstairs floorboards.

Cable prospecting

Once you have decided where you want your wall lights to be fitted, use a battery-powered cable detector (or a voltage detector) to check whether there are any existing cables buried in the wall, so that you can avoid them when running the new cables.

Keeping it legal

As explained on page 188, you only need to tell your local authority building control department if the lighting circuit you intend to extend (by installing extra light fittings) is in a kitchen or bathroom.

But for any new wiring concealed or buried in walls to meet the latest Wiring Regulations, the lighting circuit will need to be RCD protected – see page 174 for ways to do this.

❗ **Cable core colours have changed – see page 172.**

Hiding the cables

If you are installing wall lights on a stud partition wall, conceal the supply cable by running it up or down between the studs to the light position—see page 184.

On solid walls, you can run the cable on the surface until you redecorate the room; then you can bury it into a vertical chase. To disguise it for now, paint it to match the existing wall.

New lights, old switch

If you want new wall lights to come on with the existing room light, wire a spur cable into that lighting point with its cores connected to the switch return and neutral terminals. Take it on to a junction box in the ceiling void, then run a cable from this box down to each new light position.

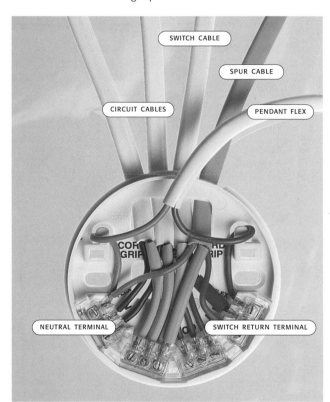

Check for overload

If you plan to power your wall lights from an existing lighting circuit, check whether the additional lights will overload the circuit. The circuit should not supply more than 12 lighting points in all, and ideally no more than eight. If an overload is likely, plan to supply the new lights through a fused spur taken from a power circuit instead (see page 197).

lighting Fitting wall lights

The perfect height

Wall lights are best sited about 1.5 m (5 ft) above floor level. However, if they're used as reading lights in bedrooms, fix them a little lower–at about 1.2 m (4 ft)–to minimise glare.

Protection for brassware

Brass light switches can be corroded by the alkalis in plaster if they are in direct contact with the wall surface. Avoid this by buying switches that come with a protective plastic mount; this fits between the switch faceplate and the wall.

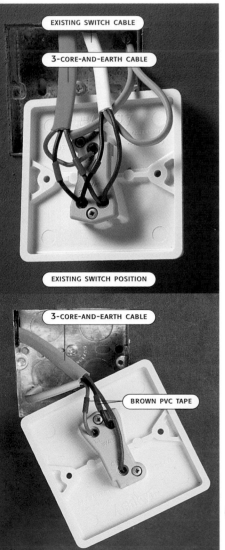

Dual control for lights

It is often useful to be able to switch a light–especially a wall light–from more than one position. If necessary, replace an existing one-way switch with a two-way switch and wire in the existing red and black switch cable cores to the L1 and L2 terminals (top left). Then fit another two-way switch at the new switch position, and run three-core-and-earth cable between the two switches. The brown cable core links the terminals marked C or COM, the black core links those marked L1 and the grey core those marked L2. The grey and black cores in the cable must be identified as live with brown PVC tape.

❶ Cable core colours have changed – see page 172.

Branching out

You can use a junction box to supply two or more wall lights from the same spur cable. Connect its cores to three terminals within the box, then connect in the branch cables as shown, with all like cores going to the same terminal in the box. Remember to sleeve each cable's bare earth core.

Replacing a light

If you want wall lights instead of an existing ceiling light, you can make use of its power supply. Disconnect and remove the existing rose or fitting, and draw the circuit and switch cables supplying it into the ceiling void. Reconnect them to a four-terminal junction box, copying the original wiring arrangement in the rose. Then wire in the spur cable and take it to a junction box as above to supply the new lights. They'll all still be controlled by the existing ceiling light switch.

EARTH LINK

Neat connections

If a wall light has a baseplate with screw fixing holes, you can fit a circular conduit box to a solid wall (see right) as an enclosure for the wiring – for stud partition walls, use a round drylining box. The alternative for solid walls is a metal architrave box (above) with the light fittings secured to the wall on either side.

Use a fused spur

Sometimes taking a power supply for new wall lights from a socket outlet involves the least upheaval and the shortest cable runs. This is especially true if there are socket outlets on the wall where you want the new lights. With the power off, open a nearby socket outlet and connect in a 2.5 mm² spur cable. Run it to a switched fused connection unit (below) fitted with a 3 amp fuse. This can act as the light's on/off switch. Then run 1 mm² cable on to the wall light.

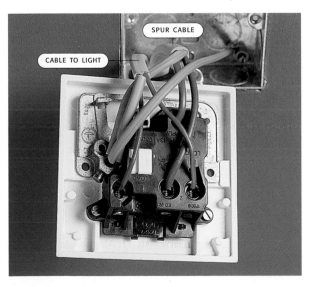

SPUR CABLE

CABLE TO LIGHT

STAGES IN
PUTTING UP A WALL LIGHT

1 Mark position of conduit box and cable run on wall, cut recesses with a cold chisel and club hammer

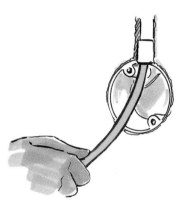

2 Fix box and conduit in place, then feed in cable to new light. Prepare cable cores for connection to the light

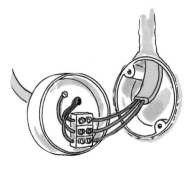

3 Connect flex tails from wall light to new cable using strip connectors. Sleeve the earth core and mount light over box

17th Edition rules See page 173 for details of the new rules for burying cable in walls.

lighting Stay on track

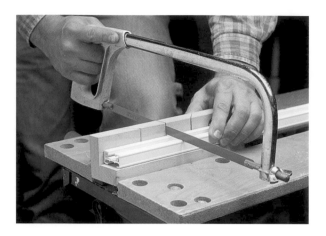

Beware of an overload

Each lighting track can supply several individual light fittings. So if you are installing one in place of a single light fitting, count up the total wattage of all the new fittings and add this to the wattage of the other fittings the circuit is already supplying. The total for the circuit must not exceed 1200 watts. If it does, you'll have to supply power to the track from an alternative source.

Earth when required

Separate transformers supplying low-voltage lights don't need an earth connection, but a combined metal track and transformer housing will. Connect the live and neutral cores of the supply cable to the transformer input terminals, and the sleeved earth core to the earth terminal provided.

Made to measure

With some track systems you can connect lengths together with push-in couplers. If you need to shorten a standard length of track to fit your plans, use a sharp hacksaw, taking care to cut cleanly through the slim copper conductor strips inside the body of the track.

TRANSFORMER HOUSING

More lights, less fuss

Track lighting allows you to install several light fittings with little change to the existing wiring. The fittings may clip into surface-mounted track or may hang from track wires (below left).

Mains-powered types get their power supply from an existing ceiling or wall lighting point, while low-voltage types run off a transformer. Once you have fixed the track or wires in position and made the power connection, you can position the lights as required to create the lighting effects you want.

Start on the floor level

Lay out track sections on the floor first. Not only does this help you to plan the track arrangement accurately, it also identifies where you will need to reduce the length of the track sections.

Using the rose

You can use an existing ceiling rose to power mains-voltage track. Just replace the existing two-core pendant flex with a length of two-core-and-earth cable, so the track will be safely earthed.

! **Cable core colours have changed – see page 172.**

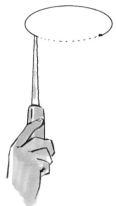

1 Mark hole for fitting, drill a hole to admit padsaw blade, and saw round. Feed in cable and prepare for connection

2 Connect cores to terminal block, linking like cores and covering the bare cable earth core with green-and-yellow PVC sleeving

3 Push light fitting up into hole in ceiling until its spring-loaded jaws grip perimeter of hole and lock it in place

lighting

lighting Spots and tubes

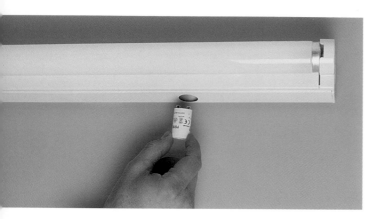

Curing a false start

If a fluorescent tube is reluctant to start, suspect a faulty starter. Locate it on the base of the fitting, push it in and twist it anticlockwise to release it from its socket. Take it to the shop so you can identify the correct replacement.

Guard against grease

Some low-voltage lighting tracks use tiny pea-shaped quartz halogen bulbs that fit into small parabolic reflectors. Always handle these with paper tissue or a handkerchief; otherwise grease from your skin can cause hot spots that will make the bulb fail prematurely. Avoid turning them on and off repeatedly too–this also shortens their life.

Get a better grip

Many spotlight bulbs are quite a tight fit in their reflector lampholders. If you have trouble undoing and removing a failed bulb, wind a couple of rubber bands around your finger and thumb to enable you to get a better grip on the smooth end of the bulb.

Recessed fittings

Use joists for planning

Plan the wiring to a row of recessed light fittings according to which way the ceiling joists run. If the row is parallel to the joists, cut the holes for the fittings and then feed the supply cables between the joists from one hole to the next, working from below. If the row is at right angles, lift a single floorboard in the room above and drill holes through the joists, so the cables can be run through them from light to light.

Protection in the loft

Make sure that loft insulation is pulled clear of recessed light fittings, so they cannot overheat and create a fire risk. If the fittings project above the tops of the joists, make open-sided protective boxes from offcuts of plywood or MDF to fit over them. Then the fitting will not be damaged accidentally by anyone moving about within the roof space.

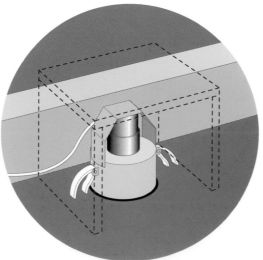

Securing light fittings

Templates make fitting simple

Use the template provided with the light fitting to mark the positions of the fixing screws. Wherever possible position the fitting directly below a joist and align its baseplate so at least two fixing screws go into the joist.

A batten between joists

If you cannot attach the light fitting to a joist, it is possible to fix it to the ceiling (providing it is lightweight) using cavity fixings such as spring toggles. Large fittings with heavy glass diffusers need screwing to timber battens secured between the joists, so you will need access to the ceiling void to fit these.

**❗ Notifiable work
– see page 172.**

outdoors
Effective lights

Find the best locations

Work out where to put outside lights by wiring up the fitting to an extension cable. Then, after dark, get a helper to hold the switched-on fitting against the house wall in a variety of positions, so you can see exactly what is lit up. Use steps or a ladder if necessary. Remember that a little light goes a long way in the dark, and over-bright lights merely dazzle. Carry out the same exercise to position lights beside paths and steps in the garden (right).

Watch the glare

Floodlights suit football stadiums more than back gardens, but if you decide you must install them, think about your neighbours and angle the fittings so the light is directed down and onto your property only. Carelessly aligned floodlights can also be a hazard if they're fitted at the front of the house, where they could dazzle drivers.

Corner positions

Cut the number of outside lights you need by positioning them on the corners of the house. Each light can then shine along two adjacent walls.

Automatic control

Your outside lights can be controlled by a simple on/off switch situated inside the house. Alternatively, they can be turned on automatically whenever anyone approaches the house, if they are wired up to a passive infra-red (PIR) sensor (left), which reacts to body heat. Some outside lights have the sensor built in. If you already have a number of outside lights, installing a separate PIR sensor to control them is a relatively straightforward wiring job.

Tilt the drill bit

Drill a hole through the house wall with a large-diameter masonry drill bit for the cable to an outside light. Check that the hole will emerge somewhere accessible indoors, and angle the drill bit so the hole runs slightly uphill from the outside, to prevent rainwater from getting in. Feed a length of round PVC conduit through the hole to protect the cable from chafing, and waterproof the exit point with exterior sealant.

outdoors
Effective lights

Choose a pick-up point
A light on the outside wall can be wired as a spur from an indoor circuit–a lighting circuit if the extra light won't overload it, a power circuit otherwise. Pick whichever is the more convenient to access. Wire a spur from a power circuit via a fused connection unit (FCU) fitted with a 3 amp fuse. The FCU can also act as the light switch. This job counts as non-notifiable work (see page 172), provided there is no additional wiring outside the house.

Easy wiring
Choose light fittings with a terminal block inside to make the wiring as easy as possible. Then all you have to do is feed the supply cable through the house wall into the back of the fitting, and connect its cores to the block. Some fittings have a waterproof rubber sleeve through which the incoming cable passes. With others you need to seal the join between the fitting's baseplate and the wall with a generous bead of exterior sealant (below).

Low voltage, low cost
Mains-voltage lights in the garden must have their own circuit, with the protection of a residual current device (RCD). Installing this circuit is **Notifiable work (see page 172)** and is a job for a professional electrician. You can save the expense of this by choosing a low-voltage lighting set powered from a transformer instead. The cable can safely be left lying on the surface of flowerbeds as it runs from light to light.

Power in the garden
❶ Notifiable work – see page 172.

Burying cable
Ordinary PVC-sheathed cable can be run underground so long as it is first threaded through impact-resistant PVC conduit, assembled with solvent-welded joints. Bury it at least 500 mm (20in) deep–more (700mm–28in) under vegetable plots or possible fence runs. For additional protection, line the trench with sand and cover the conduit with special cable covers or with paving blocks supported by bricks. A black/yellow warning tape (available from electrical wholesalers) should be laid in the back-filled trench around 150mm below ground level to alert future gardeners when they are digging.

Overhead power
Where it is impossible to bury outdoor cable (under concrete, say), it can be run overhead, but it needs to be at least 3.5m above the ground (5.2m above driveways). Normal PVC-sheathed cable can be used (but armoured or Hituf cable will last longer) and runs longer than 3m need to be supported by a steel catenary wire strung between two stout posts. You can buy all the bits you need from an electrical wholesaler.

Safety shutdown
When fitting an outside socket outlet, it is a good idea to use one with a high-sensitivity RCD built in–even if it is being connected to an RCD-protected circuit. This will trip more quickly than the circuit RCD and will offer even greater protection against electric shock.

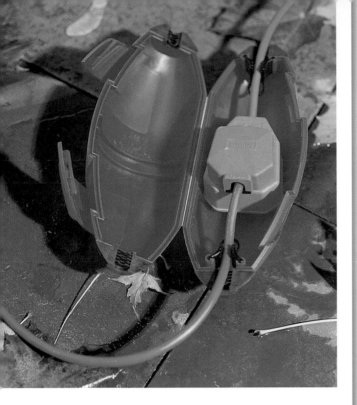

Waterproof connections

An extension lead is vital if you want to use power tools outdoors, but the plug-and-socket connection isn't waterproof and this is dangerous if conditions are damp. Make it waterproof by placing it in some kind of enclosure, such as the one above.

Extension sense

If you are using garden power tools with blades, such as lawnmowers and hedgetrimmers, always use brightly coloured leads–they are easy to see and to avoid. If you need to extend a flex with a two-piece flex connector, fit the part with the pins to the flex leading to the tool, and the part with the sockets to the flex leading to the power supply.

Tough customers

In outbuildings, fit metal-clad switches and socket outlets, set on matching surface-mounted metal boxes. These will withstand knocks and general wear and tear far better than plastic ones. Run cables in mini-trunking or conduit.

1 Drill through house wall where you want the light, and line hole with PVC conduit. Then feed in cable

2 If light fitting has a hollow baseplate, link cable to flex with strip connectors. Then screw baseplate to wall

3 If baseplate is solid, chop out recess in wall to house conduit box for connections and mount light fitting over it

4 If fitting has an internal terminal block, feed cable in through waterproof seal and make connections to it

outdoors

203

services Extra phones

Get kitted out

The simplest way to fit an extra telephone socket is to buy a telephone extension 'kit' from your local DIY store. These come with differing amounts of cable (10m, 20m or 30m, for example) - depending on how far from the main master socket the new socket will be – and include all the bits you need.

The kit includes an adaptor which you plug into the master socket (still allowing you to plug a telephone in here) and which is already attached to the length of telephone cable. You have to wire up the socket supplied (after cutting the cable to the exact length required), but a tool is supplied to make this simple.

If you want more than one socket, you can either plug the adaptor of a second kit into the socket of the first (and carry on like this if you want more than two) or take the cable of the first kit to a special junction box and then run telephone cable from this to two, three or more extra sockets. If you have too many sockets (with telephones plugged into all of them), the system won't work – four is the usual maximum number.

Strip the sheath

If you use a trimming knife to make a small cut at the end of the cable (after cutting it to length), you can use pliers to pull one of the four wires inside such that it tears the outer cable sheathing along its length. Use side cutters to remove the torn sheathing and you are ready to connect up.

Easy connections

You don't need to use wire strippers to remove the insulation from the tiny wires inside telephone cable: when you use the tool supplied with the kit to push each wire into the correct terminal, the metal jaws inside the terminal cut through the insulation such that proper electrical contact is made. Once all the wires are in place and the cable clamp fitted (as shown here), trim the wires (and the cable clamp) neatly.

It will be easier to wire the socket before you fit it to the wall (though you might want to drill the holes for your own wallplugs first); you can now secure the socket to the wall with the screws supplied and screw on the cover.

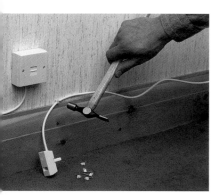

Test it out

When you have finished all the wiring for as many sockets as you want, plug the adaptor into the master socket and plug a telephone into each socket in turn, using a mobile phone to ring your own number to ensure that everything works.

Start at the master

Making sure that there is sufficient cable to allow you to plug the adaptor in (but don't plug it in yet), run cable from the master socket to the position where you want the new socket.

Telephone cable is slim enough to be run almost unnoticed along the top of skirting boards and around door architraves. Tap in a cable clip (supplied) every 250mm (10in) – at room corners, use a clip either side of the corner, not right in the corner itself. Pass the cable from room to room through holes drilled next to door frames and from floor to floor using the same routes as plumbing pipework. Keep telephone cable at least 50mm (2in) away from mains electricity cable or you may get interference on the line.

Television aerial points

Split the signal
Many people now want televisions in more rooms than just the living room, which is usually the only one with an aerial socket connected to a roof-top or loft aerial. The simplest way of providing one extra socket is to insert a device

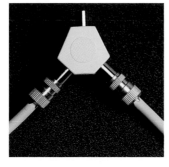

called a splitter into the existing aerial downlead. The original lead continues on to the existing socket, and you connect a new lead into the splitter to supply the second socket.

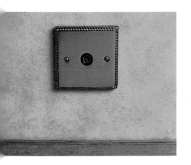

Matching accessories
Surface-mounted aerial sockets are quick and easy to install, but flush ones are much neater and you can match their style to the light switches and power points. They fit over a standard 25 mm deep metal mounting box.

Boosting the signal
You can't split the aerial downlead more than once to supply extra sockets, because the signal strength drops off rapidly. Wire the aerial to a mains-powered signal amplifier instead. This sends a boosted signal on to each new aerial socket.

Two in one
If you need an FM or DAB radio aerial as well as one for your television, you can connect both TV and FM aerial leads into a double aerial outlet in the roof space. This contains a device called a diplexer, which allows two signals to travel along a single coaxial downlead. The lead runs to a matching double outlet in your living room. The TV and radio are then connected to the relevant outlet with a short coaxial lead.

1 Make slit down outer plastic sheath, peel back and trim off about 25 mm (1 in)

2 Roll screening braid back over end of sheath and cut about 12 mm (½ in) of plastic insulation off core wire

3 Fit cap and braid grip over cable end and squeeze grip onto braid with pliers

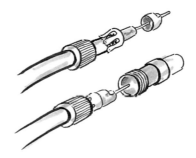

4 Slide on protective pin moulding and plug body, snip off projecting core wire and screw cap onto plug

services

205

decorating

preparation Cleaning the old surface

Use a steam stripper
Make the task of removing old wallpaper easier and quicker by using a steam stripper. A lot of hot water is generated by the equipment, so protect yourself and the floor well. If you intend to hire a steam stripper for a particular job, it is probably worth reserving it in advance—they're always in demand.

Wash with sugar soap
Clean dirt and grease off old paintwork by washing it thoroughly with sugar soap and water. The solution also takes the shine off gloss-painted surfaces, providing a good key for the new coat of paint. Rinse off the sugar soap with clean water and allow the paintwork to dry before repainting.

Dress for the job
Protect your eyes and skin from sugar soap by wearing safety spectacles and a long-sleeved top, with the cuffs tucked securely inside a pair of rubber gloves. The eye protection is especially vital when washing a ceiling.

Dust-free woodwork
After rubbing down woodwork with an abrasive paper to provide a key for new paint, wipe it with a clean rag dipped in white spirit to remove the dust.

Score and soak
Wallpaper is easier to strip if you soften it first. Score it with a wallpaper perforator or stripping knife, then soak the surface with hot soapy water. Adding a small quantity of wallpaper paste to the water thickens it slightly, so that it doesn't run down the wall quite so quickly.

Thin the first coat
Newly plastered walls must be allowed to dry out completely before painting. They will be very absorbent, so thin the first coat of emulsion by adding an extra 20 per cent of water.

Protect light fittings

Use plastic bags to guard ceiling lights and fans against paint drips. First, switch of MCB or remove fuse at the consumer unit, then unscrew the ceiling rose cover and slide it down the flex. Enclose the fitting in a bag, securing the neck of it around the flex with a freezer bag tie. Make tubes from stiff paper to slip over wall lights, removing shades and bulbs first.

Painting over wallpaper

You can save time by painting over wallpaper that is well stuck down, although doing so will make it much more difficult to remove at some future date. Test paint a small area first; if the paper bubbles, over-painting is not an option.

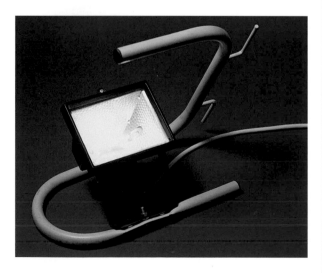

Bright idea for seeing clearly

If you are painting a poorly lit room, or have disconnected the lighting circuit for safety, consider hiring a portable work light. Plug it into a socket and angle the light so that it bounces off the ceiling—then your shadow won't be cast on the wall you're decorating. The powerful bulb will show up imperfections.

1 Remove rugs and lift fitted carpets if possible. Move the furniture to middle of room and cover with dustsheets

2 Remove curtains and blinds and prepare all surfaces

3 Use masking tape to protect glass and internal woodwork from paint splashes

4 Turn off electricity, then loosen faceplates of fittings so edges of old wallpaper can be stripped from behind them

preparation

preparation
Stripping the woodwork

Beware of melted paint

Wear long-sleeved clothing and cotton or leather gloves to protect your skin from melted paint burnt off with a hot-air gun or blowlamp. Newspaper or dustsheets laid on the floor can catch fire, so place a container of water—an old baking tray or grill pan is ideal—on the floor instead.

Dangerous lead

Any pre-1960s paintwork is likely to contain lead; DIY stores sell inexpensive kits for testing paintwork. If yours contains lead, it should be stripped with great caution. Keep children out of the way. Never use a blowlamp, hot-air gun, or abrasive paper, all of which will create lead-rich fumes and dust. Instead, wear gloves and a dust mask and use a chemical paint stripper. Seal the waste in a bag and put it in the dustbin—don't burn it.

Resisting the force of gravity

Use a gel-type paint stripper on vertical surfaces. Because it doesn't run off quickly, the chemical has more time to get to work. Alternatively, thicken the standard stripper by mixing a little wallpaper paste into it.

Stay on the move

The golden rule when stripping paint with a blowlamp or hot-air gun is to keep the tool moving. Playing too much heat on one spot will burn and char the paint rather than softening it. You also risk scorching the wood itself.

Seal the knots

Use knotting fluid to seal knots in bare wood, or apply aluminium wood primer to the whole surface, otherwise resin in the knots can show through new paint.

Follow the contours

Preserve the definition of wooden mouldings by rubbing them down as little as possible. Remove as much old paint as possible with scrapers and homemade tools—for example, a small metal washer held with mole grips for concave areas (left). Then finish with fine abrasive paper wrapped around a suitable base—for example, a piece of wooden dowel (right). Alternatively, use an abrasive sponge block.

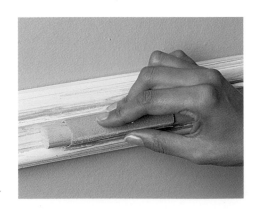

sanding floors
Stripping back to bare boards

Remove furnishings and fixtures
Sanding floorboards creates a great deal of fine dust, despite the collection bag on the machine, so take down curtains, lampshades, pictures and other removable wall and ceiling fixtures before you start. Polythene sheets pinned over door frames will help to keep the rest of the house dust free.

Protect ears, nose and throat
Drum sanders are noisy and stripping the floorboards of an average-sized room takes several hours, so wear ear protectors—and tell your neighbours what you're doing.
Avoid inhaling dust by wearing a respirator with a good filter, not just a disposable dust mask, and open the windows.
Empty the dust bag frequently because the dust—a mix of wood and old finish—is hot and can catch fire spontaneously.
Heavy work gloves help to cushion your hands against the vibration created by the sander, while those worn by mountain bikers have even more effective padding. Even so, take frequent breaks—don't wait until your hands start tingling.

Spare the belts
Carpet tacks, staples and projecting floorboard nails will shred the expensive abrasive sheets a floor sander uses. Before starting sanding, inspect the floorboards carefully. Pull out any tacks you find, and punch nail heads well below the surface of the boards.

Disguising old nail holes
Stop up all the old nail holes with a suitably coloured wood filler once the top layers of dirt have been sanded off. Then wait for the filler to dry and carry on sanding the boards.

sanding floors
Stripping back to bare boards

Reaching the edges

An edging sander is indispensable for getting right up to the face of skirting boards. In small rooms where a drum sander is heavy and unwieldy to manoeuvre, it may be the only machine you need. Hire kneepads at the same time as the sander, because you'll be working on your knees all the time.

Diagonally across hollows

Old floorboards may be cupped—hollow along their centres and curled up at the edges. As long as the cupping is not too marked, you can get rid of it by running the drum sander diagonally across the boards before you begin working along the grain (above). Use coarse abrasive.

When the dust settles

A floor sander creates a lot of dust. Once it has settled, and immediately before varnishing the floor, clean the entire room with a vacuum cleaner. Then get rid of any remaining dust by wiping the floor with a lint-free cloth dipped in white spirit.

Bottoms up

If the top surface of a floorboard is too damaged to be worth sanding, try lifting it and inspecting the underside; you might be able to re-use it if you nail it down bottom side up.

Start and stop routine

Press down on the handle or operate a special lever to raise the drum off the boards before starting or stopping. If you allow it to be in contact with the boards while building up to full speed or slowing down, they will be scarred.

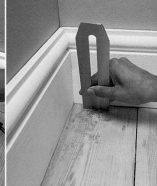

Old for old

If possible, replace badly damaged floorboards with secondhand ones of the same width and thickness, obtained from a salvage yard. Take a short length of the old board along with you for comparison. Secondhand replacements will blend in with the original boards far better than new ones.

Getting into the corners

You will need a sander with a pointed base to get right into corners (left). An alternative is to use a wide chisel or a plane blade to scrape the old finish off the boards. Hold the blade with bevel away from you and scrape in the direction of the grain (right).

A protective coating for the new-look boards

Three sorts of sealer

Polyurethane varnish is the usual choice, but it is solvent-based and takes a long time to dry. It also tends to yellow with age. Water-based varnishes and two-part catalysed lacquers provide a clearer finish, with less tendency to discolour. They dry fast, so you can apply several coats in a day, although that does mean you have to work quickly to keep a wet edge. Mix only as much of a two-part lacquer as you can use before it starts to set—usually in around an hour.

Read the instructions, because varnishes come in various grades and you need to choose one that is suitable for floors. Flooring-grade varnish may itself be graded for use according to the amount of wear and tear the floor is likely to receive.

Rub on the first coat

Thin the first coat of varnish with a little white spirit and apply it with a clean rag, rubbing it into the boards. Then use a brush for subsequent coats. Never shake the tin; the bubbles formed will appear as tiny blemishes in the dried varnish.

Buy a new brush

Don't risk getting specks of old paint or bristles in the varnish by using an old or cheap brush. Invest in a new, good-quality brush before you start. Synthetic fibre brushes are less prone to hair loss than natural bristle types.

Use a narrow brush to varnish the edge trims and the perimeter boards, then switch to a wider brush for fast coverage of the rest of the floor.

Be alert to fire risk

Open the windows, ensure gas flames—including pilot lights on a boiler or cooker—are extinguished, and don't smoke nearby when varnishing a floor. Rags used to apply varnish or oil are highly flammable and should be left outside to dry before being thrown in the bin.

Alternative to varnish

An oil polish will provide a hard-wearing alternative to varnish, and is well worth the effort if you have a beautiful old timber floor. Use a product such as Danish oil, or mix your own using 1 part raw linseed oil to 8 parts of turpentine. You can colour the oil by mixing a stain into it.

Warm the oil to make it more fluid and to help absorption. It could be 24 hours or more before the floor is dry enough for a second, more sparing coat. Keep applying coats until buffing raises a silky sheen, and water forms beads on the surface.

painting
Working outdoors

Stabilise surfaces
Test the stability of existing paint on an outside wall by rubbing it down with a dry, dark-coloured rag. If the rag collects a chalky deposit, scrub the wall with a stiff dry brush to remove loose material, then apply a stabilising solution.

Protect from splashes
Cover porch and bay window roofs, to prevent them from getting splashed as you paint. To protect paths and other hard surfaces, lay some old dustsheets or plastic sheeting along the base of walls, but don't stand a ladder on plastic sheeting in case the ladder slips.

Handiest for the job
Use a long-nap roller with a tough nylon pile or a large, synthetic-fibre brush to apply masonry paint. A medium-bristle dustpan brush with a comfortable handle is also good for the job. Apply the paint to the wall in vertical zigzags and fill in the gaps with vertical strokes.

Clearly a better choice
Painting ornamental brick surrounds of doors, windows and chimney stacks is an irreversible decision—you won't be able to get the paint off if you want to at some later date. If ornamental brickwork has deteriorated, you can protect it with a clear water-repellent silicone sealer.

Weather eye

Don't decorate outside on windy days; dust and grit is bound to get blown onto the wet paint. Cold weather can make gloss paint dry without a shine.

Stay ahead of the sun

On sunny days, try and paint walls while they are in shadow, otherwise they will dry too quickly. If you are caught in the sun's glare, protect the back of your neck, and if you're using white paint, wear sunglasses.

Exterior woodwork

Seal against rain

Position masking tape 2–3 mm (⅛ in) away from the edge of the putty when masking window glass. Paint across this gap; it seals the junction between putty and glass against rain. Remove the tape before the paint has hardened.

Let paint spots set

Use a rag dampened in white spirit or water to wipe wet paint off glass. Scrape off any spots you miss after the paint has set, but before it goes really hard.

Let the wood breathe

Microporous paints and varnishes are the best choice for exterior woodwork. They are formulated to allow any moisture trapped in the wood to escape, while at the same time preventing rain from getting through. The finish is also flexible, so it won't crack under the stress of thermal movement.

Right brush for the job

Painting windows with many small panes is a fiddly job. As an alternative to sticking masking tape around the wood to stop paint getting on the glass, use a cutting-in brush to paint glazing bars.

STAGES IN
PAINTING EXTERIOR OF A SASH WINDOW

1 Lower top sash and raise bottom one to its full extent. Then paint exposed surfaces

2 Reverse both sashes to gain access to rest of bottom sash and complete painting it

3 With both sashes closed, paint lower half of jambs and parting beads. Allow to dry

4 Lower top sash to complete painting of jambs and parting beads. Then close sashes and paint face of frame

215

painting
Exterior woodwork

Prevent windows and doors sticking

Paint windows and exterior doors early in the day, so that by evening the paint is dry enough for them to be closed. Paint surfaces where openings and frames meet first. Wedge doors open, so they can't blow shut or be closed by mistake. To ensure the joinery doesn't stick when you open it next day, smear a little petroleum jelly onto the frame rebates before shutting up for the night; it will wipe off easily in the morning.

Keep clear of grit

Pour small quantities of paint into a paint kettle when you're painting masonry and rendered walls. It prevents bits of grit from the wall being transferred to the tin (see page 225).

End on a complete board

If you cannot paint the whole of a timber-clad wall at one go, call a temporary stop when you reach the bottom edge of one complete board. Always 'feather' or blend areas of wet paint into one another with light brush strokes and little paint, otherwise you will end up with lap marks, especially if you are using gloss paint.

Gutters and downpipes

Camouflage or contrast?

Choose a colour that camouflages or highlights gutters and downpipes. Modern plastic gutters and pipes are probably best painted to blend into their background, but decorative cast-iron fittings may be worth highlighting by painting them a different colour.

Getting behind a downpipe

You can buy a special brush with an angled head for painting behind downpipes, but if you don't have one position a piece of card behind the pipe to protect the masonry.

While it's on the ground

When you take down metal guttering in order to replace a fascia board, take the opportunity to remove any rust with a wire brush and repaint the gutter before putting it back up. Make sure you use a suitable primer on aluminium.

Neighbourhood watch

Look at what your neighbours have done before choosing an exterior colour scheme for your home, espcially if you live in a terrace. Apparently simple choices, such as the colour of a front door, can have a large impact on the street scene. Do you want to stand out or blend in?

Painting plastic pipes

Plastic gutters and pipes can be left unpainted; just wash them down with water containing a little bleach. If you do want to paint them, there's no need to use an undercoat. Key the surface of new plastic with fine abrasive paper to make the paint adhere better, or wait a year before painting, by which time the weather will have taken the shine off the surface.

Primer, undercoat and finish

Stick to separate coats

Primers are designed to seal surfaces, undercoats to obliterate underlying colour and provide a strong key for the protective top coat. Using a combined primer/ undercoat may save time and money, but you will generally not get results as good as those achieved with separate coats.

Primer choice

A primer specially formulated for a particular surface–plaster, wood or metal–will last longer and produce a better finish than a universal primer. **Copper pipe needs no primer,** but an undercoat may be necessary to hide the colour of the metal.

Obliterate stains

Wax crayon and felt-tip pen marks, tar from cigarettes and water stains from plumbing leaks will all eventually show through layers of conventional paint. Smother them permanently with an aluminium primer-sealer or with a proprietary stain-block. The latter is sold in aerosol form, ideal for small areas.

Pick healthier paints

Look for the VOC (volatile organic compounds) content when choosing paint. Low VOC paints are better for the environment and for health, and are a sensible choice for children's rooms and furniture, particularly if anyone in your home has asthma. Paints range from minimal VOC content to high. You can even buy low VOC oil-based paints, manufactured using vegetable oils.

White not yellow

White paint on radiators and central-heating and hot-water pipes won't yellow if you use a proprietary radiator enamel. This gives off strong fumes as it dries, so open the windows wide.

Hide the imperfections

Gloss paint shows up every blemish in a surface. If your woodwork isn't perfect or you don't want to spend long hours on preparation, use a more forgiving matt or eggshell finish instead.

Keep mould at bay

Steamy kitchens and bathrooms can be ideal breeding grounds for mould, because of the condensation that forms on wall and ceiling surfaces. Decorate them with special kitchen and bathroom paint containing a fungicide.

Volatile combination

Polystyrene ceiling tiles and solvent-based paints make a highly combustible combination. Always paint these tiles with a water-based paint.

painting Brush, roller, pad or spray gun?

Invest in a flexible frame

It's worth buying a good-quality paint roller, with a cage that spins freely and springs back into position when you squeeze it. Look for a comfortable handle, with a threaded insert to take an extension pole. The pole will save you bending if you want to paint a floor, or climbing a stepladder to reach ceilings. A telescopic pole is the most versatile type.

Choose your sleeve carefully

Use a cheap foam roller sleeve for general painting work where the standard of the finish is not important. For a good finish on a very smooth surface, a mohair sleeve with a short pile is best. A sleeve with a long lambswool or synthetic fibre pile forces paint into every crevice on a highly textured surface. Use a long-nap sleeve with a tough nylon pile on rough exterior surfaces such as pebbledash.

Create a textured finish

A sculptured roller sleeve will add a textured finish to a flat surface. Hessian, bark, swirl, patchwork and stipple effects are among those available. Some can be used to create a repeating pattern with successive parallel passes of the roller.

What size brush?

The general rule is to use the widest brush that you can handle comfortably, and which is appropriate for the surface being painted. A 100 mm brush is ideal for applying emulsion paint to walls, while a 75 mm one is better for gloss-painting flat woodwork. The wider the brush, the quicker you can paint, making it easier to keep a wet edge as you work.

Reaching behind a radiator

Use a radiator roller or brush to paint behind a radiator. Both tools have long handles, so the new paint colour can be taken right out of sight. Be sure to remove dust and cobwebs before you start. Mask the newly painted wall with plastic sheeting or hardboard when you come to painting the radiator itself.

Get the best from a cheap brush

A cheap brush is fine if a good finish isn't important—when brightening up an understairs cupboard, for example. Try to use the brush for priming and undercoating first, so that when it's time to apply the top coat it has stopped shedding bristles.

Natural versus synthetic

Modern synthetic fibre brushes will perform as well as all but the finest hog bristle brushes, and suffer far less from 'hair loss' in use. They are also easier to clean than bristle brushes, and keep their shape better too.

Power through the job

Consider hiring a power roller if you have a large area to cover. Because paint is continuously fed along the hollow extension pole, you can finish the job much more quickly. You need to keep the roller moving to avoid drips and runs.

When a pad is best

A paint pad is the best choice for applying thin coats of paint to smooth surfaces easily and without drips. In the past, pads used to fall apart when used with solvent-based paint, but these days they last well, whether you need to clean them in white spirit or just wash off water-based paint.

Airless is best

Use an airless spray gun (right), with an electric pump that forces paint through the nozzle. It is easier to use and causes less overspray than a spray gun powered by compressed air.

Allow time for masking

Applying paint with a spray gun is faster than putting it on with a brush or roller, but remember that the time you gain from faster application has to be offset against the time it takes to mask off adjacent surfaces that won't be painted.

219

Protect your hands

Wear a pair of fabric gloves while painting, especially when using solvent-based paints. They save having to remove paint from your hands with white spirit, which can irritate the skin. A barrier cream will help to stop paint sticking to your skin if you prefer to work without gloves.

Ceiling before walls

Emulsion the ceiling first, so that any splashes on the walls are covered later. Start to paint a wall at the top right-hand corner if you are right-handed, from the opposite corner if left-handed.

Brush the margins

If you are going to paint the ceiling or adjoining walls different colours, use a brush for the edges first, then a roller to infill the rest of the surface.

Danger overhead

Wear safety spectacles when painting a ceiling. They will protect your eyes from paint splashes when you look upwards. Avoid making splashes with a roller by pushing it slowly; don't snatch it away at the end of each pass. **Try not to overload the brush** when painting a ceiling. Dip just the bottom quarter of the bristles into the paint; then it won't seep into the ferrule and run down the handle–a common problem when painting ceilings.

Bands and strips

Apply paint in horizontal or vertical bands, then blend the parallel bands together. Paint walls and ceilings in strips about 600 mm (2 ft) wide, working quickly so that the edge of the paint doesn't get a chance to dry. Finish off around door and window frames after the rest of the wall is covered. Turning the heating off and closing windows will extend the drying time–worth doing if you have a large room to paint.

Frames before paper

Paint door and window frames before hanging wallpaper, so there's no chance of getting paint on the paper. Extend the paint beyond the edge of frames and onto the walls by about 6 mm (¼ in), then any gaps you leave between the edges of the wallpaper and the frames won't show up.

Don't shoot yourself!

Keep your spare hand out of the way of the nozzle when spray-painting: the paint is forced out at high pressure and can become embedded in the skin. Wear gloves and long sleeves as a precaution. Safety goggles and a face mask or, preferably, a respirator are vital protection against fine paint droplets.

Every other tread

Paint or varnish every other tread when decorating an uncarpeted staircase, and identify which can be walked on by taping sheets of newspaper over them. Adapt the same method when painting or varnishing a floor you need to use all the time, doing half of it one day and the rest the next.

painting

Keep a spray gun on the move

Practise on a test surface with a spray gun. Always keep the gun parallel to the surface; do not swing it in an arc. Begin moving your arm before you press the trigger, and continue the movement for a moment or two after releasing it.

Check that the hose on the spray gun is long enough before you start to use it; a sudden jolt will ruin the job.

Start at the centre

Paint outwards from the centre of a door towards the edges: do the panels and the vertical surfaces separating them first, then the horizontal sections (called rails), next, the verticals (stiles) and edges. Leave the frame until last.

Connecting colours

If a door is a different colour on each side, paint the latch or lock edge the same colour as the face that opens into the room. Match the hinge edge to the other side of the door.

Remove the grit

Don't forget to wipe surfaces with a clean damp cloth or a tack rag after rubbing down between coats of paint or varnish. Otherwise, specks of grit and dust deposited by the abrasive will show in the next coat, spoiling it, and you'll have to sand it back again once it has dried.

painting Dealing with flaws and spills

Avoid overloads

Sags and runs are difficult to remove from paintwork. Sometimes you have to sand the surface back to the bare wood to get rid of them. Try to prevent them by not overloading the paintbrush. If any do form, don't try to remove them while the paint is still tacky.

Hard attack

Attack dried emulsion paint on carpets by repeatedly dampening the stain and teasing lumps of paint out of the pile with an old toothbrush.

A water-based paint stripper may remove solvent-based paint from carpets and hard floor surfaces. Test on an inconspicuous corner first. Neutralise stripper residue with water immediately afterwards.

Dab hand with spills

Act fast if you spill paint. Scrape up as much as you can with a flat-bladed tool. Then dab off what's left with dry absorbent cloths and paper before lifting the last traces with clean cloths dampened with cold water (for spilt emulsion) or white spirit (for solvent-based paint). Use washing-up liquid on a damp cloth to remove traces of white spirit from fabric.

Scrape paint off glass

The best tool for removing paint from a window pane is a plastic scraper fitted with a trimming knife blade. The blade should be inset very slightly so it cannot mark the frame.

Rub insects off dry paint

Don't try to remove small insects that become trapped on gloss paint when it is still tacky. Wait until the paint is dry, then rub them off with a rag dampened with white spirit.

Surgical removal

Unless you spot a stray bristle as soon as it appears and can lift it off the paint before it gets stuck, wait until the surface is thoroughly dry before attempting to remove it. Then use a scalpel or sharp craft knife to carefully cut it away from the new paintwork.

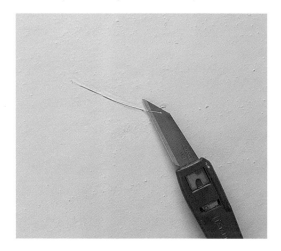

Keep equipment as good as new

Overnight break

When you take a break during painting, wrap your paintbrush tightly in either kitchen foil or cling film so air cannot get to it. The brush will then be ready for use later–or even the next day. **Keep a loaded roller** without it drying out by sliding a plastic bag over the sleeve; exclude as much air as possible before securing the neck with a wire tie.

Cleaning a spray gun

Flush a spray gun out with water or solvent as soon as you have finished using it, squirting the waste into a container (left). When the flushing liquid comes through clear, remove the nozzle from the gun and leave it to soak in clean water or solvent to get rid of any remaining paint.

painting

In suspension

Don't leave brushes soaking in white spirit unless you intend to use them again within a day or so. The way to prevent the bristles becoming bent and out of shape in the jar is to suspend the brush from a length of stiff wire or thin dowel, passed through a hole drilled just above the brush ferrule.

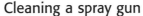

Keep bristles shapely

Wrap polythene around the bristles of cleaned brushes, secured with rubber bands, and hang them from hooks or nails. Next time you need to use them, your brushes will be clean and, most importantly, the bristles won't be misshapen.

painting Best ways to store and dispose of paint

Wrap up a roller
Make sure a roller sleeve is completely dry before storing it. Then wrap it in paper or polythene and tie up the ends to keep it clean.

Never down the drain
When you finish using a water-based paint, wipe as much of it as possible off brushes and rollers before rinsing them in the sink, so that as little as possible is washed down the drain. Never pour used white spirit or solvent-based paint down the sink or into a drain. Unwanted water-based paint can be sealed in its tin and put out for the refuse collectors. It's best to consult your local authority about getting rid of any solvent-based product; it may have special disposal facilities.

Foil the formation of a skin
Use a piece of kitchen foil to prevent a skin forming on the top of an opened tin of paint. Using the lid as a guide, cut a circle of foil just large enough to cover the surface of the paint. Press it down gently to exclude air trapped beneath it.

Decant a little at a time
Pouring paint into a paint kettle is a good idea for several reasons. For a start, large full paint tins are heavy to hold for long periods. If you pour just a little paint into the kettle at a time, you won't waste much if you upset it. And, if your brush picks up some dirt, it will contaminate only what's in the kettle, rather than the paint in the tin. Use kitchen foil to line the kettle; it cuts cleaning-up time and delays the build-up of dry paint in the container.

Give an old brush new life
Before reusing a poorly stored brush, flick the bristles against your hand to remove any dust or hardened bits of paint. Try removing any remaining paint with an old comb. Then restore life to the bristles by soaking the brush in a solution of water and hair conditioner, or a proprietary brush restorer.

Quick way to filter out grit

If there's grit in the paint, stop it getting onto your brush by tying a piece of material cut from a pair of old tights over the rim of the tin (left). Use the tip of the brush to push the material down into the paint, so that clean paint rises up through it. The same trick allows you to filter contaminated paint back into a clean container before storing it.

Recycle white spirit

Save money by recycling white spirit after using it to clean brushes and rollers. Let the paint residue settle in the spirit container, then strain the clear solvent off into a clean container with a tamper-proof lid and label it clearly. Wrap up the hardened paint residue and the dirty container in newspaper before putting them in the dustbin.

Seal the lid

Tipping a tin of paint upside down for a few seconds before storing it helps to stop a skin from forming. The paint flows around the underside of the lid to form an airtight seal when the tin is turned the right way up. Don't store the tin upside down—a skin will simply form below the paint instead of on top of it.

Dilute the waste

When you've finished painting, use newspaper to remove as much water-based paint as possible from brush bristles and roller sleeves. Then wash them out in running water to dilute the paint before it enters the drains.

Store leftovers in jars

A small amount of paint will keep better if you decant it from the tin into a jar with a screw-top lid. Make sure you have enough paint to fill the jar, or a jar small enough to just take the paint, so there's little room for air. Rub some petroleum jelly around the neck of the jar before pouring in the paint; then any that spills down the outside won't make the lid stick fast. Remember to label the jar for future reference.

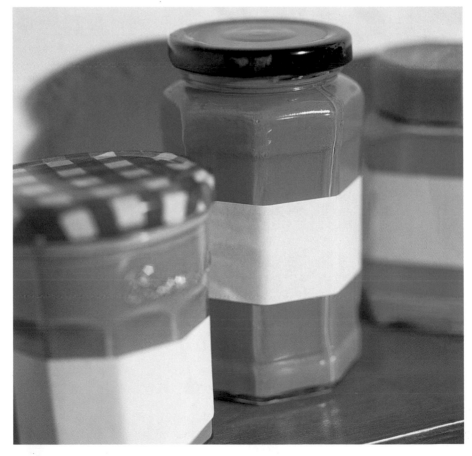

painting

tiling Keys to a strong bond

Get rough with worktops

Before tiling a laminated worktop, score it with a metal abrasive disc fitted to a power drill. Coarse abrasive paper or a file will also do the job, but will take longer.

Strip a papered wall

Don't be tempted to stick tiles over wallpaper: the paste bond will fail and the tiles will fall off. Strip the paper, then wash off any remaining paste so the tile adhesive can bond well to the plaster.

Plywood is perfect

Use 12 mm exterior grade plywood for the walls of a tiled shower cubicle. Mount it on a firm timber framework and seal it with a wood primer. Unlike plasterboard, chipboard and MDF, the plywood won't distort if it gets wet, and because it is very stable, tiles stuck to it are unlikely to crack.

Primed plaster

Tiles can be stuck straight onto bare plaster or plasterboard, but seal the surface with a plaster primer first. This makes it less absorbent, so that the adhesive does not dry too quickly.

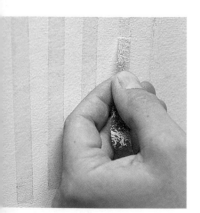

Test the paintwork

Stick test strips of adhesive tape onto a painted wall before tiling it. Leave the tape overnight; if the paint pulls away with the tape, you'll need to strip the wall before tiling. If the paint bond is strong, with no paint coming away with the tape, sand the wall surface with a coarse abrasive paper to provide a good key for the tile adhesive.

Preparing to lay the tiles

Visual effect

Large tiles are quicker to lay than small ones. However, they make a small space look even smaller, especially if a lot of cut tiles are required to cope with corners and features.

Read the pack

Check whether the number of square metres a pack of tiles will cover is printed on the box. This will save time when calculating how many packs you need to buy. Allow an extra 10 per cent for cutting and breakages. Keep any left-over tiles in case you ever have to replace any cracked or broken ones.

Match the batch

Try to buy boxes of tiles with the same batch number to reduce the possibility of colour variation. Then shuffle the tiles to disperse and hide any slight differences in colour. If there is a marked variation, try grading the tiles by shade, so that the differences in colour are 'lost' across the wall.

Edging options

The edge of a tiled area can be finished off with a coloured plastic edging trim, tiles with glazed edges (sometimes the box contains a quantity of these), slim border tiles or a hardwood moulding.

Design preview

To envisage what a tiling pattern will look like once it is on the wall, set out the tiles on the floor or a table first (below). This will give you the opportunity to work out exactly how many of each tile are needed, as well as to make changes to the design.

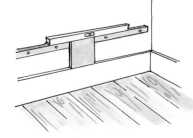

1 Cut batten and fix to wall with masonry nails. Use tile and spirit level to set batten one tile above skirting board

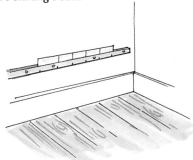

2 Use tiling gauge to work out tile joint positions, transferring marks from gauge to batten

3 Position a vertical batten on start batten so its edge coincides with first whole tile in row. Spread adhesive and start placing tiles

tiling

tiling
Preparing to lay the tiles

Make yourself a gauge
Use a straight batten to make a tiling gauge for positioning the first row of tiles. Draw evenly spaced marks on the batten—each one representing the combined width of a tile and one joint.

Tiling over tiles
As long as old tiles are firmly fixed, new ones can be stuck on top of them. This is easier than removing the old tiles, which normally results in damage to the plaster that has to be made good. Wash the old tiles with sugar soap, then use double-sided adhesive pads to fix a starting batten to them. **Arrange the new tiles** so that the joints are not directly above those of the old ones. Then if the old grouting cracks, the new grouting won't.

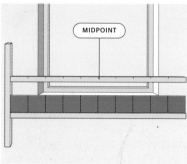

MIDPOINT

Ensuring symmetry
Using a tiling gauge to lay out tiles from the midpoint of a wall ensures equal-size cut tiles in the room corners. If the wall has a major feature such as a window, tile out from its midpoint, using the gauge to equalise the size of the cut tiles on each side of the window.

Fix a starting batten
Don't align the bottom edge of the first row of tiles with the skirting board, especially if you are tiling all round the room; it is unlikely to be perfectly level. Instead use a spirit level to position a batten horizontally so that the top edge is one tile height above the skirting board. Nail it temporarily to the wall.

Clean cuts every time

Effective nibbler
A platform tile cutter is not the best tool for cutting narrow slivers off tiles. Use it to score the line, then nibble the waste off with pliers or pincers. Be sure to protect your eyes against flying bits. Smooth the edge with a tile file.

Experiment first
The cutting wheel of a pliers-type tile cutter should make a clear whispering noise when run across the glazed surface of a tile. If it makes a dull sound instead, and the tiles won't snap cleanly in the jaws of the tool, they are too hard for this type of cutter. Buy or hire a heavy-duty platform tile cutter instead.

Saw and snap
To take a notch out of the edge of a tile—so that it fits around a pipe or bracket, for example—use a tile saw. Make the two parallel cuts at 90° to the edge, score between these, then snap out the waste with pliers. Remember to make an allowance for the grout when cutting a tile to fit around an obstacle.

Hard and harder
The platform tile cutter sold in DIY stores will cut tiles up to 6 mm thick. For thicker ones, especially quarry tiles for floors, hire a professional version (left). There will be less wastage because you'll get a clean cut every time, so the cost of hiring the tool will soon be recouped, especially if you are working with expensive tiles.

File alternative
Coarse silicon carbide abrasive paper wrapped around a sanding block is a good alternative to a proper tile file when you want to rub down cut edges.

tiling Clean cuts every time

Reduce vibration when cutting
Anchor the tile to the workbench with a G-cramp when using a tile saw (right). Use a wooden packing piece between the cramp and the tile so you don't crack the tile as you tighten the cramp. The packing piece also reduces the vibration caused by sawing. To minimise the risk of cracking the tile, position it so that it overhangs the edge of the bench as little as possible.

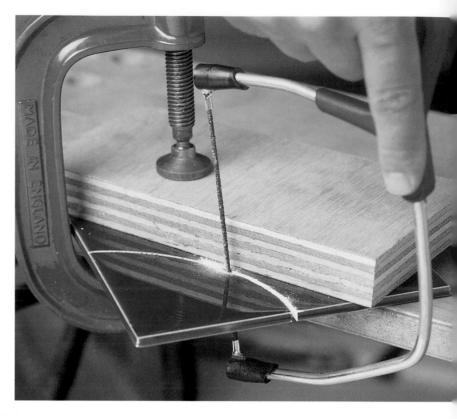

Mind the marker
Use a chinagraph pencil to mark tiles before cutting them. Felt-tip pens should never be used on tiles; they leave a stubborn smudge on the surface of the glaze, and if you use one to mark the edge of a tile where you want to make a cut, the colour can migrate into the grout and stain it.

Sticking tiles in place

Sliding into trouble
Place tiles straight down in their final position. If you slide them into place, you will create a ridge of adhesive on the edge of the tile, which will be forced up between the tile joints. Wipe adhesive off the face of tiles before it can harden.

Roll over mosaics
A paint roller is the ideal tool for bedding sheets of mosaic tiles into the adhesive. It ensures even pressure and the avoidance of high and low spots across the wall or work surface. A rolling pin makes a good alternative if you don't have a paint roller handy.

Look for daylight
Lay a straightedge, such as a spirit level, across the surface of tiles before the adhesive dries to test for hollows and high spots. Prise off the affected tiles and add or remove adhesive.

Better to butter

The general rule is to put the adhesive on the surface you are covering, not the tile. But when it comes to fixing narrow cuts and edge tiles, it's better to butter the back of the tile with adhesive, then press it into place.

Waterproof worktops

Use special angled tiles to make the edge of a homemade chipboard worktop waterproof. Stick cut tiles along the edge of the worktop first, then position the angled tiles (right) so that they overlap the face tile. Finish off by tiling the worktop from front to back, with cut tiles fitted against the wall.

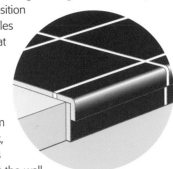

Drilling holes in tiles

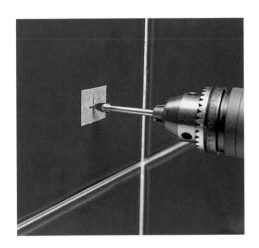

Stop drill bits from skating

Make fixings in tiled walls by drilling into the grout lines wherever possible. If you have to drill through the face of the tile, use a sharp spear-point or masonry drill bit so the glaze doesn't chip. Stop the bit from skating on the glaze by sticking masking tape on the tile where you want to drill (left); this will give the bit an initial 'bite'. Make sure the drill isn't set on hammer action and start slowly if it has variable speed control.

Neat holes for pipes

A hole-boring attachment can be fitted to a platform tile cutter to cut holes for plumbing and central-heating pipes. Bore from the back of the tile, but stop before you go right through and tap out the hole from the glazed side.

Sealed against moisture

Apply waterproof silicone sealant to the tips of screws when mounting fixtures on tiled walls that get wet. As the screw tightens in the wall plug, the sealant is forced up the threads, helping to stop water getting down the fixing and behind the tiles.

Sink the plug

If you're inserting a wall plug into a tiled wall, drill the hole at least 3 mm (⅛ in) deeper than the length of the plug so it can be pushed into the wall past the tile. Otherwise, when a screw is driven into the plug, the sideways pressure it exerts can crack the tile.

tiling Grouting the joints

Switch to a squeegee

If you've never grouted tiles, a small piece of natural sponge is the best tool to start with. Once you've gained confidence, however, a rubber squeegee (above) does a quicker job, followed by a wipe with the sponge.

External corners

Coloured plastic trims will protect tiles on external corners from damage and give the edge a neat finish. Use the trims along the edges of tiled door and window openings as well.

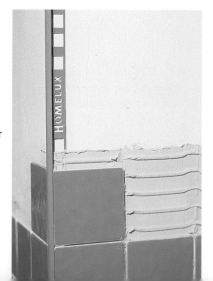

Internal corners

Lay the tiles on each side of an internal corner in pairs to achieve an even horizontal joint. In bathrooms run a bead of waterproof sealant down the corner to waterproof it, and to accommodate any slight movement.

Wipe off quickly

A combined adhesive and grout is much harder to clean off a tiled surface than ordinary grout once it has set. Mix small quantities at a time and clean up as you go. Use a kitchen scouring pad to remove the grout if it's starting to harden on the face of the tiles.

Strategy with spacers

If you're laying thin tiles and there's a risk that plastic spacers will show through the grouting, remove them before applying the grout.

Finishing touch

A ball-point pen cap makes an excellent tool for recessing grouting joints (above). A lollipop stick will also do the trick. Work while the grout is soft, carefully wiping away the surplus with a damp sponge. Don't be tempted to use your fingertip, though, grout is surprisingly abrasive and will soon rub your skin raw.

Hygienic surfaces

When you are tiling a kitchen worktop, finish the grout so that it is flush with the surface of the tiles. If you recess the joints, as you would on a wall, crumbs and grease will collect in them.

Repel mould

In rooms with a high moisture level mould thrives, causing brown or black stains on grout that won't wash off. To keep mould at bay, wipe a fungicidal wash over newly placed tiles in kitchens and bathrooms before grouting between them. Use an epoxy-based waterproof grout on tiled worktops and in bathrooms. It won't harbour mould and is easier to clean.

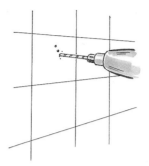

1 Make holes in centre of tile with power drill and masonry bit, then insert cold chisel into space made

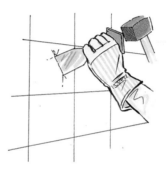

2 Wear eye protection while chipping out damaged tile. Spread adhesive on new tile and press into place

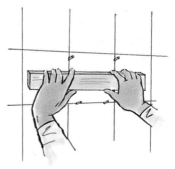

3 Lay a straightedge across repair to check that wall is flat, adding or removing adhesive as necessary

tiling

tiling Keep tiled surfaces looking good

Clean between the tiles

A toothbrush is the ideal tool for cleaning grout. Remove dirt and grease with a solution of liquid detergent in warm water or a non-abrasive cream cleaner. Don't use abrasive cleaners on tiled surfaces; they may dull the glaze and 'pit' the grout.

Getting into the groove

A trimming knife is good for scraping old grouting out of narrow joints, if you don't have a proper grout removing tool. Start at the top of the wall and take care not to chip the edges of the tiles. Use a small, stiff-bristled brush or a vacuum cleaner with a narrow nozzle attachment to remove all the debris from joints before regrouting.

Mould solution

Treat spots of mould on grout with a solution of 1 part bleach in 6 parts of clean water. Wear safety spectacles to protect your eyes from splashes. Proprietary grout cleaners containing a mould inhibitor are also available.

Disguise or display?

Choose a colour to match your tiles if you want to disguise the grout, but you can make a feature of it; for example, black grout with white tiles. Check that the tile surfaces are flat before using a contrasting grout, because it will accentuate any unevenness.

Back to white

Revive discoloured grout by painting it with a proprietary grout whitener, applied with an artist's brush. But be warned: it's a slow tedious job.

Scrape away

Dried-on grout can be removed from tiles with a glass scraper. If you squeeze a little washing-up liquid along the edge of the blade, it will glide over the tile without scratching the glaze.

Keep tiles sparkling

A solution of borax or liquid household ammonia in hot water will revive tiled surfaces discoloured by dirt and grease. Rinse the tiles with clean water then dry them off with a chamois leather.
Remove soap splashes with a mix of 1 part white vinegar to 4 parts water. Rinse the surface with clean water and then wipe it dry.

Paper polishes

Once grouting has dried, use a ball of screwed-up newspaper to remove smears of dried grout and to give the tiles a final polish (above).

Estimating grout

About 1 kg (2¼ lb) of grout is needed for every 3.5 m² (40 sq ft) of tiling; for small mosaic tiles you will need at least twice the quantity.

wallpaper Choose carefully for success

Quick change
Borders can be used on painted or papered walls. Pick a self-adhesive type or use ready-mixed border adhesive if you plan to hang one over a washable or vinyl wall covering. Ordinary powder wallpaper paste will not stick to them.

Covering an uneven wall
A textured or embossed wallpaper will help to disguise minor imperfections in a wall that is sound but slightly uneven. Smooth wallpaper tends to highlight every surface defect.

Easy-to-hang paper
The heavier the wallpaper, the easier it should be to hang. Thin, cheap wallpapers tear and crease easily, making them hard to handle. Vinyls are the strongest wall coverings of all. They consist of a tough printed plastic film bonded to a paper backing so you can hang them like ordinary wallpaper.

Consider all the options
Think about the sort of wear wallpaper will get before you buy. Uncoated papers are fine for bedrooms and living rooms, but a washable or vinyl type will resist steam and stains better in kitchens, bathrooms and children's rooms.

Best for beginners
For your first attempt at paperhanging, choose a paper with no pattern match (or with a random pattern) so you have one less thing to worry about as you hang each length.

Stagger the joins
Lining paper is a plain wallpaper used to hide minor surface defects before hanging smooth wall coverings. Start with a half-width strip, so the joins between the lining paper and the wallpaper don't coincide.

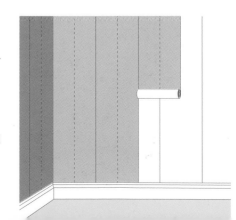

wallpaper

wallpaper How much paper to buy?

Count the widths

Use a standard 530 mm-wide wallpaper roll as a measuring stick to estimate how many strips will be needed to paper all the way round a room. Count doors and average-size windows as wall—the extra paper will be used up in trimming and pattern matching—but ignore large windows and patio doors.

Multiply the metric height of the room by the number of strips to get the total length of paper required. Divide this figure by the length of a standard roll (10 m) to find out how many rolls you'll need for the room.

Buy an extra roll

Check that all the rolls you buy have the same batch number; colours can vary from batch to batch. Buy an extra roll to be on the safe side in case your estimating is inaccurate; getting an extra roll with the same batch number at a later date may be difficult. You can usually return unused rolls for a refund.

Read the packaging first

If you are hanging wallpaper with no pattern match in a room with a typical ceiling height of around 2.3 m (7 ft 8 in), you will get four lengths from each roll. However, you may get only three (plus a lot of wastage) if the paper you have chosen has a large pattern repeat. Read the wallpaper packaging to find out what the vertical distance is between repeats.

Measuring and marking out

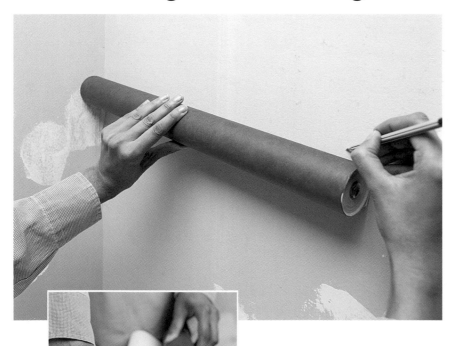

Start with a plumbed line

Mark a vertical guide on the wall before you start hanging wallpaper. Hold one end of a roll of paper into the corner, then make a mark for the line on the wall about 25 mm (1 in) from the other end, so that when you hang the paper you can turn a narrow strip round the corner and onto the adjacent wall.

Pin the top of your plumb line to the wall at ceiling level, so it hangs down over the mark. Then make pencil marks down the wall immediately behind the line and join them up with a pencil and ruler. Draw a new plumbed line when you start papering the next wall, in case the corner is not vertical.

Just fold and cut

Don't bother with a pencil and ruler to draw a cutting line through the length mark across the wallpaper. Just fold the paper at the mark with its side edges carefully aligned, and cut along the creased line. This guarantees a line at right angles to the paper's edge.

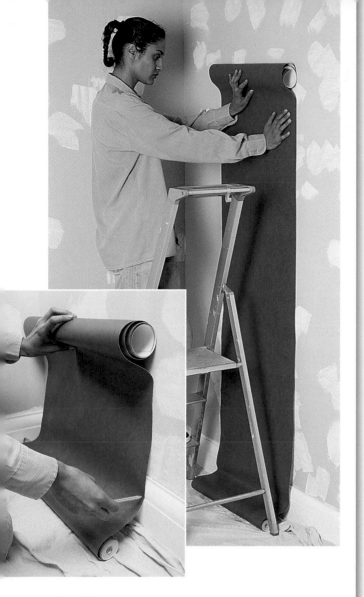

1 Use a plumb line to mark a vertical guide on wall for first length of paper

2 Press top of paper to wall so 50 mm (2 in) overlaps onto ceiling. Then slide it to guideline and brush into place

3 Press back of scissors into angles at ceiling and skirting board to make creases to cut to. Peel back paper, cut along creases and brush into place

4 Repeat procedure to hang subsequent lengths of paper. Butt adjoining edges and use seam roller to press down

The right length every time

Don't use a metal tape to measure the length of pieces of wallpaper. Instead, unwind the roll–the pattern will be the right way up–and hold the top of it against the edge of the ceiling, allowing an overlap for trimming. Then walk your hands down the wall, letting the paper roll up above them as you descend (above). When you reach skirting board level, mark the paper for cutting, again allowing a margin for trimming (above left).

Keep track of wall plugs

Use matches or cocktail sticks to mark the positions of the wall plugs once you have unscrewed and taken down wall lights, shelves and wall-mounted display cabinets. If using matches, break off the heads so they can't stain the wallpaper. As you brush the length into place, the projecting stick will pierce the paper, giving you a clear indication of the whereabouts of every wall plug.

wallpaper

wallpaper
Clever ideas with scissors, string and paste

Two tricks with string

Stop the unpasted part of the paper rolling up onto the area you've pasted by trapping it under a string loop.

Wipe excess paste off the brush onto a piece of string tied across the paste bucket. Lay the brush across the string with its handle resting on the edge of the bucket when you're not using it.

Table-top tip

Before using a new purpose-made pasting table, tap down any pins or staples sticking out of the hardboard or plywood top; they can snag and tear the wallpaper. Next, seal the table top with a couple of coats of varnish to stop it absorbing paste. The table will then be much easier to keep clean.

Use a batch at a time

You can store left-over paste in a cool place overnight. Next day, use up what's left; don't add extra water and powder to an old mix–it will go lumpy.

Guarantee a clean cut

A build-up of paste on the blades stops wallpaper scissors from cleanly. Keep a bowl of water nearby and get into the habit of dipping the blades into it every time you trim the waste from a length of pasted paper. Dry the scissors before using them again.

Pick the right paste

Choose the paste type recommended by the manufacturer of the wallpaper you're hanging. The strength of some pastes can be varied to suit the weight of the paper by increasing or decreasing the volume of water used in the mix; follow the instructions on this point. Nearly all pastes contain a fungicide to prevent mould growth; make sure you use one if you're hanging a vinyl or washable paper.

Paste up on a door

If you don't have a pasting table, take a hardboard-faced flush door off its hinges, remove one of the handles and rest the door across two trestles.

Size new plaster

Brush a coat of size or diluted wallpaper paste over new or unpainted plaster to seal its surface. Otherwise it will absorb water from the paste too quickly, and you will not be able to slide the paper into position easily as you hang it.

On painted walls, excess paste may ooze out along the edge of each length as you brush it into place. Wipe this away with a damp cloth, and make sure that no residue is left on the face of the wallpaper as it will dry in shiny smears.

Keep paste off the table

Avoid getting paste onto the pasting table—and from there onto the face of the paper, where it can cause stains—by following a simple routine. Align one edge of the paper with the far edge of the pasting table. Apply a generous daub of paste down the centre of the paper and brush it outwards to the far edge. Then slide the paper across to the near edge of the table and brush paste out to that edge too.

1 Stand water trough on newspaper next to wall where first length will be hung, and fill with cold water

2 Roll length loosely, pattern side in and top end at outside of roll. Leave immersed for recommended time, then pull top end of length upwards so water drains back into trough

3 Position top of length on wall as for ordinary pasted wallpaper and brush length into place. Use sponge to wipe off excess water. Have some mixed paste ready for sticking any dried-out edges

wallpaper

wallpaper Clever ideas with scissors, string and paste

Support from table to wall

When you've pasted a length, fold each end in on itself, paste side to paste side (below). This makes sure no paste can get onto the face of the paper. Drape the folded length over one arm and take it to the wall. Then use your free hand to draw the top edge clear, ready to be hung at the top of the wall (right).

Avoid trouble with bubbles

Allow paste to soak in

Before pasting wallpaper, read the hanging instructions to see how much time you should allow for the paste to soak in. Wallpaper expands when it gets wet, and if you hang a length while this expansion is still going on, the paper will form bubbles as it stretches and lifts away from the wall surface. The thicker and heavier the paper is, the more time will be needed for this expansion to stop—as much as 15 minutes in the case of some heavy embossed papers. Each length you paste should be left to soak for precisely the same time.

New paper over old
Don't risk trying to paper over existing wallpaper. The new paste will soak into the old paper, softening its paste, and both layers will then bubble up on the wall. Always strip old paper first.

An invisible repair

A bubble that doesn't flatten out as the paste dries is usually caused by careless pasting leaving a dry spot on the back of the paper. Make two cuts across the bubble at 90° with a sharp trimming knife or razor blade (above). Peel back the flaps and apply a little paste with a small paintbrush (above right), then press the flaps back into place with your paperhanging brush.

Wash off grease spots

Greasy marks on the walls will cause bubbles because the wallpaper can't stick properly. Wash the surfaces down thoroughly with household detergent or sugar soap before you start papering.

wallpaper Tackling the tricky bits

Turning an internal corner

Don't try to hang a full-width strip of wallpaper round an internal corner. The corner will probably not be truly square, so the edge of the turned section of paper won't be vertical and that will misalign every length on the next wall.

Measure the distance from the edge of the last full length to the corner, and cut a length of paper to that dimension, plus about 15 mm (⅝ in) for turning around the corner onto the next wall.

Measure the width of the remainder of the cut length and mark a plumbed line this distance from the corner on the next wall. Hang the length to this line so its other edge overlaps the turned strip.

Turning an external corner

Use a technique similar to that for internal corners (left) to paper round external ones. Cut the strip of paper that reaches the corner so that about 25 mm (1 in) will turn onto the next wall, and hang it. Then hang the offcut on the next wall. You'll be able to butt it to the turned edge if the corner is true. If it is not, hang it to a plumbed line so it just overlaps the turned edge, then cut through both layers, using a straightedge and a sharp trimming knife. Peel away the offcuts and finish the two edges with a seam roller.

Papering behind radiators

If you are unable (or unwilling) to remove the radiators before papering a room, cut the paper to length so you can tuck about 200 mm (8 in) down behind them. Use a radiator paint roller if you have one to press the paper into place. Otherwise improvise by taping some sponge to a slim batten.

Invisible seams

It can be difficult to get a neat butt joint between lengths of fabric wall coverings such as hessian. Overlap adjacent lengths by about 6 mm (¼ in), then cut through both layers using a sharp trimming knife and a straightedge. Peel away the waste strips and press the cut edges together for a perfect seam.

wallpaper Tackling the tricky bits

Masking a crease
Wallpaper may crease as you turn it round an out-of-square corner. If it does, tear the paper along the crease line while it's still wet, then smooth it back into place with the 'white' of the tear on the underside. The repair will be almost invisible.
Don't tear vinyl: cut the creases instead. You'll need to use overlap adhesive to stick the cut edges down.

Special treatment for vinyls
Vinyl will not stick over vinyl, whether it's ready-pasted or not, so when you overlap edges at a corner, either cut through both thicknesses to make a butt joint or stick the two together with special vinyl overlap adhesive.

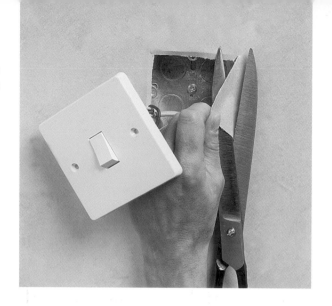

Switches and sockets
Hang wallpaper straight over a light switch or wall socket so that the fitting marks the surface of the paper. Pierce the paper over the centre of the fitting and make diagonal cuts out to the four corners. With the power off, unscrew the faceplate and pull it away from the wall. Then trim off all but about 6 mm (¼ in) of the paper triangles and trap the rest behind the faceplate.

Papering a ceiling

Extra hands make light work
Papering a ceiling is much easier if you have someone to support the concertina folds of pasted paper while you line the length up and brush it into place. Make up a T-shaped support from timber offcuts, or use a clean soft broom.

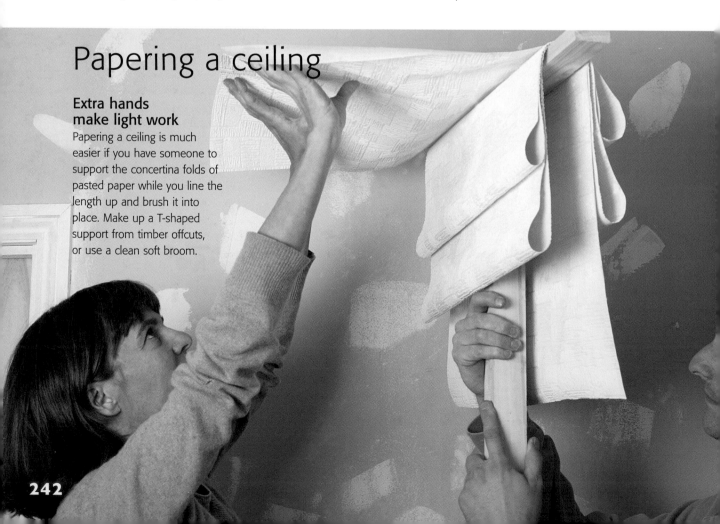

Work in comfort
Make up a work platform with scaffold boards supported on two pairs of steps, so you can reach the ceiling easily. It should span the room and leave about 75 mm (3 in) of space above your head.

Take down the lights
Turn the power off, then take down any ceiling light fittings and insulate the bare cable cores. If you have a ceiling rose, just disconnect the pendant flex from it.

Where to start
Snap a chalked string line on the ceiling to show where to position the edge of the first length of paper. Place it about 25 mm (1 in) less than the paper's width from the side wall. Then you can trim the edge of the paper to match the wall profile, which may not be straight.

Dealing with blemishes

Pencil marks
Rub away marks with an artist's soft putty rubber, which is less likely to damage the surface of the paper than a hard one. It will remove dirty finger marks too, unless they're greasy.

Water marks
To stop stains from past plumbing leaks showing through new ceiling paper, use an aerosol stain blocker to seal the surface. This product will also conceal stains left by tar from cigarette smoke.

Grease marks
You may be able to remove grease marks on printed wallpaper by dabbing them with a pad of kitchen paper dipped in white spirit. Try this on an out-of-the-way area first to check that the printing inks used are colourfast.

Invisible patches
If you have to patch badly marked or damaged wallpaper, tear rather than cut the patch so the 'feathered' edges will blend in with the surrounding paper. Then stick the patch over the damage with a little wallpaper paste. **Cut the patch** if you're repairing vinyl wallpaper. Hold an offcut over the damaged area, align the pattern and cut through both layers with a sharp trimming knife (above). Peel off the vinyl top layer, remove the backing paper with a sharp wallpaper scraper, then align the patch and stick it on.

Rust spots
Plasterboard nails are galvanised, but their coating is often damaged as they are driven in. If a ceiling or partition wall gets damp, the nail heads can rust and mark the decorations. Seal them with a dab of solvent-based paint or primer.

Glossary

Acrylic Water-based paint or glaze used for walls and ceilings.

Aggregate Small pieces of stone, gravel or similar material; coarse aggregate is mixed with cement to make concrete.

Airbrick Ventilated brick that allows air into a room or under a floor.

Airlock Blockage in a pipe caused by trapped air.

Alkyd paint Most solvent-based paints are now based on alkyd resin.

Ampere (amp) The measure of the rate at which electricity flows through a circuit.

Apron A flashing of sheet material (such as zinc) with its top edge set into a brickwork joint and its lower edge overlapping the roof below.

Architrave Decorative wooden moulding fitted round a window or door frame, to cover the join between frame and wall.

Armoured cable Electrical cable usually used underground. It is covered in steel wire to protect it from damage.

Auger Flexible steel spring wire that can be fed along wastepipes to clear blockages. Also a drilling tool, rather like a corkscrew.

Back nut Securing nut for plumbing fittings – e.g. taps and ballvalves.

Back-siphonage Water being drawn back into the mains supply from the house plumbing system, caused by a drop in mains pressure.

Balanced flue A ducting system that allows a boiler, for example, to draw fresh air from outside the house, and also to discharge gases to the outside.

Ballvalve Float-operated valve that controls the supply and level of water in a WC cistern or cold water storage cistern.

Ballast Combination of sand and coarse aggregate used for making concrete.

Bargeboard Strip of wood covering the overhanging edge of a pitched roof at a gable.

Basecoat A flat coat of paint over which a decorative coat is applied.

Blown When a surface layer such as plaster or cement render comes away from the wall behind. Also used to describe a fuse wire that has melted and broken an electrical circuit, as a result of overloading.

Bond The manner in which bricks are arranged in a wall; bond patterns are chosen to suit particular types of wall.

Cap nut The nut used to tighten a compression joint to secure pipework.

Capillary joint Soldered copper connector for joining copper pipes.

Casement Part of a window, or an entire window. Casement windows contain both fixed and opening sections.

Cavity wall A house wall made of two separate leaves, with a gap between them. They are held together with plastic or metal wall ties and the cavity can be insulated.

Cement A powdery binder that bonds with sand to form mortar and sand/coarse aggregate to form concrete.

Chase A groove cut into masonry or plaster, for a run of cable or piping.

Check valve A valve that lets water flow in one direction only.

Chipboard Man-made board made of wood fibres, supplied in sheets.

Circuit The path through which an electric current can flow.

Cistern Open-topped storage vessel for cold water, commonly known as tank.

Cladding Material used to cover a surface – usually a wall or ceiling.

Cleat A short length of timber designed to support a larger piece (e.g. gravel board).

Compression joint Brass connector for plumbing pipe, tightened with spanners.

Conductor Length of wire through which an electric current can pass. Also core.

Cornice Decorative plaster or wood moulding fitted at wall/ceiling joins.

Coving A plain moulding made of plaster or polystyrene, to cover the join between the walls and ceiling.

Cross-head Type of screw with cross-shaped recess in the head, rather than a single slot. The best type to use with a power screwdriver, because the screwdriver bit grips the head better.

Cutting in Careful painting at corners or at junctions on a wall surface, or beside door frames and windowsills.

Dado The lower part of an interior wall, often defined by a dado rail. Because it is more liable to damage it may be covered with wood panelling.

Damp-proof course (DPC) A continuous layer of impervious material (formerly slate, but now usually plastic) which prevents damp rising from the ground into walls.

Damp-proof membrane (DPM) Plastic sheeting used to form an impermeable layer in concrete floors.

Dedicated circuit A circuit which runs from the consumer unit to one appliance only, such as a cooker or freezer socket.

Detector Battery-operated electronic device for locating pipes, cables, studs, joists or the presence of electricity.

Distemper A traditional paint which feels powdery and wipes off with a wet cloth. No longer used: to redecorate, old distemper must first be washed off entirely.

Diverter valve A valve that diverts water flow from bath taps to a shower head.

Double check valve Backflow prevention device, designed to protect water supplies from contamination.

Dowel A cylindrical wooden peg used to reinforce joints in woodworking.

Dry-lining A wall lining formed by fixing sheets of tapered-edge plasterboard to a framework of timber battens. Joints are covered with tape and plastered over.

Dry rot Fungal attack on wood and other materials. First signs are small, silky threads, which spread outwards from a concealed fruiting body.

Earth The safety connection in electric wiring that links all exposed metal parts to the main earthing terminal.

Eaves The lower edge of the roof and rafters, that projects beyond the walls, to protect the walls from rainfall.

Efflorescence White, powdery deposit of soluble salts, left on a wall as it dries out. Must be brushed, not washed, off.

Eggshell Hard-wearing paint with a dull, matt finish. Acrylic or solvent-based.

Elbow Plumbing joint that forms a 90° bend in pipework.

Emulsion Water-based paint used for interior walls and ceilings.

Enamel A hard-wearing coating used on baths and sinks. Also a highly-coloured paint with a hard glossy finish.

Escutcheon Small plate used to finish off a keyhole. May have a cover for draught proofing and privacy.

Expansion joint Gap left to allow for thermal movement – in floors or guttering, for example.

Fascia A strip of wood covering the ends of rafters, to which guttering may be attached.

Feed-and-expansion cistern Water vessel that stores water to top-up central heating system. Also called header tank.

Finial Decorative piece of wood used to finish the top of a post, usually on a staircase newel. Also the decorative end of a curtain pole.

Flashing Material used to make a weatherproof join between a wall or chimney and a roof.

Flexible filler A filler for wood that sets hard, but allows slight movement.

Flexible sealant Water-based or acrylic sealant, supplied in a tube and applied with a sealant gun, to seal gaps.

Fuse Weak link in electrical circuit or plug, that fails if current is too high.

Gable The triangular end of a pitched roof.

Gate valve On-off control fitted on low-pressure pipework.

Gauge rod A timber batten marked at regular intervals used to check the positioning of tiles or bricks.

Gloss Highly decorative, shiny paint finish. Also paint for wood and metal.

Grommet A flexible ring, used to line a hole to prevent cable, for instance, from chafing against a sharp edge. Blind grommets have a thin membrane that is cut when the cable is ready to be fed through.

Grout Filling compound used in gaps between ceramic and other hard tiles.

Hawk Metal or plywood square with a handle underneath, used to hold plaster or mortar while working.

Header tank Popular name for feed-and-expansion cistern.

Hopper head Takes outflow from two rainwater downpipes and directs it into a single pipe.

Instantaneous heater A heater that heats mains-supplied water on demand, as it flows through the heater. Often gas-fired.

Inspection chamber Hole in ground where underground drains are connected or where they change direction.

Insulation Materials used to reduce the transmission of heat or sound. Also non-conductive material surrounding electrical wires or connections to prevent the passage of electricity.

Jamb The vertical side member of a window or door frame.

Jointing compound Filler used to seal gaps between sheets of plasterboard.

Jointing tape Self-adhesive tape used for covering joins between sheets of plasterboard.

Joist Wooden or steel beam used for supporting floors and ceilings.

Junction box Plastic fitting used for making connections between cables on a power or lighting circuit.

Lagging Insulating material fitted over hot-water cylinders, as well as pipes and tanks in unheated areas, to prevent freezing.

Laminated Consisting of thin layers. Applies to plywood, safety glass and worktops

Lamp Correct name for light bulb.

Laths Narrow strips of wood to which plaster is stuck, in traditional lath-and-plaster walls and ceilings.

Leading edge Vertical edge of door or window farthest from the hinges.

Lime (hydrated) Ingredient to make mortar more workable.

Live (also known as phase or line) The part of an electrical circuit that carries the flow of current to an appliance.

Lintel Supporting horizontal beam over an opening in masonry, such as a door, window or fireplace.

Manhole cover Removable lid for inspection chamber.

MDF (medium density fibreboard) Fine wood-particle board that is easily shaped to a smooth finish.

Microporous Describes a finish such as paint or woodstain that permits moisture to escape from wood, allowing it to dry out, at the same time protecting it from rainwater or damp.

Miniature Circuit breaker (MCB) A trip switch on a circuit in a consumer unit that acts automatically to break the circuit in the event of a fault. Once the fault is fixed, the MCB can be reset to restore the power.

Mineral fibre Material used for insulation.

Mitre A corner joint, made by cutting two pieces of material at a 45° angle.

Mortar Mixture of cement, sand and sometimes other additives, used in bricklaying and rendering.

Motorised valve A valve controlled by hot water cylinder and room thermostats to direct heating water as required.

Moulding Shaped wood or plaster used as a decorative feature on doors, walls and ceilings and around door frames.

Mouse A small weight used to pass a string-line through a narrow vertical space.

Mullion The vertical dividing piece of a window frame.

Muntin Central vertical frame of a door, fixed to the top and bottom rails.

Nail punch Simple tool used with a hammer, to drive nail heads below the surface of the wood.

Neutral The part of an electrical circuit that carries the flow of current from an appliance.

Olive Sealing ring in a brass compression joint for plumbing pipes.

Parting bead The strip of wood separating the two sliding sashes in a sash window.

Phase (also known as live or line) The part of an electrical circuit that carries the flow of current to an appliance.

Pilot hole Small hole drilled to allow a piece of wood to receive a larger screw or nail without splitting.

Pipe/cable detector Electronic device for detecting metal in walls.

Plasterboard Rigid wall-covering material made of gypsum plaster, sandwiched between sheets of paper.

Plumb Exactly vertical. A plumb line is used to establish vertical drops.

Pointing Shaping the mortar joints between bricks with a jointing trowel or other tool.

Pressure-treated timber Wood that has been impregnated with preservative under extreme pressure.

Primer The first coat of paint applied to protect wood and metal. It reduces the absorption of subsequent layers of paint; a metal primer prevents corrosion.

PTFE (polytetrafluoroethylene) Material used to make tape for sealing threaded plumbing fittings.

Push-fit joint Plastic or brass joint for joining pipes without tools.

Purlin A horizontal beam that provides intermediate support for rafters or sheet roofing.

PVA (polyvinyl acetate) General purpose adhesive. Often used as a bonding agent for plaster and mortar. Also used for 'white' wood adhesive.

PVC (polyvinyl chloride) A plastic used for cable insulation and corrugated roofing. The unplasticised form, PVCu, is used for plumbing pipes, exterior cladding and window frames.

Radial circuit An electrical circuit that starts at the consumer unit and runs from one outlet to another and terminates at the last one.

RCD (residual current device) Fast-acting trip-switch that cuts off the power to prevent electric shock in the event of a fault.

Reducer Plumbing joint that is used between pipes of different diameter.

Render A thin layer of cement-based mortar. It can be used as a base for plastering on an inside wall, or simply painted over when on an exterior wall.

Reveal Vertical sides of a recessed door or window opening.

Ring circuit An electrical circuit that runs from the consumer unit to each outlet in turn before returning to the consumer unit.

Rising damp Moisture entering a house from below as a result of the failure of the damp-proof course in a wall or the damp-proof membrane in a concrete floor.

RSJ (rolled steel joist) Used mainly over an opening when a load-bearing wall is removed and two rooms made into one.

Sash window A type of window with two sliding sections (sashes).

Sashlock Mortise lock fitted to back and side doors containing a handle-operated latch as well as a deadbolt.

Satin Paint with a semi-gloss finish.

Sealant See Flexible sealant.

Self-levelling compound Applied to concrete floors in order to provide a level surface for further floor covering.

Sheath The outer layer of insulation covering an electrical cable or flex.

Short circuit The accidental diversion of electricity between conductors, which increases the flow of current and blows a fuse or trips a miniature circuit breaker (MCB).

Silk Paint with a semi-gloss finish.

Size Sealer used to coat plastered or papered surfaces in preparation for wallpapering. It prevents the surface from absorbing too much paste, which makes the paper easier to hang.

Skim To apply a thin top coat of plaster to a wall surface.

Snake Common name for a plumber's auger.

Soakaway A pit filled with rubble or gravel into which rainwater is drained.

Soffit The underside of an archway or the eaves of a building.

Soil stack Large-diameter vertical pipe, vented at the top, that carries soil and waste water to the main drainage system.

Solvent-weld cement Adhesive used for joining some types of plastic waste pipe.

Spacers Small dividers used between tiles and paving slabs to keep a consistent gap between them during installation.

Spalling Flaking of the outer face of masonry, caused by moisture expanding in freezing conditions.

Spur Branch cable that extends an existing electrical circuit.

Staff bead The innermost strip of wood holding a sliding sash in a sash window frame.

Steam stripper Machine (can be hired) which aids the stripping of wallpaper by applying steam to the paper surface.

Stile The vertical side member of a door or window sash.

Stoptap On-off control fitted on mains-pressure pipework.

Striker plate Metal plate set in a door frame, containing a cut-out into which the latch fits when the door is shut.

Stud Vertical timber support in a wood-framed partition wall.

Stud detector Electronic device that detects presence of studs or joists.

Sugar soap Chemical compound used to degrease paintwork prior to redecorating.

Supplementary bonding The connecting to earth of exposed metal pipework, mainly in bathrooms.

Tail Connection between a tap and its supply pipe. Usually threaded, but plain on some mixer taps. Also connector to fit between radiator and valve.

Tank Storage vessel for cold water.

Tee Plumbing joint that connects a branch pipe to the main pipe run.

Terminals Connections to which the bared conductors of a cable or flex are attached.

Tie Piece of wood or metal that links opposing members and prevents outward movement, such as tie-beams found at the feet of rafters.

Transformer Electrical device that changes the voltage in a circuit.

Transom A horizontal dividing piece of a window frame.

Trap A U-shaped section of pipe below a bath, basin, shower tray, WC or sink. It fills with water to prevent smells coming from the drains into the house.

Trunking Rectangular-section plastic or metal duct for cables and pipes that protects them as they run along wall surfaces.

Undercoat Layer of paint used to obliterate the colour of the primer and build up a protective layer before applying the top coat.

Underlay Layer of plywood or hardboard applied over a rough floor to provide a smooth surface suitable for tiles or other floor coverings. Also a resilient layer under a carpet or a pond liner.

Valley Rainwater channel, usually of zinc or lead, between two sections of roof.

Vinyl Plastic material used for easy-to-clean floor coverings. Also protective covering on some wallpapers or an additive used in paint, to increase their hard-wearing and wipeable properties.

Vinyl emulsion Water-based paint ideal for bathrooms as it is easy to wipe down and keep clean.

VOCs Volatile Organic Compounds are chemical compounds found in paints, stains, varnishes, preservatives, carpets and laminated furniture that emit gases, contributing to atmospheric pollution. These gases can cause headaches, nausea and breathing difficulties.

Volt The measure of pressure that causes electric current to flow round a circuit.

Voltage detector Electronic device that detects the presence of electricity.

Wall plate A horizontal timber beam placed along the top of a wall to support and provide attachment for joists and rafters, and to spread their load.

Wallplug Plastic or metal sheath inserted into a pre-drilled hole in a wall to hold a screw.

Washer A flexible ring that prevents taps from leaking. Also spreads load of nut or bolt head.

Watt The measure of power consumed by an electrical appliance. 1000 watts = 1 kilowatt (kW).

Weatherboard A length of wooden moulding fixed at the base of an external door to direct rainwater away from the door.

Wet rot Fungus that attacks wood with too high a moisture content. Not as serious as dry rot, but leads to the eventual destruction of timber.

Woodworm Generic term for attacks in timber by larvae of wood-boring beetles.

index

*Main entries in the index are shown in **bold** type*

index

index

acknowledgments

The publishers wish to give their special thanks to the following organisations for equipment and help given in the preparation of this book.

HSS Hire Shops Mitcham Surrey
Robert Bosch Power Tools Buckinghamshire
Black & Decker Power Tools Slough, Berkshire
St Johns Street Cycles Bridgwater, Somerset

Thanks also to
Abru Ltd Belper, Derbyshire
Agfa Gevaert Ltd Brentford, Middlesex
Aqua-Dial Ltd Kingston upon Thames, Surrey
Armitage Shanks Ltd Rugeley, Staffordshire
Bletchley Timber Bletchley, Milton Keynes
Brian Hyde Ltd Solihull, West Midlands
Christopher Wray Lighting Ltd London SW6
Colebrand Ltd London W1
Dewalt Power Tools Slough, Berkshire
Epson (UK) Ltd Hemel Hempstead, Hertfordshire
Gainsborough Electrical Norwich, Norfolk
Greenwich Interiors London SE10
Grohe Ltd Barking, Essex
Hewlett Packard Bracknell, Berkshire
Hodgson Sealants Beverley, Yorkshire
Hunter Plastics London SE28
JD Beadmore London SW1
Kickstop Security Products Ltd London E9
Laybond Products Ltd Chester, Cheshire
Mira Showers Extreme
Paul Riley, Odell & Co Ltd Buckinghamshire
Pilkington Glass St Helens, Merseyside

Redland Roofing Systems Dorking, Surrey
Richard Burbridge Ltd Oswestry, Shropshire
Southern Motor Factors Ltd Bromley, Kent
Stanley Europe Sheffield, South Yorkshire
The Building Centre London WC1
The Sash Window Workshop Windsor, Berkshire
Thule Ltd Roof Carriers, Accessories and Roof Boxes Clevedon, North Somerset
Wednesbury Copper Tube & Fittings Bilston
Worcester, Bosch Group Bilston, West Midlands
www.DIY.com
www.dulux.co.uk/paintpod
www.screwfix.com
www.TritonShowers.co.uk
www.wickes.co.uk

Picture credits

The position of photographs and illustrations on each page is indicated by letters after the page number: *T* = Top; *B* = Bottom; *L* = Left; *C* = Centre; *R* = Right

12–29 picture frieze from Edifice except **18** *TL* Getty Images/Matthias Hauser; *CL* Superstock/imagebroker.net; *BL* Houses & Interiors by Ed Buziak

24 *BL* Houses & Interiors by David Markson

35 *CR* artwork based on photo from Skyscan

66 T The Amtico Co Ltd; *TR* Corbis/Terry Vine/Blend Images; *BL* iStock/ilbusca; *BC* Crucial Trading; *BR* Mainstream Photography © Ray Main

82 *TL* The Loft Shop Ltd

85 Room setting A.W. Champion

105 *R* Gap Interiors/Douglas Gibb

106 *TR* Getty Images/Ron Sutherland

113 *T* Rentokil Initial

131 *R* artworks based on Successful DIY © Eaglemoss Publications Ltd 1994 by Andrew Green

147 *R* artworks 1 & 3 based on Successful DIY © Eaglemoss Publications Ltd 1994 by Maltings Partnership

149 *R* artworks 1 & 2 based on The Which? Book of Plumbing & Central Heating © 1994 Which? Ltd by Tom Cross; artworks 3 & 4 based on Step-by-Step DIY © Guinness Publishing Ltd & Keith Faulkner Publishing Ltd 1994

150 *L* Getty Images/Nomadic Luxury; *L* iStock/Stuartbur

159, 161, 170 *R* artworks based on Collins Complete DIY Manual © 1993, Harper Collins Publishers

179 *R* artworks based on Step-by-Step DIY © Guinness Publishing Ltd & Keith Faulkner Publishing Ltd 1994

181 *R* artworks 1 & 2 based on a photograph by David Copsey from The Which? Book of Wiring and Lighting © 1997 Which? Ltd; artworks 3 & 4 based on an illustration by Peter Harper from The Which? Book of Wiring and Lighting © 1997 Which? Ltd

197 *R* artworks based on Step-by-Step DIY © Guinness Publishing Ltd

198 *B* Arcaid Images/Fritz vonder Schulenburg/Interior Archive. Architect: Nico Rensch

199 *R* artworks based on Successful DIY © Eaglemoss Publications Ltd 1994

201 *TR* Garden Picture Library by John Glover

204 *BR* David Holloway

205 *R* artworks based on Successful DIY © Eaglemoss Publications Ltd 1994

208 iStock/Andrew Howe

235 *L* iStock/Mark Wragg; *R* Alamy/Phovoir

Contributors

Editor Lisa Thomas
Art Editor Julie Bennett
Designer Martin Bennett
Editorial Assistant Katharine Swire
Indexer Marie Lorimer
Proofreaders Ken Vickery; Rosemary Wighton

Writers and specialist consultants Roger Bisby;
Paul Bloomfield; John Durrant; Cliff Forrest; Mike Lawrence;
Fred Milson; Mark Ramuz; John Ratcliff; Ian Williamson

FOR THIS EDITION
Editor Jo Bourne
Art Editor Sailesh Patel
Picture Researcher Elaine Denne
Consultant David Holloway

FOR VIVAT DIRECT
Editorial Director Julian Browne
Art Director Anne-Marie Bulat
Managing Editor Nina Hathway
Trade Books Editor Penny Craig
Picture Resource Manager Sarah Stewart-Richardson
Pre-press Account Manager Dean Russell
Product Production Manager Claudette Bramble
Production Controller Jan Bucil

Every effort has been made to find and credit the copyright holders of images in this book. We will be pleased to rectify any errors or omissions in future editions. Email us at gbeditorial@readersdigest.co.uk

While the creators of this work have made every effort to ensure safety and accuracy, the publishers cannot be held liable for injuries suffered or losses incurred as a result of following the instructions contained within this book. Readers should study the information carefully and make sure they understand it before undertaking any work. Always observe any warnings. Readers are also recommended to consult qualified professionals for advice.

Origination by FMG
Printed and bound in China

Fix Your Home For Less

Published in 2012 in the United Kingdom by Vivat Direct Limited (t/a Reader's Digest), 157 Edgware Road, London W2 2HR

Fix Your Home For Less is owned and under licence from The Reader's Digest Association, Inc. All rights reserved.

Material in this edition previously appeared under the title **Quick Fix DIY** © 2003

We are committed both to the quality of our products and the service we provide to our customers. We value your comments, so please do contact us on **0871 351 1000** or visit our website at **www.readersdigest.co.uk**

If you have any comments or suggestions about the content of our books, email us at **gbeditorial@readersdigest.co.uk**

Book code 400 596 UP0000 1
ISBN 978 1 78020 125 2